D0204051

Cambridge Opera Handbooks

Richard Strauss
Salome

This full-length study of *Salome* is the first in English since Lawrence Gilman's introductory guide of 1907. The book presents an informative collection of historical, analytical and critical studies of one of Strauss's most familiar operas. Classic essays by Mario Praz and Richard Ellmann cover the literary background. How Strauss adapted Wilde's play for his libretto is discussed by Roland Tenschert in a fascinating essay which has been updated by Derrick Puffett.

In three central analytical chapters, Derrick Puffett considers *Salome* in relation to Wagnerian music drama, Tethys Carpenter examines its tonal and dramatic structure, and Craig Ayrey analyses the final monologue. The last part of the book moves from analysis to criticism, with a review by John Williamson of the opera's critical reception and a new interpretative essay by Robin Holloway.

The book also contains a synopsis, bibliography and discography; Strauss's little-known scenario for the 'Dance of the Seven Veils' is reprinted as an appendix.

CAMBRIDGE OPERA HANDBOOKS
Published titles

Richard Strauss
Salome

Edited by
DERRICK PUFFETT

The right of the
University of Cambridge
to print and sell
all manner of books
was granted by
Henry VIII in 1534.
The University has printed
and published continuously
since 1584.

CAMBRIDGE UNIVERSITY PRESS

Cambridge
New York   Port Chester
Melbourne   Sydney

Published by the Press Syndicate of the University of Cambridge
The Pitt Building, Trumpington Street, Cambridge CB2 1RP
40 West 20th Street, New York, NY 10011, USA
10 Stamford Road, Oakleigh, Melbourne 3166, Australia

First published 1989

Printed in Great Britain at the University Press, Cambridge

British Library cataloguing in publication data

Richard Strauss: 'Salome'. – (Cambridge opera
handbooks)
1. Opera in German. Strauss, Richard, 1864–
1949. Salome
I. Puffett, Derrick
782.1'092'4

Library of Congress cataloguing in publication data

Richard Strauss, Salome / edited by Derrick Puffett.
      p.   cm. – (Cambridge opera handbooks)
Bibliography.
Discography.
Includes index.
ISBN 0-521-35172-3. – ISBN 0-521-35970-8 (pbk.)
1. Strauss, Richard, 1864–1949. Salome. I. Puffett, Derrick.
II. Title: Salome. III. Series.
ML410.S93R52 1989
782.1'092'4 – dc 19   89–500 CIP

ISBN 0 521 35172 3 hard covers
ISBN 0 521 35970 8 paperback

Contents

Criticism

Illustrations

General preface

This is a series of studies of individual operas written for the opera-goer or record-collector as well as the student or scholar. Each volume has three main concerns: historical, analytical and interpretative. There is a detailed description of the genesis of each work and of the collaboration between librettist and composer. A synopsis considers the opera as a structure of musical and dramatic effects, and there is also a musical analysis of a section of the score. The analysis, like the history, shades naturally into interpretation: by a careful combination of new essays and excerpts from classic statements the editors of the handbooks show how critical writing about the opera, like the production and performance, can direct or distort appreciation of its structural elements. A final section of documents gives a select bibliography, a discography, and guides to other sources. Each book is published in both hard covers and as a paperback.

Acknowledgements

The publishers gratefully acknowledge permission to reprint the following: Chapter 1 (Oxford University Press); Chapter 2 (Mrs Mary D. Ellmann); Chapter 3 (© copyright 1960 by Boosey & Hawkes GmbH. Reprinted by permission of Boosey & Hawkes Music Publishers Ltd.); the English translation of Strauss's scenario for the 'Dance of the Seven Veils' given in Appendix A (Office du Livre, Fribourg, and Phaidon Press); and Appendix B (Rudy Shackelford). Music from the score is © copyright 1905 by Adolph Furstner. Copyright assigned 1943 to Boosey & Hawkes Ltd., for all countries excluding Germany, Danzig, Italy, Portugal and the U.S.S.R. Reprinted by permission of Boosey & Hawkes Music Publishers Ltd.

The Editor thanks Alfred Clayton and Michael Gordon, for help with translations; John Williamson, for advice on illustrations; and Monica Buckland, for typing the manuscript.

For S.

Introduction

I

This is the first full-length study of *Salome* in English (and perhaps in any language) since Lawrence Gilman's introductory guide of 1907.[1] How one of Strauss's most popular works could have escaped sustained critical attention for so long is a subject for a separate book, though it will be returned to briefly later in this Introduction. There have of course been distinguished shorter studies. Ernest Newman, one of the earliest champions of Strauss's music in Britain (though by no means uncritical), included a chapter on it in *More Opera Nights*.[2] This provided a prototype for later writers such as William Mann and Norman Del Mar, whose well-known books on Strauss[3] are essential reading for any devotee of the work. The approach in all three studies is similar: the author begins with a short history of the composition, together with a certain amount of literary background; then comes an 'analysis' (in fact, a synopsis of the action interspersed with music examples and comments of a critical-analytical type, rather than what is now understood as analysis proper); finally a brief summing-up. Other distinguished contributions have appeared as chapters in books not exclusively devoted to Strauss. Gary Schmidgall's essay on *Salome*, despite its musical limitations, is valuable for the way in which it relates the work to the Symbolist and Decadent movements, a subject rarely tackled by musicologists.[4] Peter Conrad's account is more contentious but still worth reading.[5] And the work of Anna Amalie Abert, Alan Jefferson, Michael Kennedy, Romain Rolland, Willi Schuh, Richard Specht and Roland Tenschert[6] should not be forgotten.

Not to mention the numerous remarks of Strauss himself. Though a reluctant writer, he left behind vivid comments on historical, technical and aesthetic aspects of the work (as well as a wealth of lively anecdotes), notably in his reminiscences of the first

1

performance.[7] These have been plundered heavily by other writers, as they will be again in the course of the next two hundred pages. An account of the origins of *Salome* ought to begin not with Strauss, however, but with the author on whose play it was based: Oscar Wilde.

II

Wilde's play was first produced in 1896. But he had been fascinated by Salome ever since Walter Pater, one of his Oxford mentors,[8] had lent him Flaubert's *Trois contes* (containing the story *Hérodias*) in 1877.[9] Wilde admired Flaubert enormously.[10] He copied shamelessly from *Hérodias* and affected not to understand when the older man failed to appreciate the compliment.[11] Curiously, however, it was another 'Herodias' that provided the immediate stimulus for the composition of Wilde's play. Mallarmé's poem was still unfinished after many years, in Richard Ellmann's words 'the best known unfinished poem since "Kubla Khan"':

> Wilde determined to use the same subject, the beheading of John the Baptist at the instigation of Herodias. Whether or not he intended to compete directly, he did so, and Mallarmé, in his futile effort to complete 'Hérodiade', had to take note of Wilde's efforts, and said he would retain the name of Herodias to differentiate it from that other (*Salome*) 'which I shall call modern'.[12]

Wilde began the play in 1891, the year of *Lady Windermere's Fan*, his political essay 'The Soul of Man under Socialism' and four other major works. He was then living in Paris. As Ellmann has written, his knowledge of the iconography of Salome was immense:

> He complained that Rubens's Salome appeared to him to be 'an apoplectic Maritornes'. On the other hand, Leonardo's Salome was excessively incorporeal. Others, by Dürer, Ghirlandaio, van Thulden, were unsatisfactory because incomplete. The celebrated Salome of Regnault he considered to be a mere 'gypsy'. Only Moreau satisfied him, and he liked to quote Huysmans's description of the Moreau paintings.[13] He was eager to visit the Prado to see how Stanzioni had painted her, and Titian, about whom he quoted Tintoretto's comment, 'This man paints with quivering flesh [*carne molida*].'

He seemed torn between two opposing conceptions of her character. On the one hand she must be the embodiment of sensuality:

> If he passed the rue de la Paix, he would examine the jewelry shops for proper adornment of her. One afternoon he asked, 'Don't you think she

would be better naked? Yes, totally naked, but draped with heavy and ring-
ing necklaces made of jewels of every colour, warm with the fervour of her
amber flesh. I don't conceive of her as unconscious, serving as a mute
instrument [that is, for Herodias' hatred of John]. No, her lips in
Leonardo's painting disclose the cruelty of her soul. Her lust must needs be
infinite, and her perversity without limits. Her pearls must expire on her
flesh.' He began to imagine Sarah Bernhardt dancing naked before the
Tetrarch . . .

On the other hand she must be chaste:

She would dance before Herod out of divine inspiration . . . 'Her body, tall
and pale, undulates like a lily. There is nothing sensual in her beauty. The
richest lilacs cover her svelte flesh . . . In her pupils gleam the flames of
faith.' The image was suggested to him by a painting of Bernardo Luini.[14]

All sorts of other images contributed to the character: the bust of a
decapitated woman, a Rumanian acrobat dancing on her hands, the
playing of a gypsy orchestra, even phrases from the Song of Songs.[15]
    The play was finished in January 1892 (Wilde had now returned
to England). Rehearsals began in June. But after two weeks the
Lord Chamberlain's office banned the work, on the grounds that
representations of biblical scenes were not allowed. (Massenet's
Hérodiade (1881), based on Flaubert, and Saint-Saëns' *Samson et
Dalila* were also prohibited.) Despite protests from Shaw and
William Archer, the only established critics to defend the play, it
became clear that it would not be staged publicly in Britain (there
were some private performances).[16] Wilde threatened to emigrate
to France, simultaneously advancing his plans to have the play published in English. It had, of course, been written in French, and the
translation was entrusted to Lord Alfred Douglas, the notorious
'Bosie'. The ensuing row was almost the cause of a rift between
them: Wilde later wrote of the 'schoolboy faults of your attempted
translation of *Salome*',[17] and revised it heavily before it was published.[18] At all events, it was only in 1896, while the author was in
prison, that *Salomé* was given its first public hearing, at the Théâtre
de l'Œuvre in Paris.
    'The rest is history.' Mario Praz has written eloquently about its
subsequent fortunes. It had a massive success in Germany,[19] where
Strauss soon heard about it. Let him take up the story:

Once, in Berlin [Strauss was conductor at the Royal Court Opera there], I
went to Max Reinhardt's 'Little Theatre' in order to see Gertrud Eysoldt in
Oscar Wilde's *Salome*. After the performance I met Heinrich Grünfeld,
who said to me: 'My dear Strauss, surely you could make an opera of this!'

I replied: 'I am already busy composing it.' The Viennese poet Anton Lindtner [*sic*] had sent me this exquisite play and had offered to turn it into a libretto for me. When I agreed, he sent me a few cleverly versified opening scenes, but I could not make up my mind to start composing until one day it occurred to me to set to music *Wie schön ist die Prinzessin Salome heute Nacht* straight away. From then on it was not difficult to purge the piece of purple passages to such an extent that it became quite a good libretto.[20]

The performance Strauss describes was a private one given on 11 November 1902 (not in 1903, as is sometimes stated);[21] in any case he had been familiar with the play since 1901. Reinhardt, who was then at the beginning of his directorial career, was later to collaborate with Strauss on numerous projects, notably *Ariadne auf Naxos*. Gertrud Eysoldt (who was to be the first Elektra in Hofmannsthal's play) has been described as 'boyish, rather plain, though with fascinating eyes and an extremely expressive face'.[22] Anton Lindner was known personally to Strauss, having provided the text for his 'Hochzeitlich Lied', Op. 37, No. 6 (1889). Strauss, however, preferred the translation by Hedwig Lachmann,[23] the one used by Reinhardt. (Still another translation, by one Dr Kiefer, had been performed in Breslau in 1901.)[24]

Composition began in earnest in August 1903. As Walter Panofsky has pointed out, most of the sketching was done not in Berlin but in a house in Marquartstein, Upper Bavaria. The house belonged to Strauss's in-laws, and Strauss himself was banished to an ironing room, with nothing more than an upright piano, a writing-desk and the jingle of cow-bells from the Alpine pastures outside. *Salome*, like *The Rite of Spring*, another of the noisiest scores of the twentieth century, was composed in a room the size of a broom-cupboard.[25]

This is as good a point as any to mention an idea first put forward by Ernest Newman and repeated by countless writers since, namely that Strauss 'began by composing the Dance of the Seven Veils and the long closing scene'. Newman supports this idea by referring to 'a remark made by Strauss towards the end of his life'.[26] What this remark was (like the five words that Elgar is supposed to have whispered to Newman on his death-bed) will never be known. It is plain from the catalogue of sketches published by Franz Trenner, however, that the 'Dance' was composed *after* the rest of the score, indeed after the finishing date of '20 June 1905' which Strauss wrote on his manuscript.[27] The position with the closing scene (actually

Salome's final monologue, since the 'closing scene' proper begins with Herod's entry) is less clear. Trenner lists individual sketches for the monologue, in their correct 'chronological' placing,[28] but it is uncertain at what point the monologue was sketched as a whole. Newman's hypothesis, though interesting, remains unproven.

The composition sketch was finished in September 1904. Strauss then embarked upon the orchestration, putting his signature to the score, as we have seen, on 20 June the following year (the 'Dance' would be completed during August). Meanwhile he began his machinations for the première. These have been described in detail by Mann and others,[29] and it is scarcely worth going over the same ground again. Clearly Strauss had decided that a première at the Vienna Court Opera (where the censors were notoriously severe) was unlikely and that his best chance lay with Dresden, which had mounted *Feuersnot* in 1901. The conductor there, Ernst von Schuch, was an artist whom he admired.[30] Nevertheless Strauss threatened to take the première to Vienna (under Mahler) or to Leipzig (under Nikisch) if Schuch did not meet his deadline of 9 December 1905. The problems caused by this timetable were amusingly described by Strauss himself:

. . . during the first reading rehearsal at the piano, the assembled soloists returned their parts to the conductor with the single exception of Mr [Carl] Burian, a Czech, who, when asked for his opinion last of all, replied: 'I know it off by heart already.' Good for him. After this the others could not help feeling a little ashamed and rehearsals actually started. During the casting rehearsals Frau [Marie] Wittich, entrusted the part of the sixteen-year-old Princess with the voice of Isolde (one just does not write a thing like that, Herr Strauss: either one or the other), because of the strenuous nature of the part and the strength of the orchestra, went on strike with the indignant protest to be expected from the wife of a Saxon Burgomaster: 'I won't do it, I'm a decent woman', thereby reducing the producer [Willi] Wirk, who was all for 'perversity and outrage'[,] to desperation.[31]

Nevertheless the première was a triumph (more than one review called it a 'sensation').[32] The artists took thirty-eight curtain calls. By the end of 1907 the opera had been heard in more than fifty German and foreign cities, and fifty times in Berlin alone by 9 November of that year.[33] The income resulting from this success enabled Strauss to terminate his contract with the Berlin Opera and devote himself full-time to composition.[34]

But all this lay in the future. At the time of the première it must have seemed as if *Salome*'s troubles were only just beginning:

Plate 1: Salome pleads for the head of Jochanaan: from the first Dresden production, with Marie Wittich (Salome) and Carl Burian (Herod), Dresden, December 1905

Three weeks later it had, I think, been accepted by ten theatres and had been a sensational success in Breslau with an orchestra of seventy players. Thereupon there was a hullabaloo in the papers, the churches objected – the first performance in the Vienna State Opera took place in October 1918, after an embarrassing exchange of letters with Archbishop Piffl – and so did the Puritans in New York, where the opera had to be taken off the repertoire at the instigation of a certain Mr [J. Pierpont] Morgan. The German Kaiser only permitted the performance of the opera after Hülsen [Georg Hülsen-Haeseler, the Intendant] had had the bright idea of signifying the advent of the Magi at the end by the appearance of the morning star![35]

The Vienna debacle is of particular interest because of the involvement of Mahler. Although initially ambivalent about the work, Mahler soon came to regard it as Strauss's masterpiece. In 1905 he hoped to conduct it in Vienna. But he was told that the Censorship Board had refused permission 'on religious and moral grounds'. Despite some wheeling and dealing Mahler was unable to get the decision reversed. The letter he eventually received from the Censor (31 October 1905) is worth quoting at length:

The first objection arises . . . from the repeated explicit or implicit references to Christ in the text [examples are cited]. All these passages would need to be cut or radically altered.

A further difficulty is the presentation of John the Baptist on the stage. The poet admittedly gives him the Hebrew name Jochanaan, but just as this change of name is unable to create the illusion that it is not the person honoured as Christ's forerunner, so equally would the choice of any other name fail to have this effect.

But also, quite apart from these textual reservations I cannot overcome the objectionable nature of the whole story, and can only repeat that the representation of events which belong to the realm of sexual pathology is not suitable for our Court stage.[36]

This verdict led Mahler to revise his views on morality in art.[37]

III

Could it be that some lingering *moral disapproval* is at the root of *Salome*'s critical neglect (there are more books on *Elektra*, *Der Rosenkavalier* and even *Ariadne*)? Certainly British critics seem to feel guilty about enjoying it. Ernest Newman wrote quaintly in 1910: 'In *Salome* the subject is a trifle unpleasant, but Strauss has given us a marvellous study of the diseased woman's mind.'[38] William Mann, who must have led a sheltered life, calls it 'the nastiest opera in existence'.[39] And Norman Del Mar, a superb

Strauss *conductor*, cannot write of it without distaste: 'a horrible display of hysterical triumph . . . after a performance of *Salome* one is left with a very nasty taste in the mouth'.[40]

A different sort of puritanism afflicts German writing about the work. Theodor W. Adorno, usually so acute, becomes surprisingly intemperate where Strauss is concerned, writing of his 'boastful banality' and 'helpless incoherence';[41] he even denies his technical mastery.[42] It is easy to see why Strauss does not fall into Adorno's scheme of things ('Had Richard Strauss never existed, contemporary music might have long ago ceased to call itself "new"').[43] By any Marxist–historicist criterion, let alone one so totally committed to modernism, his music must fail. Adorno's enormous influence on post-war German musicology – his book *Philosophie der neuen Musik* (1949), glorifying Schoenberg at the expense of Stravinsky, became the Bible of the Darmstadt summer schools – is probably the reason why hardly anyone in Germany writes about Strauss nowadays.[44] His attitude has even influenced Carl Dahlhaus, the leading present-day German musicologist, who writes dismissively of Strauss in his essay 'Neo-Romanticism'.[45] (Dahlhaus's writings on Wagner, nevertheless, are of crucial importance for an understanding of the later composer, as I shall demonstrate in Chapter 5.)

The attitude of these censorious Schoenbergians contrasts markedly with that of Schoenberg himself. Though certainly no friend of Strauss, who remained in Germany during the Third Reich, he defended him in 1946: 'Works like *Salome, Elektra, Intermezzo* and others will not perish.'[46] Forty years earlier he had kept the score of *Salome* on his music stand, marvelling at the harmony of the opening page.[47] This admiration for the *music* (shared, incidentally, by Berg and Webern) transcended petty personal, or even major political, considerations.

The music of *Salome* is at the centre of this book. Not morals, not religion, not even politics, but music. It is after all the music that an opera-lover goes to hear! And yet this prudishness, this unwillingness to enjoy (or to admit to enjoyment of) a work that is so manifestly popular, has prevented critics from taking it seriously as art. *Salome* is too often treated as 'light music', presumably as a result of some sort of defence mechanism ('if we cannot face up to it, make light of it'). This alone is testimony to its disturbing power. But both the ability to please and the ability to disturb are functions of the music, that is, of an *artistic* quality. We must confront what we fear if we want to understand it. And trying to understand it will provide new kinds of pleasure.

What follows, though a collection of essays, should be read as a book; it has a shape and a coherence which (I hope) outweigh any sense of 'bittiness'. Some of the essays are old, some new, just as the authors vary from the established to the less well-known. The authors of the first three chapters are unfortunately all dead. Mario Praz's account of Salome, though familiar, is nevertheless so brilliant that it seemed worth reprinting (and none of the several efforts to follow his path is anything like as good). Richard Ellmann, taking up where Praz leaves off, offers an *interpretation* of Wilde's play rather than a mere introduction to it – and an interpretation, moreover, whose resonances are felt throughout the book. Roland Tenschert, a distinguished Strauss scholar of the older generation, was one of the few to have seen Strauss's marked-up copy of the play – though I have taken the liberty of trying to bring his work up to date, in an editorial postscript.

With the second part of the book, *Salome* itself comes to the fore. After a brief synopsis I consider its relation to Wagnerian music drama. Tethys Carpenter then examines its tonal and dramatic structure. Finally Craig Ayrey analyses the final monologue, for many the crowning glory of the work. In the last part of the book we move from analysis to criticism, first with a review by John Williamson of the opera's critical reception and then with a new interpretative essay by Robin Holloway. My little postlude is not intended as a summary (I would not attempt to summarise work so diffuse), merely as a few final thoughts in the light of what has gone before. The discography, as usual in this series, is by Malcolm Walker.

That *Salomé* was originally written in French is, for Peter Conrad, 'the first defining oddity of Wilde's play', evoking parallels as diverse as Beckford (*Vathek*) and Beckett.[48] It also creates editorial problems. Any attempt to impose linguistic consistency on a work involving a character called Jochanaan – the German version of an English transliteration of the Hebrew form of the name of a character in a German opera based on a play written in French by an Irishman – is probably doomed from the outset. Nevertheless I have tried to maintain a distinction between *Salomé*, referring to the play (and the heroine of the play), and *Salome*, referring to the opera (and *its* heroine).[49] Similarly Jokanaan refers to the character in the play, Jochanaan the character in the opera. Such distinctions are hardly worth making and in any case break down in the course of the many quotations from secondary sources. But it still seemed worth making the effort. *All* translations from the libretto are given in Wilde's (or Douglas's) English version.

Note: The orchestral and vocal scores of *Salome* are published by Boosey and Hawkes (1943). References to specific passages take the form 'four bars after Fig. 126', sometimes abbreviated to 'Fig. 126/4'. In such references the bar headed by the rehearsal number is always included.

OVERTURES TO *SALOME*

1 *Salome in literary tradition*

MARIO PRAZ

> Time and again he had opened the old Bible of Pierre Variquet,[1] translated by the Doctors of Theology of the University of Louvain, and read the Gospel of St Matthew which recounts in brief, naive phrases the beheading of the Precursor; time and again he had mused over these lines:
>
> 'But when Herod's birthday was kept, the daughter of Herodias danced before them, and pleased Herod.
> 'Whereupon he promised with an oath to give her whatsoever she would ask.
> 'And she, being before instructed of her mother, said, "Give me here John Baptist's head in a charger."
> 'And the king was sorry: nevertheless for the oath's sake, and them which sat with him at meat, he commanded it to be given her.
> 'And he sent, and beheaded John in the prison.
> 'And his head was brought in a charger, and given to the damsel: and she brought it to her mother. [Matthew 14: 6–11]'
>
> Huysmans, *A rebours*[2]

[Praz's remarks on Salome occur in the context of a discussion of the painting of Gustave Moreau. For Praz, it was precisely in such painting, 'at the same time sexless and lascivious', that the spirit of the Decadent movement was most vividly expressed. 'Nor was it for nothing that the discoverer of Moreau should have been Huysmans, creator of the character of des Esseintes . . . ']

I

Huysmans imagines des Esseintes as having acquired the two masterpieces of Gustave Moreau, the artist above all others 'who sent him into raptures of delight'[3] – the oil-painting called *Salomé* (in the Mante Collection) and the water-colour *L'Apparition* (now in the Luxembourg Museum),[4] both of which were exhibited at the

1876 Salon, which marked the success of this painter in the same way in which the Pre-Raphaelite Exhibition of 1856 had marked the success of D. G. Rossetti. Huysmans' faithful description helps one to trace the type of literature to which Moreau's *soi-disant* anti-literary painting was related. He describes *Salomé* as follows:

This painting showed a throne like the high altar of a cathedral standing beneath a vaulted ceiling – a ceiling crossed by countless arches springing from thick-set, almost Romanesque columns, encased in polychromic brickwork, encrusted with mosaics, set with lapis lazuli and sardonyx – in a palace which resembled a basilica built in both the Moslem and the Byzantine styles.

In the centre of the tabernacle set on the altar, which was approached by a flight of recessed steps in the shape of a semi-circle, the Tetrarch Herod was seated, with a tiara on his head, his legs close together and his hands on his knees . . .

Round about this immobile, statuesque figure, frozen like some Hindu god in a hieratic pose, incense was burning, sending up clouds of vapour through which the fiery gems set in the sides of the throne gleamed like the phosphorescent eyes of wild animals. The clouds rose higher and higher, swirling under the arches of the roof, where the blue smoke mingled with the gold dust of the great beams of sunlight slanting down from the domes.

Amid the heady odour of these perfumes, in the overheated atmosphere of the basilica, Salome slowly glides forward on the points of her toes, her left arm stretched out in a commanding gesture, her right bent back and holding a great lotus-blossom beside her face, while a woman squatting on the floor strums the strings of a guitar [see Plate 2].[5]

In Flaubert's *Tentation* we read:

And Antony sees in front of him an immense basilica.

Light is projected from the far end, as if from a marvellous multicoloured sun . . . And he [Hilarion] pushes him towards a golden throne with five steps, where . . . the prophet Mani sits – beautiful as an archangel, still as a statue, wearing an Indian robe, carbuncles in his plaited hair, in his left hand a book of painted images, under his right a globe . . . Mani revolves his globe; and timing his words to the crystalline sounds coming from a lyre . . . [6]

Huysmans is describing Salome's appearance:

With a withdrawn, solemn, almost august expression on her face, she begins the lascivious dance which is to rouse the aged Herod's dormant senses; her breasts rise and fall, the nipples hardening at the touch of her whirling necklaces; the strings of diamonds glitter against her moist flesh; her bracelets, her belts, her rings all spit out fiery sparks; and across her triumphal robe, sewn with pearls, patterned with silver, spangled with gold, the jewelled cuirass, of which every chain is a precious stone, seems to be ablaze with little snakes of fire, swarming over the mat flesh, over the tea-

Plate 2: Gustave Moreau, *Salomé*

rose skin, like gorgeous insects with dazzling shards, mottled with carmine, spotted with pale yellow, speckled with steel blue, striped with peacock green.[7]

This Salome is sister of the Queen of Sheba in the *Tentation*:

Her gown of golden brocade, cut across at regular intervals by falbalas of pearl, jet, and sapphire, pinches her waist in a tight bodice, enriched with coloured appliqué to represent the twelve signs of the Zodiac . . . Her wide sleeves, garnished with emeralds and birds' feathers, allow a bare view of her little round arm . . . A flat golden chain passing under her chin runs up along her cheeks, spirals around her blue-powdered hair, and then dropping down grazes past her shoulder and clinches over her chest on to a diamond scorpion, which sticks out its tongue between her breasts.[8]

Huysmans sees in Moreau's Salome the type of Fatal Woman [described in Chapter 4 of *The Romantic Agony*]:

The character of Salome, a figure with a haunting fascination for artists and poets, had been an obsession with him for years . . . Neither St Matthew, nor St Mark, nor St Luke, nor any of the other sacred writers had enlarged on the maddening charm and potent depravity of the dancer. She had always remained a dim and distant figure, lost in a mysterious ecstasy far off in the mists of time, beyond the reach of punctilious, pedestrian minds, and accessible only to brains shaken and sharpened and rendered almost clairvoyant by neurosis . . . she had always passed the comprehension of the writing fraternity, who never succeeded in rendering the disquieting delirium of the dancer, the subtle grandeur of the murderess.

In Gustave Moreau's work, which in conception went far beyond the data supplied by the New Testament, des Esseintes saw realized at long last the weird and superhuman Salome of his dreams . . . She had become, as it were, the symbolic incarnation of undying Lust, the Goddess of immortal Hysteria, the accursed Beauty exalted above all other beauties by the catalepsy that hardens her flesh and steels her muscles, the monstrous Beast, indifferent, irresponsible, insensible, poisoning, like the Helen of ancient myth, everything that approaches her, everything that sees her, everything that she touches . . .

Moreover, the painter seemed to have wished to assert his intention of remaining outside the bounds of time, of giving no precise indication of race or country or period, setting as he did his Salome inside this extraordinary palace with its grandiose, heterogeneous architecture, clothing her in sumptuous, fanciful robes, crowning her with a nondescript diadem like Salammbo's, in the shape of a Phoenician tower, and finally putting in her hand the sceptre of Isis, the sacred flower of both Egypt and India, the great lotus-blossom.[9]

Des Esseintes dilates upon the meaning of this emblematic flower: is it a phallic symbol, or an allegory of fertility, or was the painter thinking of 'the dancer, the mortal woman, the soiled vessel, ultimate cause of every sin and every crime',[10] or was he remembering the embalming custom of ancient Egypt by which lotus-petals were inserted in the sexual organs of corpses for the purpose of purification?

However, even more disquieting than this to des Esseintes was the water-colour called *L'Apparition*, in which the severed head of the saint appears, after the crime, to a half-naked, terrified Salome, less majestic and proud 'but more seductive than the Salome of the oil-painting':

> Here she was a true harlot, obedient to her passionate and cruel female temperament; here she came to life, more refined yet more savage, more hateful yet more exquisite than before; here she roused the sleeping senses of the male more powerfully, subjugated his will more surely with her charms – the charms of a great venereal flower, grown in a bed of sacrilege, reared in a hot-house of impiety.[11]

He concludes with a comprehensive appreciation of the art of Moreau, in which he discovers only a vague affinity with Mantegna, Jacopo de' Barbari, Leonardo, Delacroix, but above all a unique originality:

> Going back to the beginnings of racial tradition, to the sources of mythologies whose bloody enigmas he compared and unravelled; joining and fusing in one those legends which had originated in the Middle East only to be metamorphosed by the beliefs of other peoples, he could cite these researches to justify his architectonic mixtures, his sumptuous and unexpected combinations of dress materials, and his hieratic allegories whose sinister quality was heightened by the morbid perspicuity of an entirely modern sensibility. He himself remained downcast and sorrowful, haunted by the symbols of superhuman passions and superhuman perversities, of divine debauches perpetrated without enthusiasm and without hope.
>
> His sad and scholarly works breathed a strange magic, an incantatory charm which stirred you to the depths of your being like the sorcery of certain of Baudelaire's poems . . .[12]

II

Moreau was a forerunner of Maeterlinck. [And] it was, in fact, from the plays of Maeterlinck (particularly *La Princesse Maleine*, 1889, and *Les sept Princesses*, 1891: Maeterlinck became famous as a result of an article by Mirbeau in the *Figaro* of 24 August 1890) that Oscar Wilde derived the childish prattle employed by the characters in his *Salomé* (written in French in 1891, published in 1893),[13] which reduces the voluptuous Orient of Flaubert's *Tentation* to the level of a nursery tale. It is childish, but it is also humoristic, with a humour which one can with difficulty believe to be unintentional, so much does Wilde's play resemble a parody of the whole of the material used by the Decadents and of the stammering mannerism of Maeterlinck's dramas – and, as a parody, *Salomé* comes very near to being a masterpiece. Yet it seems that Wilde was not quite aiming at this . . .

It was Wilde who finally fixed the legend of Salome's horrible passion. There is no suggestion of this to be found in Flaubert's tale (*Hérodias*), in which Salome is merely the tool of her mother's vengeance and after the dance becomes confused in repeating the instructions of Herodias:

. . . lisping a little, [she] said with a childish air:
'I want you to give me, in a dish, the head . . . ' She had forgotten the name, but went on again, smiling: 'The head of Jokanaan!'[14]

Wilde repeats this repartee on the part of Salome, but in quite a different sense. Salome denies that she had made the request at her mother's instigation. 'It is for mine own pleasure that I ask the head of Jokanaan in a silver charger.'[15] And, having obtained the head, she fastens her lips upon it in her vampire passion. Yet not even here can Wilde be given credit for originality.[16] He did not take the idea of Salome's monstrous passion from Flaubert, where it did not exist, nor yet from the pages of *A rebours* devoted to the paintings of Moreau – pages and pictures which certainly had their influence upon the play, but in an incidental manner: in them, in any case, the idea of sensual cruelty remained vague. Heinrich Heine, in 'Atta Troll' (written in 1841), had been the first to introduce into literature this theme, which he derived from popular tradition.[17] Herodias appears in the cavalcade of spirits seen from the witch Uraka's window (Caput 19):

And the third of those fair figures,
Which thy heart had moved so deeply,
Was it also some she-devil
Like the other two depicted?

If a devil or an angel,
I know not. With women never
Knows one clearly, where the angel
Leaves off and the devil begins.

O'er the face of glowing languor
Lay an Oriental magic,
And the dress recalled with transport
All Sheherazade's stories.

Lips of softness like pomegranates,
Lily-white the arching nose,
And the limbs, refreshing, taper,
Like a palm in some oasis.

High she was on white steed seated,
Whose gold rein two Moors were holding,
As along the way they trotted,
At the Princess' side afoot.

Yes, she was indeed a princess,
Was the sovereign of Judaea,
Was the beauteous wife of Herod,
Who the Baptist's head demanded.

For this deed of blood was she too
Execrated; and as spectre
Must until the day of Judgement
Ride among the goblin hunt.

In her hands she carries ever
That sad charger, with the head of
John the Baptist, which she kisses:
Yes, the head with fervour kisses.

For, time was, she loved the Baptist –
'Tis not in the Bible written,
But there yet exists the legend
Of Herodias' bloody love –

Else there were no explanation
Of that lady's curious longing –
Would a woman want the head of
Any man she did not love?

Was perhaps a little peevish
With her swain, had him beheaded;
But when she upon the charger
Saw the head so well beloved,

Straight she wept and mad became,
And she died of love's distraction –
Love's distraction! Pleonasmus!
Why, love is itself distraction!

Rising up at night she carries,
In her hand, as now related,
When she hunts, the bleeding head –
Yet with woman's maniac frenzy

> Sometimes, she, with childish laughter,
> Whirls it in the air above her,
> Then again will nimbly catch it,
> Like a plaything as it falls.
>
> As she rode along before me,
> She regarded me and nodded,
> So coquettish yet so pensive,
> That my inmost soul was moved.[18]

Heine's Herodias had a success in France. Banville was inspired by it to write one of the sonnets in his *Princesses* (1874), of which the epigraph is the passage from 'Atta Troll': 'Yes, she was indeed a princess / Was the sovereign of Judaea, / Was the beauteous wife of Herod, / Who the Baptist's head demanded'; he had already described the Salome of the picture by Henri Regnault[19] (now in the Metropolitan Museum, New York) in a sonnet, called 'La Danseuse' (January 1870, in *Rimes dorées*) – 'the eye was bewitched by the jewels – the smiling, bright red knife and bowl', concluding:

> . . . How great is your joy, o fragile dolls!
> For you always naively loved
> The flaming toys and severed heads.

In *La Forêt bleue* (1883), Jean Lorrain also was inspired by Heine's lines for his medallions of Diana, Herodias and Dame Habonde. Lorrain, however, merely described 'the Herodias hunt', without spending any time over the details of the legend.

A reflection of Heine's poem seems to be visible in Wilde, when he makes Herod say:

Come, Salomé, be reasonable . . . Surely, I think thou art jesting. The head of a man that is cut from his body is ill to look upon, is it not? It is not meet that the eyes of a virgin should look upon such a thing. What pleasure could you have in it? None. No, no, it is not what you desire.[20]

One thinks of the witty lines:

> Else there were no explanation
> Of that lady's curious longing –
> Would a woman want the head of
> Any man she did not love?

In one of the *Moralités légendaires* (published in *La Vogue* for June–July 1886, then, with alterations, in the *Revue indépendante* edition, 1887), Jules Laforgue improved upon Heine's ironical attitude by presenting an exquisite caricature of Salome – almost as she might be presented in a musical comedy by another Offenbach bent on toying with suggestions of the sinister, or as she actually appears in the illustrations which Beardsley later devised for Wilde's play. This is Laforgue's Salome:

Her bare shoulders, held erect in the centre of the chemise of mother-of-pearl, had the roundness of a miniature peacock, with a shifting depth of moire, azure, gold and emerald. From this halo there arose her guileless, superior head, which she was sincerely unconcerned with considering unique; her exposed neck, her eyes broken up in sparkling expiations, her lips revealing, behind their pale pink circumflex accent, a set of teeth and paler gums, with the most mortified smile . . . She staggered on her anaemic feet with their splayed toes, covered only by a ring of pegs from which flowed dazzling fringes of yellow moire . . . Who would have been capable of mortifying the little Immaculate Conception's smile? . . .

After uttering a little throaty laugh, perhaps especially to pretend she did not take herself seriously, Salome plucked her black lyre until she drew blood, and continued improvising with the timbreless, sexless voice of a sick person who complains about his medicine, no longer with any need of you or me . . .

'And now, father, I want you to have brought to me, on any dish, the head of Jokanaan.[21] I have spoken; I am waiting for it.' . . .

And there, on a cushion, amid the remains of the ebony lyre, John's head (as once that of Orpheus) glistened, coated in phosphorus. It was washed out, painted, twisted, with a fixed grin aimed at those twenty-four million heavenly bodies.

No sooner was the object delivered, than Salome, in a spirit of scientific enquiry, tried those famous post-decapitation experiments which are so often discussed; she waited, but the electric currents drew nothing but grimaces from the face.

Finally Salome 'kissed that mouth mercifully and hermetically, sealed it immediately with her corrosive stamp', and died, as a result of losing her balance while throwing the head of Jokanaan from a promontory into the sea, 'less the chance victim of ill-education than from having wanted to live by imitation and not in simplicity, like every one of us'.

Therefore, even before Wilde made use of the story of Salome, both Heine and Laforgue had emptied it of all tragic content by their ironical treatment of it. Yet, as generally happens with specious second-hand works, it was precisely Wilde's *Salomé* which became popular.[22] In 1896 the play, originally written for Sarah Bernhardt – who had been prevented from performing it by the censor – had a moderate success at the Théâtre de l'Œuvre; in 1901, a year after Wilde's death, it was given in Berlin, and since then – thanks also to the music of Richard Strauss – it has continued to figure in the repertories of European theatres. In Germany it has held the boards for a longer period than any other English play, including the plays of Shakespeare. It has been translated into Czech, Dutch, Greek, Hungarian, Polish, Russian, Catalan, Swedish and even Yiddish. In Italy it became part of the repertory of Lyda Borelli, and I still remember with what enthusiasm the gentlemen's opera-glasses were levelled at the squinting *diva*, clothed in nothing but violet and absinthe-green shafts of limelight. The Salomes of Flaubert, of Moreau, Laforgue and Mallarmé are known only to students of literature and connoisseurs, but the Salome of the genial comedian Wilde is known to all the world.

2 Overtures to Wilde's 'Salomé'

RICHARD ELLMANN

I

Salome, after having danced before the imaginations of European painters and sculptors for a thousand years, in the nineteenth century turned her beguilements to literature.[1] Heine, Flaubert, Mallarmé, Huysmans, Laforgue and Wilde became her suitors. Jaded by exaltations of nature and of humanism, they inspected with something like relief a biblical image of the unnatural. Mario Praz, bluff, and sceptical of Salome's allurements, seeks to limit them by arguing that she became the type of no more than the *femme fatale*. By type he means, he says, something 'like a neuralgic area. Some chronic ailment has created a zone of weakened resistance, and whenever an analogous phenomenon makes itself felt it immediately confines itself to this predisposed area, until the process becomes a matter of mechanical monotony.'[2] But like most medical metaphors, this one doesn't apply easily to the arts, where repetition of subject is not a certain contraindication to achievement. Most of these writers were conspicuous for their originality, and if they embraced so familiar a character from biblical history, it was to accomplish effects they intended to make distinctive. As there are many Iseults, many Marys, so there were many Salomes, without monotony.

The fact that Wilde's *Salomé* is a play, and a completed one, distinguishes it from other versions and helps to make it more original than Mr Praz would have us believe. Mallarmé was not merely flattering when he congratulated Wilde on the 'definitive evocation' of Salome,[3] or when he took care to avoid seeming to copy Wilde when he returned to work on his own 'Hérodiade'.[4] Wilde's simple sentences and repeated words may indeed owe something to Maeterlinck or even (as a contemporary critic suggested) to Ollendorff; but they have become so habitual in modern drama as to seem

21

anticipatory rather than derivative. The extreme concentration upon a single episode which is like an image, with a synchronised moon changing colour from pale to blood-red in keeping with the action, and an atmosphere of frenzy framed in exotic chill, confirms Yeats's oblique acknowledgement that he had learned as much from Wilde as from the Noh drama for his dance plays.[5] A torpid tetrarch (three Herods telescoped into one)[6] lusting yet inert, a prophet clamouring from a well below the floorboards, are more congenial figures now that Beckett has accustomed us to paralysis, senile drivelling, voices from ashcans and general thwart.

Mr Praz, quick to deny Wilde any novelty, insists that the play's culminating moment, when Salomé kisses the severed head of Jokanaan, is borrowed from Heine's 'Atta Troll'.[7] But in Heine's version kissing the head is a punishment after Herodias' death, not a *divertissement* before it, and the tone of caricature is quite unlike that of perverted horror which Wilde evokes. If some source has to be found – and it always has – I offer tentatively a dramatic poem called *Salome* published in Cambridge, Massachusetts, in 1862, by a young Harvard graduate named J. C. Heywood,[8] and subsequently republished during the 1880s in London in the form of a trilogy. I have to admit that in Heywood as in Heine, it is Herodias, not Salome, who kisses the head, but at least she does so while still alive, and in a sufficiently grisly way. Wilde knew one part of Heywood's trilogy – he reviewed it in 1888, three years before writing his own play[9] – and he may well have glanced at the other parts. Still, he is not really dependent on Heywood either, since he exchanges mother for daughter and, unlike Heywood, makes this monstrous kissing the play's climax.[10]

To read Heywood or other writers about Salome is to come to a greater admiration for Wilde's ingenuity. The general problem that I want to enquire into is what the play probably meant to Wilde and how he came to write it. Villainous women were not his usual subject, and even if they had been, there were others besides Salome he could have chosen. The reservoir of villainous women is always brimming. The choice of Salome would seem to inhere in her special relationship to John the Baptist and Herod. The sources offer little help in understanding this, and we have to turn to what might be called praeter-sources, elements which so pervaded Wilde's imaginative life as to become presences. Such a presence Amadis was for Don Quixote, or Vergil for Dante. In pursuing these I will offer no *explication de texte*, but what may well appear a divagation; perhaps to give it critical standing I should write it *divagation*, though I hope to show its clandestine relevance. It includes, at any rate, those fugitive associations, often subliminal, which swarm beneath the fixed surface of the work, and which are as pertinent as is that surface to any study of the author's mind.

II

It will be necessary, therefore, to retrace certain of Wilde's close relationships. If Rilke is right in finding a few moments in a writer's life to be initiatory, then such an initiatory experience took place when Wilde left Ireland for England. He later said that the two turning-points in his life occurred 'when my father sent me to Oxford, and when society sent me to prison'.[11] Wilde matriculated at Magdalen College, Oxford, on 11 October 1874, just before he was twenty. The two men he had most wanted to know at that time, he said, were Ruskin and Pater,[12] both, conveniently enough, installed at the same place. He managed to meet Ruskin within a month, and though he did not meet Pater so quickly, during his first three months at Oxford he made the acquaintance of Pater's *Studies in the History of the Renaissance*,[13] which he soon called his 'golden book',[14] and subsequently referred to in a portentous phrase as 'that book which has had such a strange influence over my life'.[15]

Three weeks after Wilde arrived, Ruskin gave a series of lectures on Florentine painting. During one of them he proposed to his students that, instead of developing their bodies in pointless games, in learning 'to leap and to row, to hit a ball with a bat',[16] they join him in improving the countryside. He proposed to turn a swampy lane near Ferry Hinksey into a flower-bordered country road. Such muscular effort would be ethical rather than narcissistic, medieval rather than classical.[17] Although Oscar Wilde found rising at dawn more difficult than most men, he overcame his languor for Ruskin's sake. He would later brag comically that he had had the distinction of being allowed to fill 'Mr Ruskin's especial wheelbarrow' and even of being instructed by the master himself in the mysteries of wheeling such an object from place to place. At the end of term Ruskin was off to Venice, and Wilde could again lie late abed, comfortable in the thought that, as he said, 'there was a long mound of earth across that swamp which a lively imagination might fancy was a road'.[18] The merely external signs of this noble enterprise soon sank from sight, but Wilde remembered it with affectionate respect, and his later insistence on functionalism in decoration and in women's dress, and on socialism based upon self-fulfilment in groups, were in the Ferry Hinksey tradition.

The road proved also to be the road to Ruskin. Wilde met his exalted foreman often during the ensuing years. In 1888, sending him a book, he summed up his feelings in this effusive tribute:

> The dearest memories of my Oxford days are my walks and talks with you, and from you I learned nothing but what was good. How else could it be? There is in you something of prophet, of priest, and of poet, and to you the gods gave eloquence such as they have given to none other, so that your message might come to us with the fire of passion, and the marvel of music, making the deaf to hear, and the blind to see.[19]

That (like this prose) the prophet had weaknesses, made him if anything more prophetlike. Wilde was as aware of Ruskin's weaknesses as of his virtues. His letter of 28 November 1879, by which time he had taken his Oxford degree, mentions that he and Ruskin were going that night to see Henry Irving play Shylock, following which he himself was going on to the Millais ball. 'How odd it is,' Wilde remarks.[20] The oddity lay not only in attending this particular play with the author of *The Stones of Venice*, but in proceeding afterwards to a ball which celebrated the marriage of John Everett Millais' daughter. Mrs Millais had for six years been Mrs Ruskin, and for three of those years Millais had been Ruskin's friend and protégé. The details of Ruskin's marriage and annulment were no doubt as well known at that time at Oxford by word of mouth as they have since become to us by dint of a dozen books. It was the fact that Ruskin and the Millaises did not speak to each other that obliged Wilde to leave Ruskin with Irving and proceed to the ball alone.

To call the Ruskin ambience merely odd was Oxonian politeness. As soon as Ruskin was married, he explained to his wife that children would interfere with his work and impede necessary scholarly travel. Consummation might therefore be deferred until later on, perhaps in six years' time when Effie would be twenty-five. Few of us could claim an equal dedication to learning. In the meantime Effie need have no fear about the possible sinfulness of their restraint, since many early Christians lived in married celibacy all their lives. Effie tried to accommodate herself to this pedantic view, and Ruskin in turn was glad to oblige her on a lesser matter: that they go to live in Venice, since he was already planning to write a book about that city.

In Venice, while Ruskin sketched, Effie survived her boredom by going about with one or another of their friends. Ruskin encouraged her, perhaps (as she afterwards implied) too much. If he accompanied her to dances and masked balls, he often left early without her, having arranged that some gentleman friend escort her home. If she returned at 1:30 in the morning, he duly notified his parents in England, at the same time adding that he was completely at rest about her fidelity.[21] Yet her obvious pleasure in pleasure, her flirtatiousness, her impatience with his studies, her delight in frivolity and late hours, struck Ruskin sometimes – however much he repudiated the outward thought – as forms of misconduct and disloyalty. He said as much later. That Effie was not sexually unfaithful to him did not of course prevent Ruskin, any more than it prevented Othello before him, from considering her so, or from transposing her mental dissonance into larger, vaguer forms of betrayal.

The Stones of Venice will always stand primarily as a work of art criticism. But criticism, as Wilde said, is the only civilised form of autobiography,[22] and it is as a fragment – a large fragment – of Ruskin's autobiography that the book claims an added interest. In novels and poems we take for granted that some personal elements will be reflected, but in works of non-fiction we are more reluctant, and prefer to postulate an upper air of abstraction in which the dispassionate mind contemplates and orders materials that already have form and substance. Yet even the most impersonal of writers, Thucydides, writing about the fortunes of another city, shaped his events by preconceptions absorbed from Greek tragedy. Ruskin made no pretence of Thucydidean impersonality, and the influence of his reading of the Bible is manifest rather than latent. But some problems of his own life also were projected onto the Venetian scene. Rather than diminishing the book's value, they merge with its talent and add to its intensity.

It may be easier to be convinced that *The Stones of Venice* is in part autobiographical if we remember Ruskin's candid admission that *Sesame and Lilies*, a book he wrote a few years later, was a reflection of one particular experience. His preface expressly states that the section in it called 'Lilies' was generated by his love for Rose La Touche. This love impelled him to idealise women, he says, even though

the chances of later life gave me opportunities of watching women in states of degradation and vindictiveness which opened to me the gloomiest secrets of Greek and Syrian tragedy. I have seen them betray their household charities to lust, their pledged love to devotion; I have seen mothers dutiful to their children, as Medea; and children dutiful to their parents, as the daughter of Herodias.

His love for Rose La Touche also covertly leads him to quarrel in the book with pietism because Rose was that way inclined. *The Stones of Venice* deals less obviously, but with the same insistence, on the virtues and defects of the feminine character. As Ruskin remarks in *Sesame and Lilies*, 'it has chanced to me, untowardly in some respects, fortunately in others (*because it enables me to read history more clearly*), to see the utmost evil that is in women . . . ' (my italics).[23] To Ruskin Venice is always *she*, and the gender is not merely a form of speech but an image to be enforced in detail.

Accordingly Ruskin distinguishes two stages, with medieval Venice as virgin and Renaissance Venice as whore. The moment of transition is, apparently, the moment of copulation, and the moment of copulation is therefore (as in a familiar view of the Garden of Eden) the fall. When Ruskin describes the fallen state, he attributes to the city the very taste for masqued balls and merriment which he had ostentatiously tolerated in his wife. 'She became in after times,' he declares, 'the revel of the earth, the masque of Italy: and *therefore* is she now desolate, but her glorious robe of gold and purple was given her when first she rose a vestal from the sea, not when she became drunk with the wine of her fornication.'[24] At the end of the first volume he again asserts, 'It was when she wore the ephod of the priest, not the motley of the masquer, that the fire fell upon her from heaven.'[25] After that fire came another which changed the virgin city to its contrary:

Now Venice, as she was once the most religious, was in her fall the most corrupt, of European states; and as she was in her strength the centre of the pure currents of Christian architecture, so she is in her decline the source of the Renaissance. It was the originality and splendour of the Palaces of Vicenza and Venice which gave this school its eminence in the eyes of Europe; and the dying city, magnificent in her dissipation, and graceful in her follies, obtained wider worship in her decrepitude than in her youth, and sank from the midst of her admirers into her grave.[26]

Ruskin cannot bring himself to sketch out

the steps of her final ruin. That ancient curse was upon her, the curse of the cities of the plain, 'pride, fulness of bread, and abundance of idleness.' By the inner burning of her own passions, as fatal as the fiery reign of Gomorrah, she was consumed from her place among the nations, and her ashes are choking the channels of the dead salt sea.[27]

Just how passions should burn except inwardly may not be clear, especially since we cannot suppose that Ruskin favoured the translation of sensual thought into sensual action, but pride, gluttony and sloth secure a more sinister confederate in the unnamable sin of lust, whose self-generated fire is contrasted with that fire which had earlier fallen on the city from heaven.

Ruskin's stridency shows how much he had this problem at heart. In fact, consummation and defilement were irrevocably united for him, in his life as in his criticism. The Renaissance (a new term then but already favourable in its connotations)[28] was for him not a rebirth but a relapse. (In *De Profundis* Wilde accepted this view.) Ruskin's revulsion extended from coupling to begetting to having been begot. He had more trouble than most people in allowing that he was himself the product of his parents' intercourse. A small indication is to be found in an epitaph which he wrote for his mother (who already had an epitaph) long after her death, consecrating a memorial well, as he writes, 'in memory of a maid's life as pure, and a mother's love as ceaseless . . . '[29] In Ruskin's mind his mother had immaculately passed from maid to mother without ever becoming a wife.

Margaret Ruskin's marriage had made her a mother, while Effie Ruskin's 'dissolute' behaviour in Venice had made her – in fancy if not in fact – an adulteress. Moral blame, from which his mother was freed, was shunted to his wife. Ruskin's own later summary of *The Stones of Venice* confirms that he had this theme in mind. In *The Crown of Wild Olive* (1866) he wrote, '*The Stones of Venice* had, from beginning to end, no other aim than to show that the Renaissance architecture of Venice had arisen out of, and in all its features indicated, a state of concealed national infidelity, and of domestic corruption.'[30] The trip to Scotland which Ruskin, his wife and Millais took in 1853 strengthened the metaphors, and in later life he accused Millais of infidelity – artistic infidelity he called it[31] – to the Pre-Raphaelite principles as Ruskin had earlier enunciated them. Venice, his wife and his friend were all guilty of the same crime.

Necessary as Ruskin found it to think of himself as wronged, there were moments when he recognised his own culpability. After the annulment of his marriage he came, by a series of mental leaps, to try a revision of his character. In 1858, while looking at Veronese's *Solomon and Sheba* in Turin, he suddenly felt a wave of sympathy for the 'strong and frank animality' of the greatest artists.[32] He disavowed his earlier religious zeal, and became (though at the urging of his father and of Rose La Touche's mother he did not publicly say so) quite sceptical. Then, as Wilenski points out, he began to acknowledge that his theory of history in *The Stones of Venice* was mistaken. Writing to Froude in 1864, he stated firmly, 'There is no law of history any more than of a kaleidoscope. With certain bits of glass – shaken so, and so – you will get pretty figures, but what figures, Heaven only knows . . . The wards of a Chubb's lock are infinite in their chances. Is the Key of Destiny made on a less complex principle?'[33] This renunciation of historical law was intellectually daring, and emotionally as well, for it meant that he was trying to alter those 'pretty figures' which earlier had enabled him to lock his own conception and marriage into the history of Venice. As part of this change, he resolved to propose marriage to Rose La Touche, and in 1866 he at last did so. Rose La Touche, no mean calendar-watcher herself, said she could not answer for two years, or perhaps for four. Ruskin abided by her verdict with desperation; his diary records the passing of not only these anniversaries but, since she died soon after, of year after year following her death.[34] No one will mock Ruskin's pain, or his struggle to overcome his fears and become as animal as Veronese.

III

Rose La Touche had been dead less than a year when Ruskin and Wilde met and took walks together. Neither professor nor pupil was reticent, and Wilde probably divined the matters that Ruskin was unwilling to confide. At any rate, the moral law as imparted by Ruskin, even with the softenings he now wished to introduce, was for Wilde sublime – and berserk. In Ruskin, whom everyone called a prophet, the ethical life was noble and yet, in its weird chastity, perverse. Against its rigours life offered an antidote, and what life was had been articulated by Pater, who saw it not in terms of stones but of waters, not of monuments but of rivery passions. Pater was like Wilde in that, at the same age of nineteen, he too had fallen under Ruskin's sway. He soon broke free; his conscience unclenched itself. He surprised a devout friend by nonetheless attempting, although he had lost his faith, to take orders in the Anglican Church. His friend complained to the bishop and scotched this diabolic ordination. The *Studies in the History of the Renaissance*, Pater's first book, does not mention Ruskin by name, but uses him throughout as an adversary. Pater's view of the Renaissance did not differ in being more detached; in its way it was just as personal, and it ended in a secular sermon which ran exactly counter to that of *The Stones of Venice*. It is Ruskin inverted. Pater is all blend where Ruskin is all severance. He calls superficial Ruskin's view that the Renaissance was 'a fashion which set in at a definite period'. For Pater it was rather 'an uninterrupted effort of the middle age'.[35] One age was older, one younger; they encountered each other like lovers.

An atmosphere of suppressed invitation runs through Pater's book as an atmosphere of suppressed refusal runs through Ruskin's. The first essay of *Studies in the . . . Renaissance* recounts at length how the friendship of Amis and Amile (in the thirteenth-century story) was so full and intense that they were buried together rather than with their respective wives. Later essays dwell with feeling upon such encounters as that of young Pico della Mirandola, looking like a Phidian statue, with the older Ficino, or as that – planned but prevented by murder – of Winckelmann and the still callow Goethe. For Ruskin the Renaissance is an aged Jezebel, while for Pater it is a young man, his hair wreathed in roses more than in thorns, such a youth as Leonardo painted as John the Baptist. In describing this painting, Pater lingers to point out that the saint's body does not look as if it had come from a wilderness, and he finds John's smile intriguingly treacherous and suggestive of a good deal[36] – which may be Victorian hinting at the heresy, a specially homosexual one, that Christ and John (not to mention Leonardo and his model) were lovers.[37]

Whatever Ruskin says about strength and weakness, Pater opposes. The decay against which *The Stones of Venice* fulminates is for Pater 'the fascination of corruption';[38] and images of baleful female power, such as Leonardo's Medusa and other 'daughters of Herodias', are discovered to be 'clairvoyant' and 'electric',[39] when Ruskin had found the daughter of Herodias monstrously degraded. Instead of praising the principle of *Noli me tangere*, so ardently espoused by Ruskin, Pater objects to Christian asceticism that it 'discredits the slightest sense of touch'. Ruskin had denounced 'ripe' ornamentation in terms which evoked elements of the adult female body:

I mean [he said] that character of extravagance in the ornament itself which shows that it was addressed to jaded faculties; a violence and coarseness in curvature, a depth of shadow, a lusciousness in arrangement of line, evidently arising out of an incapability of feeling the true beauty of chaste forms and restrained power. I do not know any character of design which may be more easily recognized at a glance than this over-lusciousness . . . We speak loosely and inaccurately of 'overcharged' ornament, with an obscure feeling that there is indeed something in visible Form which is correspondent to Intemperance in moral habits.[40]

But for Pater overcharged ornament is rather an 'overwrought delicacy, almost of wantonness', or 'a languid Eastern delicious-ness'.[41]

Ruskin strenuously combated what he considered to be a false fusion of classicism and Christianity in the Renaissance. 'It would have been better,' he said, 'to have worshipped Diana and Jupiter at once than have gone through life naming one God, imagining another, and dreading none.'[42] Galleries had no business placing Aphrodite and the Madonna, a Bacchanal and a Nativity, side by side.[43] But this juxtaposition was exactly what Pater endorsed. For him European culture was what he called, following Hegel to some extent, a synthesis. To countervail Ruskin's diptych of Venice as virgin of the Adriatic and whore of Babylon, he offered as his Renaissance altarpiece the Mona Lisa of Leonardo. His famous description begins, 'The presence that rose beside the waters', and it is clear that he is summoning up not only Lisa, but Venus rising like Ruskin's favourite city from the sea. Lisa has, according to this gospel of Saint Walter, mothered both Mary and Helen, exactly the indiscriminateness, as well as the fecundity, which Ruskin condemned. Pater's heroine, as Salvador Dali has implied by giving her a moustache more suited to Pater, is an androgyne: the activities attributed to her, dealing with foreign merchants and diving in deep seas, seem more male than female. She blends the sexes, she combines sacred and profane. Like Saint John, she has about her something of the Borgias.

Against Ruskin's insistence upon innocence, Pater proffers what he bathetically terms, in the suppressed and then altered and reinstated conclusion to the *Renaissance*, 'great experiences'. He urges his readers to seek out high passions, only being sure they are passions; later, only being sure they are high. The Renaissance is for him the playtime of sensation, even its spiritual aspects being studies in forms of sensation. W. H. Mallock parodied this aspect by having Pater, as the effete 'Mr Rose' in *The New Republic*, lust for a pornographic book. Something of the extraordinary effect of Pater's *Renaissance* comes from its being exercises in the seduction of young men by the wiles of culture. And yet Pater may not have seduced them in any way except stylistically. When Wilde presented Lord Alfred Douglas to him, the flagrancy of the homosexual relationship was probably, as Lawrence Evans suggests, the cause of the rift between Pater and Wilde which then developed.

IV

Ruskin and Pater were for Wilde at first imagined, and then actual figures; then they came to stand heraldically, burning unicorn and uninflammable satyr, in front of two portals of his mental theatre. He sometimes allowed them to battle, at other times tried to reconcile them. A good example is his first long published work. This was an ambitious review of the paintings in a new London gallery; he wrote it in 1877, his third year at Oxford, for the *Dublin University Magazine*. The article takes the form of a rove through the three rooms, which had been done, Wilde said admiringly, 'in scarlet damask above a dado of dull green and gold'. (Ruskin, who also attended, complained that this decor was 'dull in itself' and altogether unsuited to the pictures.) Upon entering, Wilde immediately belauds Burne-Jones and Hunt as 'the greatest masters of colour that we have ever had in England, with the single exception of Turner' – a compliment to Ruskin's advocacy of Turner and to the sponsorship of the Pre-Raphaelites by both Ruskin and Pater. Wilde then, to praise Burne-Jones further, quotes Pater's remark that for Botticelli natural things 'have a spirit upon them by which they become expressive to the spirit', and as he sweeps through the gallery he finds occasion to savour the same sweet phrase again. He also manages to mention the portrait of Ruskin by Millais, though it was not on exhibition. Reaching the end, he salutes 'that revival of culture and love of beauty which in great part owes its birth to Mr Ruskin, and which Mr Swinburne and Mr Pater and Mr Symons and Mr Morris and many others are fostering and keeping alive, each in his peculiar fashion'. He slipped another quotation from Pater into this final paragraph, but a watchful editor slipped it out again.

Wilde's review of the exhibition is not so interesting as Ruskin's, in *Fors Clavigera* 79, which roused Millais to fury and Whistler to litigation. But it did result in Wilde's finally meeting Pater, who, having been sent a copy of the review, invited him to call. Their subsequent friendship, though hardly close, afforded Wilde the chance to study the student of the Renaissance. He did not lose his admiration, as we can surmise from the poem 'Hélas!' which he wrote a

little later. In it he invokes both of his mentors as if they were
contrary forces tugging at him. After owning up to frivolity, Wilde
says:

> Surely there was a time I might have trod
> The august[44] heights, and from life's dissonance
> Struck one clear chord to reach the ears of God.

The chief reference is to Gothic architecture, celebrated by Ruskin
because, though fraught with human imperfection – 'life's
dissonance' – it reached towards heaven. In the next lines Wilde
confesses to having fallen away a little:

> Is that time dead? Lo, with a little rod,
> I did but touch the honey of romance.
> And must I lose a soul's inheritance?

Here he is quoting Jonathan's remark to Saul, 'I did but taste a little
honey with the end of the rod that was in mine hand, and lo! I must
die', which Wilde remembered Pater's having conspicuously quoted
and interpreted in the *Renaissance* in his essay on Winckelmann.
For Pater Jonathan's remark epitomises 'the artistic life, with its
inevitable sensuousness', and is contrasted with Christian asceticism and its antagonism to touch.[45] If the taste for honey is a little
decadent, then so much the better. Wilde is less sanguine about this
appetite here. But as Jonathan was saved, so Wilde, for all his
alases, expected to be saved too, partly because he had never
renounced the Ruskin conscience, only foregone it for a time.

The tutelary presences of Pater and Ruskin survived in Wilde's
more mature writings. In *The Picture of Dorian Gray*, for example,
Pater is enclosed (like an unhappy dryad caught in a tree trunk) in
Lord Henry Wotton. Lord Henry's chief sin is quoting without
acknowledgement from the *Renaissance*. He tells Dorian, as Pater
told Mona Lisa, 'You have drunk deeply of everything . . . and it has
all been to you no more than the sound of music.' He predicts,
against the 'curious revival of Puritanism' (a cut at Ruskin), a new
hedonism, the aim of which will be 'experience itself, and not the
fruits of experience'. It will 'teach man to concentrate himself upon
the moments of a life that is but a moment'. These are obvious tags
from the Conclusion to the *Renaissance*. Lord Henry's advice to
Dorian, 'Let nothing be lost upon you. Be always searching for new
sensations,' was so closely borrowed from the same essay that Pater,
who wrote a review of the book, was at great pains to distinguish

Lord Henry's philosophy from his own. Wilde seems to have intended not to distinguish them, however, and to offer (through the disastrous effects of Lord Henry's influence upon Dorian) a criticism of Pater.

As for Ruskin, his presence in the book is more tangential. The painter Hallward has little of Ruskin at the beginning, but gradually he moves closer to that pillar of aesthetic taste and moral judgement upon which Wilde leaned, and after Hallward is safely murdered, Dorian with sudden fondness recollects a trip they had made to Venice together, when his friend was captivated by Tintoretto's art. Ruskin was of course the English discoverer and champion of Tintoretto, so that the allusion is specific. The ending of *Dorian Gray* executes a Ruskinesque repudiation of a Pateresque career of self-gratifying sensations. Wilde defined the moral in so witty a way as to content neither of his mentors: in letters to newspapers he said *Dorian Gray* showed that 'all excess, as well as all renunciation, brings its own punishment'.[46] Not only are Hallward and Dorian punished by death, but, Wilde asserted, Lord Henry is punished too. Lord Henry's offence was in seeking 'to be merely the spectator of life. He finds that those who reject the battle are more deeply wounded than those who take part in it.'[47] The phrase 'spectator of life' was one that Wilde used in objecting to Pater's *Marius the Epicurean*.[48] However incongruous his conception of himself as activist, with it he lorded it over his too donnish friend. For Pater, while he touted (sporadically at least) the life of pleasure, was careful not to be caught living it. He idealised touch until it became contemplation. He allowed only his eye to participate in the high passions about which he loved to expiate. Dorian at least had the courage to risk himself.

In *Dorian Gray* the Pater side of Wilde's thought is routed, though not deprived of fascination. Yet Hallward, when his ethical insistence brings him close to Ruskin, is killed too. In 'The Soul of Man under Socialism', also written in 1891, Wilde superimposes Ruskin's social ethic upon Pater's 'full expression of personality', fusing instead of destroying them. In *Salomé*, to which I come at last, the formulation is close to *Dorian Gray*, with both opposites executed. Behind the figure of Jokanaan lurks the image of that perversely untouching, untouchable prophet John whom Wilde knew at Oxford. When Jokanaan, up from his cistern for a moment, cries to Salomé, 'Arrière, fille de Sodome! Ne me touchez pas. Il ne faut pas profaner le temple du Seigneur Dieu' ['Back, daughter of

Sodom! Touch me not. Profane not the temple of the Lord God'],[49] a thought of Ruskin, by now sunk down into madness, can scarcely have failed to cross Wilde's mind. By this time Wilde would also have recognised in the prophet's behaviour (as in Ruskin's) something of his own, for after his first three years of marriage he had discontinued sexual relations with his wife. Jokanaan is not Ruskin, but he is Ruskinism as Wilde understood that pole of his character. Then when Salomé evinces her appetite for strange experiences, her eagerness to kiss a literally disembodied lover in a relation at once totally sensual and totally 'mystical'[50] (Wilde's own term for her), she shows something of that diseased contemplation of life for which Wilde had reprehended Pater. Her adaptation, or perversion, of the Song of Songs to describe a man's rather than a woman's beauty also is reminiscent of Pater's *Renaissance* as well as of Wilde's predisposition. It is Salomé, and not Pater, who dances the dance of the seven veils, but her virginal yet perverse sensuality is related to Paterism.

Admittedly the play takes place in Judaea and not in Oxford. Wilde wanted the play to have meaning outside his own psychodrama. Yet Wilde's tutelary voices from the university, now fully identified as forces within himself, seem to be in attendance, clamouring for domination. Both Jokanaan and Salomé are executed, however, and at the command of the Tetrarch. The execution of Salome was not in the Bible, but Wilde insisted upon it.[51] So at the play's end the emphasis shifts suddenly to Herod, who is seen to have yielded to Salomé's sensuality, and then to the moral revulsion of Jokanaan from that sensuality, and to have survived them both. In Herod Wilde was suggesting that *tertium quid* which he felt to be his own nature, susceptible to contrary impulses but not abandoned for long to either.

Aubrey Beardsley divined the autobiographical element in Herod, and in one of his illustrations gave the Tetrarch the author's face. Herod speaks like Wilde in purple passages about peacocks or in such an epigram as, 'Il ne faut pas regarder que dans les miroirs. Car les miroirs ne nous montrent que les masques' ['Only in mirrors should one look, for mirrors do but show us masks'].[52] Just what Wilde thought his own character to be, as distinct from the alternating forces of Pater and Ruskin, is implied in a remark he made in 1883 to George Woodberry, who promptly relayed it to Charles Eliot Norton. Wilde told Woodberry that Ruskin 'like Christ bears the sins of the world, but that he himself was "always like Pilate, washing his hands of all responsibility" '.[53] Pilate in the story of Christ occupies much the same role as Herod in the story of John the Baptist. In other letters Wilde continues to lament his own weakness, yet with so much attention as to imply that it may have a certain fibre to it. In March 1877 he wrote, 'I shift with every breath of thought and am weaker and more self-deceiving than ever,'[54] and in 1886 he remarked, 'Sometimes I think that the artistic life is a long and lovely suicide, and am not sorry that it is so.'[55] What he more and more held against both his mentors was a vice they shared equally, that of narrowness. To keep to any one form of life is limiting, he said in *De Profundis*, and added without remorse, 'I had to pass on.'[56]

Herod too passes on, strong in his tremblings, a leaf but a sinuous one, swept but not destroyed by successive waves of spiritual and physical passion, in possession of what Wilde in a letter calls 'a curious mixture of ardour and of indifference. I myself would sacrifice everything for a new experience, and I know there is no such thing as a new experience at all . . . I would go to the stake for a sensation and be a sceptic to the last!'[57] Here too there is martyrdom and abandonment, with a legal right to choose and yet stay aloof. Proust had something of the same idea when he said of Whistler's quarrel with Ruskin that both men were right.[58] In that same reconciling vein Wilde in *De Profundis* celebrates Christ as an artist, and the artist as Christ. And in Wilde's last play, when Jack declares at the end, 'I've now realized for the first time in my life the vital Importance of Being Earnest', he is demonstrating again that Ruskin's earnestness, and Pater's paraded passionateness, are for the artist not mutually exclusive but may, by wit, by weakness, by self-withholding, be artistically, as well as tetrarchically, compounded.

3 Strauss as librettist

ROLAND TENSCHERT

I

The fact that Richard Strauss,[1] after having seen some introductory scenes in verse, decided not to set a *Salome* libretto planned by the Viennese author Anton Lindner, turning instead to Hedwig Lachmann's German translation of the French original, is widely taken to mean that the composer set Lachmann's text to music 'lock, stock and barrel'. After all, the literature repeatedly states that this is a rare example of a spoken drama which has been set to music unaltered. That this is not the case will be shown with reference to Strauss's own 'adaptation' of Lachmann's libretto, which Franz Strauss[2] kindly permitted me to examine. Although the composer's alterations consist mainly of cuts, which are of course not irrelevant to the elucidation of his intentions, the relatively few changes that he made to the diction are in a variety of ways characteristic of his clarity of vision. Over and above this a number of annotations which directly anticipate the composition offer certain insights into Strauss's creative process. So it is worth examining in greater detail the libretto that he himself arranged.

His copy, in contrast to one in the Theatre Collection of the Austrian National Library (629.094-B Th.), which is the second edition, has no pagination, though in addition to the two title pages it contains ten drawings by Marcus Behmer in place of the two in the later edition.[3] In the copy used by Strauss the page with the dramatis personae is missing, and the composer has entered them in by hand. Yet the Lachmann text (in the second edition) still mentions Tigellinus, a young Roman; a Nubian; Salome's slaves; and one Mannai, the Executioner.[4] [None of these characters appears in the opera, except for the Executioner, who has merely a walk-on part.]

The extent of the cuts to Lachmann's original text is fairly considerable, comprising just under half of the work. The excisions serve primarily to streamline the plot for musical purposes. Thus on a number of occasions they apply to repetitions of short sections of the text. Furthermore their purpose is to simplify the action through the elimination of more or less inessential subplots.

Above all Strauss restricts the dramatic delineation of the Young Syrian solely to the fact that he helps Salome to fulfil her wish to be allowed to see Jochanaan. In Wilde/Lachmann the character is elaborated in much greater detail. We learn that Narraboth (though the name does not yet appear)[5] is the son of a king who has been driven from his kingdom by the Tetrarch, Herod, and whose wife has become a slave of Herodias. The Young Syrian himself has only been a captain of the Tetrarch's bodyguard for three days, and the latter has a certain sympathy for him. The love of the Page for Narraboth, who is rather narcissistic, is only touched upon lightly by Strauss. After Narraboth's suicide Lachmann furnishes a short description of the unfortunate man, a passage which is given to the mourning Page. It includes the following lines:

Er war mein Bruder, ja er war mir näher als ein Bruder. Ich gab ihm eine kleine Nardenbüchse und einen Achatring, den er immer an der Hand trug. Abends gingen wir oft am Fluss spazieren und unter den Mandelbäumen, und er erzählte mir gern von seiner Heimat. Er sprach immer sehr leise. Der Klang seiner Stimme war wie der Klang der Flöte, wie wenn einer auf der Flöte spielt. Er hatte auch grosse Freude daran, im Fluss sein Bild zu betrachten. Ich habe ihn oft darum getadelt.

He was my brother, and nearer to me than a brother. I gave him a little box full of perfumes, and a ring of agate that he wore always on his hand. In the evening we used to walk by the river, among the almond trees, and he would tell me of the things of his country. He spake ever very low. The sound of his voice was like the sound of the flute, of a flute player. Also he much loved to gaze at himself in the river. I used to reproach him for that.

The original also describes in greater detail the fate of Herod's elder brother, the first husband of Queen Herodias, who was held captive for twelve years in the cistern in which Jochanaan is now imprisoned, and then strangled on the Tetrarch's orders. Together with the latter's brother Strauss also excises a quarrel between the royal couple relating to Jochanaan's accusation that the Tetrarch's marriage is sinful. Herod accuses his wife of infertility, whereupon she retorts:

Ich bin unfruchtbar, ich? . . . Du sprichst wie ein Narr. Ich habe ein Kind geboren. Du hast kein Kind gezeugt, nicht mit einer einzigen deiner Sklavinnen. An dir liegt es, nicht an mir!

I am sterile, I? . . . It is absurd to say that. I have borne a child. You have gotten no child, no, not even from one of your slaves. It is you who are sterile, not I.

Herod answers:

Still, Weib! Ich sage du bist unfruchtbar. Du hast mir kein Kind geboren, und der Prophet sagt . . . dass es eine Ehe der Blutschande ist . . .

Peace, woman! I say that you are sterile. You have borne me no child, and the prophet says . . . that it is an incestuous marriage . . .

Wilde/Lachmann repeatedly refers to Herod's hatred of the King of Cappadocia; this too fell victim to Strauss's red pencil. At one point we read:

Caesar, der der Herr der Welt ist, Caesar, der der Herr über alles ist, liebt mich gar sehr. Er hat mir höchst kostbare Geschenke übersandt. Auch hat er mir versprochen, den König von Cappadocien, der mein Feind ist, nach Rom vorzuladen. Kann sein, dass er ihn in Rom ans Kreuz schlagen lässt, denn er ist imstande, alles zu tun, wonach ihm der Sinn steht . . .

Caesar, who is lord of the world, who is lord of all things, loves me well. He has just sent me most precious gifts. Also he has promised me to summon to Rome the King of Cappadocia, who is my enemy. It may be that at Rome he will crucify him, for he is able to do all things that he wishes . . .

Herod later explains his grievance as follows:

Der König von Cappadocien trug immer Lügen im Mund, aber er ist kein echter König. Er ist ein Wicht. Er schuldet mir auch Geld, das er nicht heimzahlt. Er hat sogar meine Gesandten beleidigt. Er hat Worte gesprochen, die kränkend waren . . .

The Kind of Cappadocia always lies, but he is no true king. He is a coward. Also he owes me money that he will not repay. He has even insulted my ambassadors. He has spoken words that were wounding.

It is easy to see that this motive is not of essential importance for the streamlined plot of the opera. Nor is the discussion of the types of wine favoured by Herod:

Der Tetrarch liebt den Wein sehr. Er hat drei Sorten Wein. Den einen bringt man von der Insel Samothrake, er ist purpurn wie der Mantel des Caesar . . . Der zweite kommt aus einer Stadt namens Cypern und ist gelb wie Gold . . . Und der dritte ist ein Wein aus Sizilien. Dieser Wein ist rot wie Blut.

The Tetrarch is very fond of wine. He has wine of three sorts. One which is brought from the island of Samothrace, and is purple like the cloak of Caesar . . . Another that comes from a town called Cyprus, and is yellow like gold . . . And the third is a wine of Sicily. That wine is red like blood.

Much the same is true of the conversation in which the Nubian and the Cappadocian discuss their gods, of the quarrel among a Nazarene, a Sadducee and a Pharisee about the existence of angels, and of the gout plaguing Caesar. Not to mention the much more exhaustive 'collection of minerals and animals' in the original text with which Herod tries to change Salome's mind after she has demanded Jochanaan's head. As is well known, Strauss's considerably shortened version of this section was later subjected to even greater cuts.[6]

Certain passages in the text of Salome's final monologue seem to have been of some importance for the musical conception,[7] even though Strauss omitted them. They refer to the virginity of the Tetrarch's daughter. After 'Hättest du mich gesehen, so hättest du mich geliebt!' ('If thou hadst seen me thou wouldst have loved me'), Lachmann continues: 'Ich sah dich und ich liebte dich. O, wie liebte ich dich . . . ' ('I saw thee . . . and I loved thee. Oh, how I loved thee!'); and after 'nicht Wein noch Äpfel können mein Verlangen stillen . . . ' ('neither wine nor fruits can appease my desire'), we read:

Ich war eine Fürstin, und du verachtetest mich! Ich war eine Jungfrau, und du nahmst mir meine Keuschheit. Ich war rein und züchtig, und du hast Feuer in meine Adern gegossen . . .

I was a princess, and thou didst scorn me. I was a virgin, and thou didst take my virginity from me. I was chaste, and thou didst fill my veins with fire . . .

It may be that these passages were omitted in deference to the figure of Jochanaan.[8] Yet they surely had some influence on the musical conception of the opera's final scene.[9]

II

The cuts and changes also indicate Strauss's dislike of subordinate clauses, which impaired the precision and flow of the diction. The following comparisons show this quite clearly:

Lachmann:	Strauss:
Sie ist wie eine Taube, die sich verirrt hat . . .	Sie ist wie eine verirrte Taube . . .
auf dem Felde, das nie Sichel berührt hat . . .	auf einem Felde, von der Sichel nie berührt . . .

Nicht die Füsse der Dämmerung, wenn sie auf die Blätter herabsteigt . . .	Nicht die Füsse der Dämmerung auf den Blättern . . .
Das Schweigen, das im Walde wohnt . . .	Des Waldes Schweigen . . .
Der Purpur, den die Könige von ihnen haben . . .	Der Purpur der Könige . . .
Dein Mund ist wie ein Korallenzweig, den die Fischer in der Dämmerung des Meeres gefunden haben . . .	. . wie ein Korallenzweig aus der Dämmerung des Meeres . . .
kein König, der Pfauen hat, wie meine Pfauen sind . . .	kein König, der solche Pfauen hat . . .

Strauss also omitted the bracketed words in the following phrases:

. . . wie der Schnee[, der] auf den Bergen Judäas [liegt] . . .

. . . die Brüste des Mondes[, wenn er] auf dem Meere [liegt] . . .

. . . Büschel schwarzer Trauben[, die] an den Weinstöcken Edoms [hängen] . . .

. . . Granatäpfelblüten[, die] in den Gärten von Tyrus [wachsen], [die] glüh[e]nder [sind] als Rosen . . .

. . . eine sehr gefährliche Lehre[, die] aus Alexandria [kommt] . . .

Bei einer Hochzeit[, die in einer kleinen Stadt] in Galiläa [stattfand] . . .

. . . zwei Aussätzige[, die vor dem Tore] von Capernaum [sassen] . . .

. . . Topase[, die sind] hellrot wie die Augen einer Waldtaube und grüne Topase[, die sind] wie Katzenaugen . . .

. . . mit einem Feuer, [das] kalt wie Eis [ist] . . .

Those who remember the relevant Straussian vocal phrases will instinctively find the original form of Lachmann's text halting and uneven. In the passages cited above there are also instances where Strauss avoids the perfect tense. Two further examples of this should be mentioned: 'Jochanaan, der gerufen hat' ('Jochanaan who cried out') is changed to 'Jochanaan, der rief', and 'Sie hat der immer schlechten Rat gegeben' ('She [was] ever giving you evil counsel') to 'Sie gab dir . . . '

To achieve a better basis for a flowing melodic line, Strauss often reordered the words. The following passages are typical:

Strauss: 　　　　　　　2　　3　　4　　　1
Lachmann: Wie eine Frau, die aus dem Grab aufsteigt.
Strauss: 　　　　　　　　3　　4　　5　　6　　　7　　　1
Lachmann: Ich bin nicht wert, ihm die Riemen an seinen Schuh[e]n[10] zu
　　　　　　　2
　　　　　lösen.
Strauss: 　　　　　　3　　4　　2　1
Lachmann: Wie süss die Luft hier ist!
Strauss: 　　　11　10　　1　　2　　　3　　　4　　　5　　　6　　7　　8
Lachmann: Ich seh[e] den Abdruck deiner kleinen weissen Zähne in einer
　　　　　　　9　12　13
　　　　　Frucht so gern.
Strauss (in Lachmann's text): 　1　　2　3　　4　　　　　　　　　　　　10
Strauss (in final version): 　　　1　　2　3　　11　　　　　　　　　　　16
Lachmann: 　　　　　　　　　Wo ist sie, die vor den gemalten Männer-
　　　　　　　5　　　6　　7　　8　　　　　9
　　　　　　12　　　13　14　　　　　　　15
　　　　　bildern gestanden hat, vor den buntgemalten Bildern der
　　　　　　11　　12　　13　　14　　15　　16　　17　　18
　　　　　　4　　5　　　6　　　7　　　8　　9　　10　　17
　　　　　Chaldäer, die sich hingab der Lust ihrer Augen und
　　　　　19
　　　　　18
　　　　　Gesandte . . . [11]

Personal preference probably prompted other cuts. To this category I assign the following eliminated passages: 'Wie die Hand einer toten Frau, die das Laken über sich ziehen will' ('like the hand of a dead woman who is seeking to cover herself with a shroud') (the moon!); 'Sie sind, als ob schwarze Löcher mit Fackeln in einen tyrischen Teppich gebrannt worden wären' ('They are like black holes burned by torches in a Tyrian tapestry') (Jochanaan's eyes!); and 'Er ist röter als die Füsse des Mannes, der aus dem Walde kommt, wo er einen Löwen erschlagen und goldfarbige Tiger erblickt hat' ('It is redder than the feet of him who cometh from a forest where he hath slain a lion, and seen gilded tigers') (Jochanaan's mouth!). It is also quite understandable that Jochanaan's disagreeably theatrical exclamation 'Diese Hure! Ha!' ('The harlot! Ah!') found no favour with Strauss.

Although Strauss excises textual repetitions that impede the flow of the music, as has been emphasised, he gladly makes use of corresponding passages to facilitate formal organisation. For example, he makes a note of the following lines in the libretto by writing numbers in the margin:[12]

I Salome: Ich bin nicht durstig, Tetrarch.
II Salome: Ich bin nicht hungrig, Tetrarch.
III Salome: Ich bin nicht müde, Tetrarch.

In Jochanaan's first arioso the composer actually creates a framework for the formal organisation by means of a repetition he himself has introduced, one which is linked with an accentuated motive [ ]. Lachmann writes:

Wenn er kommt, werden die verödeten Stätten frohlocken. Sie werden aufblühen wie die Rosen. Die Augen der Blinden werden den Tag sehen und die Ohren der Tauben werden geöffnet.

When He cometh, the solitary places shall be glad. They shall blossom like the lily. The eyes of the blind shall see the day, and the ears of the deaf shall be opened.

Strauss restructures and at the same time simplifies this by changing it to: '*Wenn er kommt*, werden die verödeten Stätten frohlocken. *Wenn er kommt*, werden die Augen der Blinden den Tag sehn. *Wenn er kommt*, die Ohren der Tauben geöffnet' (my italics). The motive to the words thus repeated acquires even greater significance in the ensuing dialogue.

When one considers how much in Strauss's *Salome* music derives from Wilde/Lachmann's continually changing moods of the moon, which could almost claim to be mentioned in the list of characters,[13] one is happy to accept that even here the composer deemed certain cuts necessary. And in the choice of the excisions, too, Strauss had an infallible sense of what was right. Besides certain extravagant passages, which fell victim to the red pencil, he cut the following: 'Wie eine tote Frau, man könnte meinen, sie blickt nach toten Dingen aus' ('She is like a dead woman. You would fancy she was looking for dead things').[14] The Page interprets Narraboth's suicide as evidence that the moon was indeed seeking a dead thing:

Ach, warum barg ich ihn nicht vor dem Mond! Hätte ich ihn in einer Höhle verborgen, dann hätte er ihn nicht gesehen.

Ah! why did I not hide him from the moon? If I had hidden him in a cavern she would not have seen him.

The comparison of the moon with a madwoman who is 'seeking everywhere for lovers' is further elaborated in the original:

Und nackt ist es, ganz nackt. Die Wolken wollen seine Nacktheit bekleiden, aber das Weib lässt sie nicht. Es stellt sich nackt am Himmel zur Schau . . .

She is naked, too. She is quite naked. The clouds are seeking to clothe her nakedness, but she will not let them. She shows herself naked in the sky . . .

Wilde's spoken drama may be said to have made too liberal a use of moon imagery. Nevertheless Strauss took over much of this, and substantially elaborated it with his music, something that was not possible to the same extent for the mere word or the stage designer. Such limitations notwithstanding, modern lighting technique makes it less justifiable than ever to go so far as to ignore completely onstage the moon 'prop' that is so important in *Salome* and, as happens at the Vienna State Opera, simply to presume the existence in the auditorium of the satellite that repeatedly plays a role in the plot both visually and symbolically – a policy which relieves the producer of the duty of representing it pale or bloodred, clear or cloud-covered, and whatever else the work requires.[15] The very first bars of Strauss's music categorically demand this companion, interpreter and even disposer of the fates of the operatic characters in the night sky. The opening stage direction says: 'Der Mond scheint sehr hell . . .' ('The moon shines very brightly'),[16] and the final direction, after the disc has disappeared behind a large cloud during Salome's fateful kiss, states: 'Der Mond bricht wieder hervor und beleuchtet Salome' ('A moonbeam falls on Salomé covering her with light').

III

Let us turn now to some of Strauss's annotations in Lachmann's text, annotations which already relate to the musical creative process in its incipient stages. There are only a handful of short jottings, cues and musical sketches which permit us to observe the composer at work. Some of these were either not elaborated or later changed, but everything exudes the fresh immediacy of inspiration. In particular it seems that Strauss was attracted by the beginning, which was of course most important for the discovery of a new style appropriate to this particular work. The introductory key of C sharp minor, which is so characteristic of *Salome*, is established at once, and the first sentence of the Young Syrian, 'Wie schön ist die

Prinzessin Salome heute Nacht!' ('How beautiful is the Princess Salome tonight!'), appears precisely delineated in terms of its vocal rhythm through the insertion of barlines (see Plate 3). Here, and in some of the following sentences, the musical treatment of line-beginnings that avoid the strong beat is hinted at by means of strokes. The significance that Strauss accorded to the tonal, or merely chordal, definition of certain words is shown by many short jottings of this kind. Of course the first sketch does not always have to be identical with the final result. In addition to the famous C sharp minor beginning, Strauss jotted down the D minor chord on 'Sie streiten über ihre Religi*on*' ('They are disputing about their religion'),[17] the C minor chord on 'Wie *blass* die Prinzessin ist' ('How pale the Princess is!'),[18] the D major chord on 'wie abgezehrt er *ist*!' ('How wasted he is !') and the D flat major chord at the end of the same sentence: 'Gewiss ist er keusch wie der *Mond* . . . ' ('I am sure he is chaste as the moon is').[19] However, the jottings in the libretto envisage C minor, D minor and E flat minor chords for Jochanaan's repeated exclamation 'Sei verflucht' ('Cursed be thou!') or 'Du bist verflucht' ('Thou art accursed'), whereas the work itself has F minor, B minor and C sharp minor chords at this point.[20] I conclude this series of examples with the C sharp major chord on ' . . . du hättest mich ge*liebt*' ('thou wouldst have loved me') and the 'E flat minor' on ' . . . das Geheimnis des *To*des' ('the mystery of death').[21] In both cases these harmonies for Salome's closing monologue occurred to Strauss while he was reading Lachmann's text.

Here and there Strauss jotted down the time signature and changes of metre; furthermore, in places he makes a noticeable effort to sketch in the melodic line, allowing us to see that in certain cases the final result was destined to be still more precise. Strauss originally wrote Jochanaan's phrase as shown in Ex. 1, but then changed it to the form shown in Ex. 2.[22]

All in all an examination of Strauss's copy of Hedwig Lachmann's translation of *Salomé* provides a welcome insight into the earliest stage of the composer's musical elaboration of a literary work, especially as there are quite a number of short musical

Example 1

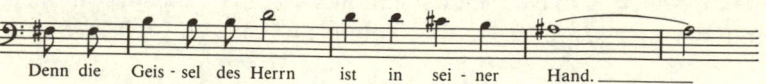

Denn die   Geis - sel des Herrn   ist   in   sei - ner   Hand.

Example 2

Denn die Geis - sel des Herrn ist in sei - ner Hand.

sketches which immediately attempt to render certain features in musical form.

Postscript by the Editor

Tenschert's description breaks off just as it is beginning to get really interesting! Most readers would want to know more about Strauss's musical annotations than about the minutiae of his cuts. And in some respects Tenschert is tantalisingly vague: it is impossible to tell how extensive the musical annotations are (at one point he says there are 'only a handful', at another point 'quite a number'); whether the examples he has chosen are typical or the most interesting; or indeed whether much thought has gone into the selection at all. Nevertheless his essay is important because it constitutes the only detailed description of this source we have, a source which is not available for general consultation. (Eight pages, however, have been published in a recent documentary volume,[23] and one of those pages – the first – in the book by Kurt Wilhelm.)[24]

Before going any further it is necessary to be clear exactly what this source is. It is not a working copy (or *Handexemplar*)[25] of a libretto, in the sense of Strauss's working copies of Hofmannsthal libretti. Lachmann's text was not designed as a libretto but as a translation of a spoken play, for performance in the theatre. In reading it Strauss had therefore to take different decisions (particularly with regard to form and proportion) from those he would normally have taken when faced with a libretto. But his musical responses were clearly similar, and we can draw a little more knowledge from the examples Tenschert provides.

Strauss's working methods have been the object of several valuable studies, notably those of Willi Schuh (concentrating on *Der Rosenkavalier*), Charlotte E. Erwin (concentrating on *Ariadne auf Naxos*) and Bryan Gilliam (who discusses a variety of works, including *Der Rosenkavalier*, *Elektra* and the *Symphonia Domestica*).[26] Of these the most relevant to our purposes is the article by Erwin.

Plate 3: The first page of Strauss's working copy of Oscar Wilde's *Salomé* in the translation by Hedwig Lachmann; the illustration (by Marcus Behmer) shows Narraboth gazing at Salome

She establishes that the 'presketch-stage marginal glossing of a text or a literary programme was a fundamental part of [Strauss's] working method', even extending to songs whose texts were annotated in detail but never actually set.[27] (The subsequent stages of composition are described by Gilliam.) According to Erwin, the annotations are basically of two kinds. A 'predominance of harmonic over other kinds of designation is typical' (this is equally true of non-vocal works), but there are also 'metric indications'. Her conclusion is that 'the degree of integration of musical ideas prior to sketching can be very high'.[28]

Turning back to Strauss's *Salome* copy, we see that Tenschert's examples of purely musical annotation (which occupy only the last part of his essay) fall into three types: harmonic–tonal, metric and a type which for want of a better name can be called 'formal'. In the first category we have the C sharp minor of the beginning, which as Tenschert says is 'established at once':[29] Strauss's marking here seems to be at variance with his usual practice, which was *not* to write down the opening tonality.[30] Then there are the D minor of 'Religion' and the D major of 'wie abgezehrt'. In the opera as a whole D minor is associated with the Jews,[31] while the D major is an obvious reference back to Fig. 68 (the *fortissimo* statement of Jochanaan's theme). Even from these marginal jottings, then, we can see that Strauss was thinking in terms of 'associative tonality', the technique of dramatic key association he had inherited from Wagner.[32] In other words, his entire tonal scheme was implicit in his earliest, pre-sketch annotations to the play; it only remained for him to work it out in detail.

But the most interesting of these tonal 'associations' has to do with the D flat major of the moon. D flat is the enharmonic equivalent of C sharp, which is associated with Salome herself. Almost the very first thing she says, on entering, is 'Wie gut ist's, in den Mond zu sehn' ('How good to see the moon!', six bars after Fig. 29), and her voice rises to a high A flat on 'sehn'. This is supported by a D flat chord, a curious way of notating C sharp in an A major context. Her next thought is to compare the moon with herself – 'Ja, wie die Schönheit einer Jungfrau, die rein geblieben ist' ('Yes, she is a virgin. She has never defiled herself') – and here flats give way to sharps, with a dominant seventh of C sharp minor, Salome's key, on the word 'Jungfrau'. The phrase cited by Tenschert, 'Gewiss ist er keusch wie der Mond . . . ' ('I am sure he is chaste as the moon is'), is an obvious reference back to the earlier passage, with the same high A flat, now on 'Mond', as well as the D flat chord. Strauss thus establishes a network of associations between Salome, the moon and Jochanaan, who is identified with the heroine through his chastity as surely as he is with the moon; indeed the composer seems to be telling us that it is precisely Jochanaan's chastity Salome finds attractive, and that when she sees the moon in him she is only seeing herself.

Our second category of annotations, the metric one, is limited to a single example. Tenschert reports that the first sentence in the play, Narraboth's 'Wie schön ist die Prinzessin Salome heute Nacht!', appears 'precisely delineated in terms of its vocal rhythm through the insertion of barlines', and that Strauss continues this form of annotation into some of the following sentences. Not only that, but he actually writes the numbers of the bars above the text, as we can see from the page reproduced as Plate 3.[33] This shows that he had the metrical outline of the first thirty or so bars of the opera (the numbers do not correspond exactly with those in the score) clear in his mind.

The third category of annotation pertains to formal organisation, and here there are two examples: the insertion of 'I', 'II' and 'III' besides Salome's 'Ich bin nicht durstig, Tetrarch', etc., and the symmetry that Strauss creates for himself through the threefold introduction of 'Wenn er kommt'. Both show the predilection for grouping events in threes that Tethys Carpenter notes in her chapter on 'Tonal and dramatic structure'. It is also worth mentioning that the three chords Strauss originally intended to accompany Jochanaan's curse – C minor, D minor and E flat minor – form an ascending stepwise progression analogous to that of 'Wenn er kommt'.

All this may be to speculate too much on the basis of slender information. Yet a little more speculation on Tenschert's part would surely have been welcome. He might also have been more critical. Some of Strauss's cuts obscure the sense of the original. For example, Salome's 'Ah!', when she first sees Narraboth, is an 'Ah!' not of deviousness but of understanding, since it comes in response to the First Soldier's comment, 'And indeed, it is not of us that you should ask this thing' (that is, to bring the Prophet out of the cistern). The reference to 'Des Waldes Schweigen' is likewise obscured by a cut, since the full sentence says that 'the silence that dwells in the forest is not so black [as thy hair]'. And later the First Nazarene's 'But', in 'But He hath healed blind people also', seems illogical because the contradiction applies to a remark that has been cut ('. . . it was blind men that He healed at Capernaum.' 'Nay; they were lepers. But . . . ').

Nor is only the immediate sense affected. Important information is lost, as William Mann has observed,[34] when Strauss cuts the discussion of the cistern in which Salome's father was imprisoned for twelve years. The order that he should finally be strangled was conveyed by the delivery of Herod's ring to the Executioner. We remember this fact, or should remember it, when Herodias draws the ring from Herod's finger towards the end. Similarly it is interesting to know that the Veil of the Sanctuary has disappeared (Herodias says to Herod, 'It was thyself didst steal it').[35] Perhaps more important than any of these cuts is the omission of two sentences in Salome's first speech. In the play, after saying, 'It is strange that the husband of my mother looks at me like that', Salome adds, 'I know not what it means. In truth, yes, I know it.' This cut results in a drastic simplification of Salome's character, reducing her sexual awareness and concentrating attention on her 'virginity' – though Strauss, as we have seen, gives the virginity theme new resonances by purely musical means. Other cuts are less serious. It is a pity to lose the Pinteresque humour of Herod's entrance, immediately after the First Soldier has said, 'The Tetrarch will not come to this place. He never comes on the terrace'; but the Wildean epigrams ('You must not find symbols in everything you see. It makes life impossible') surely had to go.

On the other hand, Strauss creates symmetries by repeating remarks that are not repeated in the original. Not only in his treatment of 'Wenn er kommt', but in the way he brings back the Page's 'Something terrible may happen' just before the voice of Jochanaan is heard for the first time (this would otherwise have been part of a larger cut further on) and then again, in the mouth of Herod, just before the slaves finally put out the torches: this last is operatic rhetoric at its most sublime. Equally rhetorical, though opinions may differ as to whether it is sublime, is the addition of an extra 'I have kissed thy mouth' at the end of Salome's last speech. This is a case of restoring what has previously been taken away. After the Baptist storms back to the cistern in the play, Salome murmurs, 'I will kiss thy mouth, Jokanaan; I will kiss thy mouth', but in the opera these thoughts are represented orchestrally, in the interlude (where erotic desire is transformed into something much more threatening). By transposing Salome's words to the end, Strauss turns what had been lascivious anticipation into gloating after the event. The division of the action into 'scenes' is also his own.

The effect of Strauss's cuts on the *structure* of the work will be discussed by Tethys Carpenter. Meanwhile some final speculation may be in order. At the biographical level, Strauss's treatment of his libretto sheds light on his development as an opera composer. There is of course no 'libretto' to *Salome* as such, only his marked-up copy of Wilde/Lachmann.[36] His choice of a pre-existing play constitutes a tacit criticism of his earlier libretti. He had been his own librettist for *Guntram* (1887–93); the text of *Feuersnot* (1900–1) had been supplied by Ernst von Wolzogen. Both use a form of verse, Wagnerian *Stabreim* in the first case, comic doggerel in the second. Neither is completely successful. For all its Wagnerian aspirations, *Guntram* is still rooted in the conventions of early nineteenth-century 'scene opera':[37] the quality of the musical ideas (there are several near-quotations from *Tristan*) is at odds with the formal framework. *Feuersnot* embraces those conventions, half affectionately, half satirically, but clearly no further progress was possible along the same lines. With *Salome* Strauss evidently intended to write what was for him a new kind of opera. 'With the best will in the world,' says Anna Amalie Abert, 'a dialogue such as that at the beginning [of *Salome*] could not have been set to music in the style of *Guntram* or even *Feuersnot*, quite apart from its content.'[38] A prose text became the means of creating musical prose, that is, music drama.[39] That is why Strauss's rejection of Lindner's 'cleverly versified . . . scenes'[40] in favour of Lachmann's sober translation was of such importance. His entire future development as an opera composer lay in the balance.

4 *Synopsis*

I

The opening of *Salome* is one of the most evocative in all opera.[1] No overture; not even a prelude; just a rising scale on the clarinet, leading to a shimmering wind chord and *tremolando* violins. We are immediately in a strange world, one which will gradually take on the 'oriental' characteristics associated with it.[2]

The scene is the great terrace of Herod's palace.[3] On the right there is a huge staircase, on the left an old cistern, or watertight tank, surrounded by a wall of green bronze. The moon is shining brightly. Some soldiers are leaning over the balcony. Their captain, a young Syrian called Narraboth, is talking to the Queen's Page. 'How beautiful is the Princess Salome tonight!' he says. But the Page is staring at the moon, the first of several characters in the work to be 'moonstruck'. He compares it to a woman rising from a tomb. For Narraboth, however, it resembles 'a little princess who has white doves for feet' (each character sees in it what he or she wants to see).

The atmosphere is broken by a sudden noise from the banqueting-hall below. It is the Jews, one soldier explains to another. 'They are always like that. They are disputing about their religion.' But Narraboth is still lost in his admiration for Salome. 'You look at her too much', says the Page. 'It is dangerous to look at people in such fashion. Something terrible may happen.' This last sentence becomes a verbal leitmotive, returning many times in the course of the work.[4]

The conversation of the soldiers now turns to Herod. He too is staring at something (or someone), but we cannot see what (or whom). Narraboth is still fixated on Salome. 'You must not look at her', the Page persists. 'Something terrible may happen.' At this point a voice comes booming from the cistern (complete with bathroom acoustic: a tamtam provides the right muffled sound). It is Jochanaan, or John the Baptist, announcing the coming of the Lord. We learn from the soldiers that he has come from the desert, where a great multitude used to follow him. Herod has forbidden him to be seen. Their conversation is interrupted by Narraboth, who has observed Salome leave the table. She is coming this way!

II

To a flurry of movement in the orchestra, Salome enters. 'I will not stay. I cannot stay. Why does the Tetrarch look at me all the while . . . ? It is strange that the husband of my mother looks at me like that.' She pauses to breathe in the night air. What a relief to escape from those Jews, 'who are tearing each other to pieces', those 'silent, subtle Egyptians' and those 'brutal', 'coarse' Romans. (She particularly hates the Romans.) While Narraboth stares at her, to the evident distress of the Page, she greets the moon. 'She is like a little silver flower, cold and chaste. She has a virgin's beauty.'

As if in response, Jochanaan's voice booms out again: 'The Lord hath come.' Salome is immediately excited. 'Who was that who cried out?' The prophet. 'Ah, the prophet! He of whom the Tetrarch is afraid?' Narraboth tries to change the subject by offering to have her litter brought out. Salome, however, is already thinking of the terrible things Jochanaan says about her mother. 'Yes; he says terrible things about her,' she repeats. A slave enters, conveying a message from Herod, who wants her to return to the feast. Salome refuses. 'Is he an old man, this prophet?' Narraboth, perhaps already sensing doom, offers to escort her back inside. 'This prophet . . . is he an old man?' 'No, Princess', one of the soldiers answers, 'he is quite young' – and again the voice booms out, prophesying disaster.

Salome now begins to become obsessed. First she wishes to speak to this strange man. The soldiers tell her it is impossible: the Tetrarch will not permit anyone to speak to him. Salome persists. She approaches the cistern and peers down into it. 'How black it is, down there! . . . It is like a tomb. Did you not hear me? Bring out the prophet.' The soldiers still refuse. Then she sees Narraboth ('Oh! what is going to happen?' says the Page). She wheedles; Narraboth protests. She tries again; he is desperate. 'Look at me, Narraboth, look at me. Ah! you know that you will do what I ask of you.' Narraboth's fate is sealed. With an abrupt gesture, he orders one of the soldiers to bring the prophet out of the cistern.

III

Now comes the first of the two orchestral interludes. The mood of agitation serves for both Salome and Narraboth – her excitement, his apprehension – while a theme for four horns portends the approach of the prophet. At last he appears (to the sound of six horns, not four), and Salome, for a moment, is silent.

'Where is he whose cup of abominations is now full? Where is she who having seen the images of men painted on the walls, gave herself up unto the lust of her eyes . . . ? Bid her rise up from the bed of her abominations, from the bed of her incestuousness, that she may hear the words of him who prepareth the way of the Lord . . . ' Only Salome understands that he is talking about her mother. The reference to incestuousness concerns the fact that Herodias had married her first husband Philip's brother; it is because Jochanaan has denounced this union that Herod has imprisoned him.[5] Narraboth begs Salome not to stay, but she is fascinated by the prophet's eyes. 'They are like black lakes troubled by fantastic moons . . . I am sure he is chaste as the moon is. I would look closer at him.'

Jochanaan begins to perceive that someone is looking at him. His imprecations are turned upon Salome, but she wishes only to hear more (Strauss changes her remark, 'Thy voice is wine to me', to 'Thy voice is as music to mine ear', thus providing the opportunity for some gorgeous orchestral textures). Narraboth begins to lose control. The more Jochanaan tries to hold her back, the more she presses herself on him. Then she launches into her threefold hymn of praise, a parody of the Song of Songs: 'Jochanaan, I am amorous of thy body! . . . It is of thy hair that I am enamoured . . . It is thy mouth that I desire.' Each time she is repulsed, and each time she comes back for more. Finally, 'I will kiss thy mouth, Jochanaan. I will kiss thy mouth.'

This is more than Narraboth can take, and, in Wilde's immortal stage direction, 'He kills himself and falls between Salomé and Jokanaan.' (Strauss's use of leitmotive at this point is discussed in Chapter 5.) Salome of course is quite oblivious to this. She merely repeats her desire to kiss Jochanaan's mouth. The prophet makes one last, rather feeble, effort to save her, urging her to seek an unnamed man 'in a boat on the sea of Galilee'. His advice goes unheeded. Salome repeats her request, and, cursing her, Jochanaan retreats to his cistern.

IV

As was observed in the last chapter, Salome's next remark in the play is cut by Strauss. Left alone, she muses, 'I will kiss thy mouth, Jokanaan; I will kiss thy mouth.' Strauss transforms this remark into the centrepiece of his second interlude. After the orchestral ravings accompanying the prophet's exit have died away, the brass intone a theme which we later recognise as Salome's demand for his head. Without a word being said, the musings of disappointed love are turned into a deadly threat.

Herod and Herodias now appear with all the court (even the Executioner moves around with them, it seems). 'Where is Salome?' he asks. 'Why did she not return to the banquet as I commanded her? Ah! there she is!' Herodias reproaches him for looking at her too much. But Herod's attention has already wandered. 'The moon has a strange look tonight. Has she not a strange look? She is like a mad woman who is seeking everywhere for lovers.' 'No', returns Herodias, the realist in this ménage; 'the moon is like the moon, that is all. Let us go within.' (This passage is discussed in Chapter 5.) 'I will stay here!' Herod decides, and orders carpets for his guests.

Suddenly Herod slips in blood. He notices the body of Narraboth for the first time. The young man's suicide seems strange to him: 'I remember that I saw he looked languorously at Salome.' The soldiers remove the body. Herod is immediately troubled by a mysterious wind; he feels cold, and hears the beating of wings. Herodias of course hears nothing.

And so Herod settles down to the serious business of the evening, ordering wine (and offering some to Salome, who is not thirsty, or so she says) and fruit (she says she is not hungry). He even offers Salome her mother's throne, but the offer is not taken up. As he tries to remember what else it is he desires, the voice of Jochanaan is heard again, provoking Herodias to call for him to be silenced. She of course has particular reason to hate him. Herod, on the other hand, talks of him with respect. 'I think you are afraid of him', taunts his wife; otherwise, 'why do you not deliver him to the

Jews, who for these six months past have been clamouring for him?' This is enough to start a theological argument among the Jews, whose differences are worked out by Strauss in a long scherzo. Despite Herodias' repeated cries for silence, they are halted only by the voice of Jochanaan: 'I hear upon the mountains the feet of Him who shall be the Saviour of the world.' What this can mean is discussed at length by two Nazarenes. They describe certain miracles which have been performed by the man from Galilee, including the raising of the dead. 'He raises the dead?' says Herod, with sudden alarm; 'I forbid him to do that . . . It would be terrible if the dead came back.'

The voice of Jochanaan is heard again: by now it begins to sound like a terrible refrain. He denounces Salome: 'Let the war captains pierce her with their swords, let them crush her beneath their shields.' On he drones, prophesying ever worse misfortunes. The Queen's complaints – 'Command him to be silent' – go unheeded.

Then Herod has a bright idea. 'Dance for me, Salome.' Naturally she does not want to dance. But as he persists, and as the voice of Jochanaan drones forth again, she senses her advantage. 'Will you indeed give me whatsoever I shall ask?' 'Everything, even the half of my kingdom.' She makes him swear on it. Herod thinks he is in luck: 'Thou wilt be passing fair as a queen, Salome.' For a moment he feels the icy wind again, and hears the beating of wings. But now the wind is not cold, it is hot. In a panic he tears the wreath of flowers from his head and throws it on the table. 'Now I am happy. Will you not dance for me, Salome?' 'I will dance for you, Tetrarch.'

And she dances the dance of the seven veils.

Wilde left no instructions as to how it should be danced,[6] and there are only two stage directions (apart from those for the onstage musicians) in Strauss's score: towards the end, 'Salome seems to tire for a moment, but then she summons up new strength'; and, later still, 'Salome remains for an instant in a visionary attitude near the cistern where Jochanaan is kept prisoner', before throwing herself at Herod's feet. Twenty years after composing the dance, Strauss wrote a scenario setting out his intentions in detail.[7]

As the dance is in progress, however, it is Salome who decides how things go. When she has finished, Herod is exultant. 'Ah! wonderful! wonderful! . . . Come near, Salome, come near, that I may give you your reward.' Everyone knows the byplay that follows. 'I would that they presently bring me in a silver charger . . .' 'In a silver charger? Surely yes, in a silver charger. She is charming, is she not? What is it you would have in a silver charger, O sweet and fair Salome, you who are fairer than all the daughters of Judaea?' And so on. Eventually back comes the response: 'The head of Jochanaan.'

Herod is thunderstruck. Herodias laughs. Her husband tells Salome not to listen to her mother's voice. 'She is ever giving you evil counsel. Do not heed her.' 'It is for mine own pleasure that I ask the head of Jochanaan in a silver charger'; and she reminds him of his oath. Herod pleads with her. He offers her half his kingdom; an emerald; the beautiful white peacocks in his garden; jewels that even Herodias has never seen – if only she will release him from his oath. 'This man comes perchance from God. He is a holy man.' Every offer is refused with the same words: 'Give me the head of Jochanaan.' Increasingly desperate, Herod offers her the mantle of the high priest. He even offers her the Veil of the Sanctuary, scandalising the Jews. But she is obdurate. Sinking back in his seat, he accepts defeat: 'Let her be given what she asks! Of a truth she is her mother's child!'

As the next few minutes pass, Herod might well have reflected, like another monarch contemplating the murderous instincts of her children, 'Every family has its little ups and downs.' Instead he remains in a stupor, while Herodias slips the ring of death from his finger and passes it to the Executioner. Herod wakes up again: 'Who has taken my ring?' The Executioner goes down into the cistern (the order of events is slightly different in Wilde). 'There was a ring on my right hand. Who has drunk my wine? There was wine in my cup. Oh! Surely some evil will befall someone.'[8]

Salome leans over the cistern, listening intently. First she hears nothing (Strauss's music for this, with its insistent solo double bass note, is the most notorious in the opera).[9] Then she hears something fall. Thinking the Executioner has dropped his sword, she urges the Page and the soldiers to do what the Executioner has failed to do. They recoil. She screams at Herod to order his soldiers to bring her Jochanaan's head.

Like a restaurant waiter delivering a steak, the huge black arm of the Executioner appears, bearing the head on a silver shield. Salome seizes it and, as Herod hides his face with his cloak, plunges into her final monologue (discussed in detail in Chapter 7).[10] Recalling her love for him, and imagining the love he might have had for her, she sates her longing by kissing his dead mouth.

Herod, appalled, rises to go inside. Herodias naturally decides to stay. Fearing some terrible retribution, the Tetrarch orders the torches to be extinguished. 'Some terrible thing will befall.' The slaves put out the torches; the stars disappear; a great black cloud crosses the moon, covering it completely. Herod begins to climb the staircase. Salome's voice is heard in the darkness: 'Ah! I have kissed thy mouth, Jochanaan, I have kissed thy mouth. There was a bitter taste on thy lips. Was it the taste of blood? No! But perchance it is the taste of love. They say that love hath a bitter taste. But what of that? what of that? I have kissed thy mouth, Jochanaan. I have kissed thy mouth.'

A moonbeam falls on Salome, covering her with light. Turning abruptly on the staircase, Herod orders his stepdaughter to be killed. The soldiers crush her under their shields.

5 'Salome' as music drama

Gentlemen, there are no difficulties or problems. This opera is a scherzo with a fatal conclusion!

Strauss, at the first rehearsal for the première[1]

I

Salome proclaims its genre on the title-page: 'music drama in one act'.[2] When it was first performed, it was widely perceived as the ultimate extension of Wagner's operatic methods; indeed, critics 'fell over themselves' in the rush to evaluate Strauss's debt to his predecessor.[3] Eighty-five years later, the dust has settled. Strauss's place in music history is firmly established, and to call him a 'Wagnerian' composer is no more controversial than to recognise the Brahmsian (or Schubertian, or Mendelssohnian) elements in his style. No more illuminating, either: composers as disparate as Wolf, Mahler, Schoenberg and Pfitzner have all been termed 'Wagnerian' at one time or another. Yet the matter of genre is interesting. If a composer around the turn of the century calls a work a 'music drama', he is making an artistic statement, just as a present-day composer is who chooses to write a symphony. The manner in which *Salome* is a music drama – in other words, the extent to which it observes the conventions of the genre – bears investigation precisely *because* it has always been recognised as such. Pigeonholes obscure; we imagine we have explained something merely by giving it a name, but all we have done is create an excuse not to think about it.

Music drama is a notoriously slippery concept. 'In 19th-century and current usage, the meanings attached to the term . . . derive from the ideas formulated in Wagner's *Oper und Drama* [1851]; it is applied to his operas and to others in which the musical, verbal and scenic elements cohere to serve one dramatic end.'[4] Thus the *New Grove*, summing up a lifetime's work in a sentence (why did Wagner bother to write all those books?). The basic point is valid: the drama

58

is served through the creation of a 'total work of art', the *Gesamt-kunstwerk*, in which music is merely one element among many. Yet the definition glosses over a vital distinction. Wagner's music dramas are *not* operas. Indeed his book is largely concerned with trying to distinguish between the two (as its title implies). The trouble with opera, in his view, was that a means of expression (music) had been made an end, while the end of expression (drama) had been made the means.[5] What was needed was a new type of work, whose ideal subject was myth; dramatic music would be renewed by infusing it with the symphonic methods of Beethoven; and the vehicle for this transformation would be libretti that avoided end-rhyme and regular stress-patterns in favour of *Stabreim* and text-lines of variable length. The result, as everyone knows, was the incomparable series of music dramas from *Das Rheingold* to *Parsifal* (only these works, written after *Oper und Drama*, qualify as music dramas in the strict sense). Wagner's practice in these works varied greatly. But in every case he achieved a new kind of continuity. The old formal categories were dissolved (except where it was important for them to be retained on dramatic grounds, as in *Die Meistersinger*), giving way to a mixture of closed and open forms. The regular periodicity that had been standard since the middle of the eighteenth century was replaced by irregular patterns, or 'musical prose'. And with the balance of interest now divided between voice and orchestra (it would be going too far to say that it had passed exclusively to the latter), the orchestra too could play a part in shaping the form, no longer merely accompany-ing the singer but maintaining a type of symphonic development through the use of the leitmotive.[6]

Strauss was no theorist. Whenever he felt the need to pronounce on aesthetic matters, as in the Preface to *Intermezzo* (1924), the result is a mixture of anecdotes and practical advice. Nevertheless he had a clear instinctive understanding of Wagner's aims.[7] Writing about the Bayreuth Festival Theatre in 1940, he commented (with characteristic hyperbole):

[Wagner's] attractive idea that the chorus of the ancient drama, which accompanied the action as critic, interpreter and guide, had been replaced by the orchestra as created by our classical symphonic composers is only partly correct. A superficial examination will show that the expressive range of the modern orchestra, more especially since Weber and Berlioz [in other words, in Wagner], is far greater than that of the descriptive explana-tory chorus of a tragedy by Aeschylus or Sophocles.[8]

And this from the composer of an *Elektra*! (Strauss might almost have been writing about himself. It should be remembered, however, that the decision to omit the chorus in that work was Hofmannsthal's, not the composer's.) Almost fifty years earlier he had written: 'To Richard Wagner the highest problem of the opera was the achievement of balance between its dramatic and musical tendencies . . . '[9] These words are a reminder that Strauss had just read *Oper und Drama*.[10] But they also anticipate his Foreword to Berlioz's *Treatise on Instrumentation*, which he was revising while at work on *Salome*. In the Foreword, after citing Wagner's 'magnificent interpretations [of the history of the orchestra] in his writings' (and again he refers to *Oper und Drama*), he distinguishes between 'two main roads of orchestral development: the *symphonic* (*polyphonic*) and the *dramatic* (*homophonic*) roads' (Strauss's italics). The former culminated in the symphonies of Haydn, Mozart and Beethoven, the latter in the operas of Gluck and Weber. Wagner of course achieved a synthesis: 'He combined the *symphonic* (polyphonic) technique of composition and orchestration with the rich expressive resources of the *dramatic* (homophonic) style.' And Strauss emphasises that the 'phenomenal sound combinations which a Berlioz or Wagner drew from the orchestra' were a means, not an end: 'These masters used them for giving expression to unheard-of, great, poetic ideas . . . '[11]

Strauss, echoing Wagner, sees the 'dramatic' and 'musical' tendencies of opera as being in opposition. This is worth bearing in mind when reading his comments on his own works. Two particular remarks come to mind. In a letter to Hofmannsthal of 4 May 1909, after acknowledging receipt of the text for Act I of *Der Rosenkavalier*, he says: 'The final scene is magnificent. I've already done a bit of experimenting with it today. I wish I'd got there already. But since, *for the sake of symphonic unity*, I must compose the music from the beginning to the end I'll just have to be patient' (my italics).[12] In other words, the work must possess a purely musical coherence, irrespective of its dramatic or musico-dramatic qualities. The second remark directly concerns *Salome*: 'It is the symphony in the medium of drama . . . '[13] In other words, it is not a symphonic poem. Fauré seems to have been the first to suggest that *Salome* was a symphonic poem with voice parts added, a view endorsed by many later writers (notably Ernest Newman and Joseph Kerman).[14] Yet Strauss's remark makes it clear that the music is there to serve the drama. Putting these two, apparently contradictory, remarks together, we obtain a coherent Wagnerian viewpoint. Music must have its own autonomous unity, which is best achieved by symphonic means. Yet in a dramatic work – and even in a non-dramatic work, if we accept that the expression of 'great, poetic ideas' is paramount – music is only a means, not an end. 'Symphonic unity' is of no interest in itself.

In a remarkable article on Wagner's musical influence, Carl Dahlhaus lays down seven points to be borne in mind when such matters are discussed, adding: 'The significance we accord to a certain factor, e.g. the choice of subject-matter, the dramaturgical structure or the leitmotif technique, is dependent upon the aesthetic position we adopt.'[15] Or upon the nature of the work. Since by no stretch of the imagination can the subject-matter of *Salome* be described as mythological, and the dramaturgy of the opera is basically that of the play, it makes sense to concentrate on the leit-motive.[16]

II

Once again, the classic statement on the subject comes from Dahlhaus:

The idea of a leitmotif[17] . . . as a fixed, recurrent, musical formula . . . is simplistic to the point of falsity. Unchanged recurrence is the exception rather than the rule, even in the *Ring*, let alone in *Parsifal* (as long as the musical form and the dramatic significance are always considered conjointly). To counterbalance Debussy's and Stravinsky's malicious references to 'visiting-cards' and 'check-room numbers', amusing though they may be, it should be remembered that the themes and motifs are unceasingly varied, taken apart and merged with or transformed into each other, and that they move gradually closer together or further apart as they are modified. (A 'theme' differs from a 'motif' in its greater extent and complexity . . .) It is seldom wise to take the earliest form in which a theme or motif appears as necessarily its primary form, from which all subsequent forms derive as secondary variations. Rather, they are all different impressions of the same material, and all principally equal in status; but each impression throws one particular feature of a situation, one trait of a character or one element of an idea into musical relief, without admitting of the motif as 'really' corresponding to one thing and only 'approximately' to another . . . Naming the motifs is not completely arbitrary; but it reduces the intended configuration, which requires quite a lengthy description, to an over-simple object or idea that can be identified by a single word.[18]

This is the modern, 'relativist' view (I shall return to its contentious aspects later), and of course it applies to the Wagnerian use of the leitmotive. Unfortunately it has not yet penetrated Strauss studies, which, with one or two exceptions, are still bogged down in literalism. Take the following passage from Norman Del Mar:

> The function of Ex. 20 [= Ex. 1a below] . . . is of the greatest interest. When the whole section [Figs. 132ff.] recurs later in the work the opening figure of this melody is retained, but with a different continuation. In each case the marked repetition of the tonic rising to the mediant is the focal point of the entries and this connects up with Jochanaan's 'Wenn er kommt', Ex. 7 [= Ex. 1b]. Since it is this very looked-for coming of Jesus that we are now dealing with, the allusion is plain and can be pursued to include the opening of Ex. 22 [= Ex. 1c], the interval now justifiably being major, since we are in the presence of the Divine. What is less plain is why Ex. 20, the theme of Salome's passion for Jochanaan, should from the first have been connected in the same way. Specht in his analysis of the opera discusses the point at length and offers a number of alternative explanations, including Jochanaan's hope for the expiation of Salome's sin through Jesus. It is possible that Strauss may indeed have intended to give point to Jochanaan's line 'ask of Him the remission of thy sins', not only by sublimating in Jesus's music the theme of her terrible lust, but by linking it motivically with that of His coming.[19]

Example 1

What Strauss's intentions were will never be known, but that is the wonderful thing about this type of analysis. The argument can be extended indefinitely. Del Mar goes on to relate Ex. 1a to Salome's 'Ich will den Kopf' (his Ex. 25: see Chapter 6, Ex. 12e below), which in turn generates new motives (e.g. his Ex. 25a). However, in order to do justice to the richness of motivic relationships one would also have to relate 'Ich will den Kopf' to the Page's 'Du siehst sie immer an' (Fig. 7), or, for that matter, Jochanaan's 'Wenn er kommt' (first heard over a diminished-seventh chord on B flat, Fig. 13) to the Page's 'Schreckliches kann geschehen' (Fig. 11), an absurd connection. Having said which, I will not breathe another word against Del Mar, whose book is a heroic achievement.

Another confirmed literalist is William Mann, who is always offering lame explanations. Of the solo violin line at Fig. 24, for instance, he says: 'The accompanying motif is not concerned with balmy breezes [why not?] . . . but with Salome herself. Later this theme . . . will seem to denote Salome's relationship to her mother Herodias, or her own dawning sexuality.'[20] That music can denote so much and yet so little! A 'relativist' interpretation would allow it to denote all these things, the breezes as well as Salome's tremulous longings. To do Mann justice, he says in a footnote:

Even if we try to associate the main themes with particular states of mind, or more rarely with particular characters, we should remember that they are primarily symphonic materials which may and often do appear to change their precise meaning according to the symphonic context.[21]

This is the relativist position *par excellence*. Unfortunately he never allows it to influence his analysis.[22]

The literal approach is unsatisfactory, partly because it is often so badly executed in itself, but also because it limits the meaning of the music. As Arnold Whittall has observed (apropos of *Parsifal* rather than Strauss), ' . . . the extent to which words can adequately translate the expressive quality and dramatic significance of themes and motives is bound to vary very greatly, not only according to the changing contexts in which the material occurs' – the Dahlhaus view – 'but also according to the predispositions of each individual listener'.[23] He prefers an approach based on tonal and harmonic relations. For Carolyn Abbate, however, writing on *Elektra*, the motivic approach is 'one [voice] among the many', which has its place in a rounded interpretation. It simply requires more sensitive handling:

Long experience with Wagner's works has taught us that even in the most lexical of his operas (*The Ring*) the referential meaning of motives is by no means immanent in the score. Rather, the motives may begin with specific associations, then quickly slide away from their symbolic nexus to become 'symphonic' or 'purely musical' matter; or they may begin as musical gestures and occasionally don masks of extramusical meaning.[24]

In other words, motives and meaning form a continuum, with specific associations at one end and 'purely musical' values at the

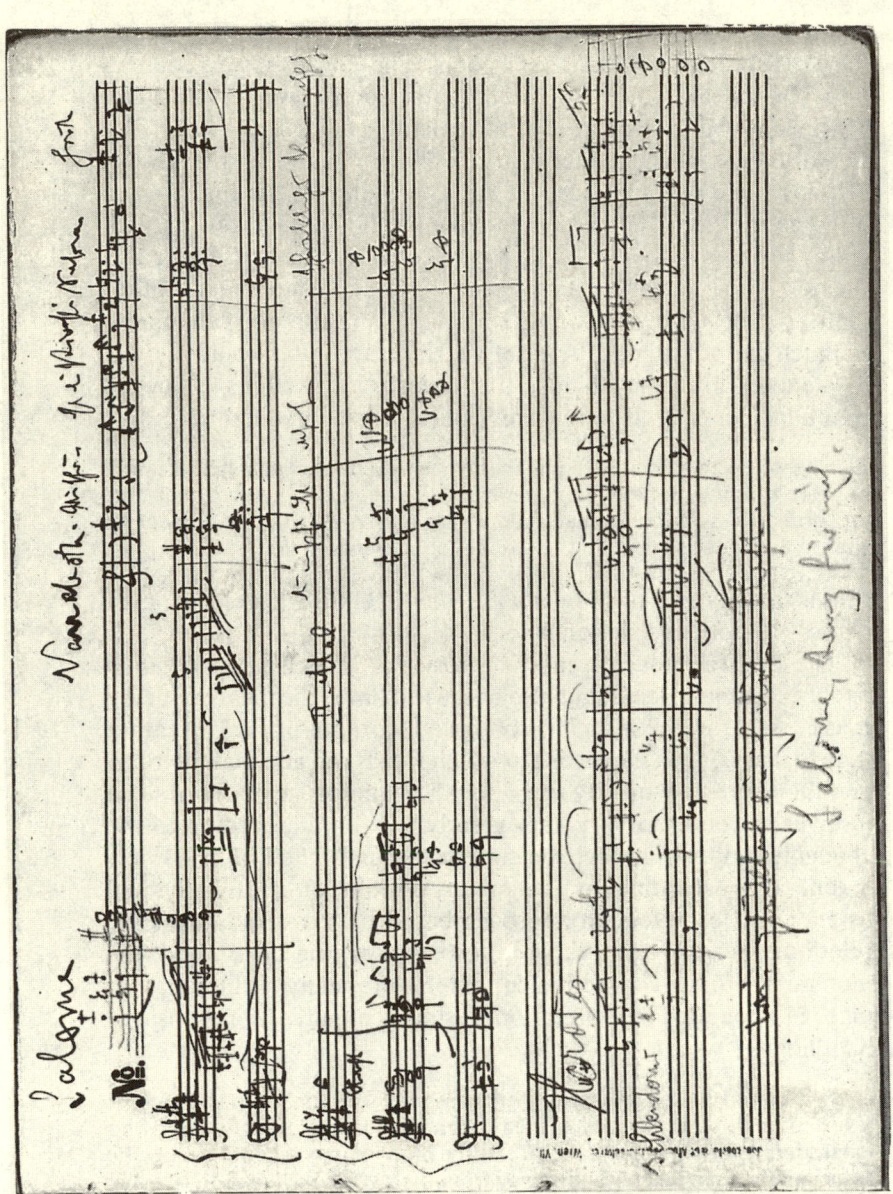

Plate 4: The first page of Strauss's sketches for *Salome*, Sketchbook 11, folio 1 (see pp. 65; 184, n. 48)

other. Literal meaning has its place, but it is not inherent in the music: what begins with a clear-cut association may become more abstract, and vice versa. To extend the argument, the literal approach fails because it remains fixed at one end of the continuum. A more successful approach might start with the score – the one stable element among so many unstable ones – deriving its interpretations of meaning from the analysis of 'purely musical' relationships rather than predicating the musical analysis on assumptions about the meaning.

Strauss's own position in all this is curious. While it will never be possible to know his 'intentions' in any particular case, there is a certain amount of evidence regarding his views on the leitmotive in general. The 'literal' interpretations familiar from Mann, Del Mar and the rest have their origins in the leitmotivic guides compiled as introductions to the operas at the time of their first performance. (The guide to *Salome* by Lawrence Gilman is a well-known example in English.)[25] These publications could only have been issued with Strauss's approval; Willi Schuh maintains that 'the well-known guides to the orchestral works, compiled by Herwarth Walden, and to the music dramas, compiled by Georg Göhler . . . were compiled with his collaboration, or at the very least with his consent'.[26] Now, these 'well-known guides' are based on the very same aesthetic assumptions that Dahlhaus criticises when he writes that 'the idea of a leitmotif . . . as a fixed, recurrent, musical formula . . . is simplistic to the point of falsity'. A guide in my possession, by Otto Roese, lists motives beneath the headings 'Hauptthema der Salome', 'Thema des Narraboth', 'Entschluss der Rache', and so on.[27] In other words, the 'simplistic' idea of the motive was a widespread aspect of Wagner reception at the time when *Salome* was composed.[28] Not only that, but it seems that Strauss himself thought in this way. His sketches for *Salome* bear titles such as 'Salome', 'Herodes Begehrlichkeit' ('Herod's covetousness') and 'Das Todesurteil' ('the death sentence' – this is the motive usually referred to as 'Herod's command') (see Plate 4).[29] Thus reception influences composition.[30]

Strauss's *practice*, however, as opposed to the view of the leitmotive revealed by his sketches, is complex. In order to interpret it adequately we need to adopt a 'relativist' approach such as I have outlined above. Before doing so, however, it is worth reflecting that the 'literal' analyses I have castigated are themselves an example of reception, though Strauss reception, now, rather than Wagner. So criticism of Strauss, beginning with the early leitmotive guides, which have their roots in a piece of dubious Wagner reception, has evolved by applying these dubious ideas (to which it seems Strauss himself subscribed) to the later composer *while somehow bypassing his actual practice.*[31] To use the language of music semiology: Strauss's poietics (his working methods) were influenced by a simplistic idea of the motive; at the neutral level (the level of the work itself) his use of the motive is complex; yet, at the level of esthesics (reception), our response is still conditioned by that earlier, simplistic idea.[32]

III

The continuum metaphor may be illustrated by two examples. One of the simplest musical images in the opera (it hardly qualifies as a motive, since no pitches are involved) is provided by the tamtam strokes that accompany Jochanaan's offstage pronouncements. The tamtam is an instrument traditionally associated with religious ceremony, and therefore with the Divine.[33] When Jochanaan's voice first booms out from the cistern, the tamtam booms out with it; and with almost comic literalism Strauss makes sure that each of its booms coincides with a reference to God or Christ (italicised words indicate tamtam strokes):

[Fig. 11/5] Nach mir wird *Einer* kommen, *der* ist stärker als ich . . . Wenn er *kommt*[34] . . . werden die Augen der Blinden den *Tag* sehen . . . die Ohren der *Tau*ben geöffnet.

After me shall come *another* mightier than I . . . When He *cometh* . . . The eyes of the blind shall see the *day* . . . the ears of the *deaf* shall be opened.

(Even here, with the tamtam stroke on 'Tauben', there is a tendency for the association to become diffused.) This association is maintained throughout Jochanaan's second speech:

[Fig. 30/9] *Siehe*, der *Herr* ist gekommen, des Menschen *Sohn* ist nahe.

[*See*,] The *Lord* hath come. The *Son* of Man hath come.

But in his third speech the association breaks down:

[Fig. 39] *Jauch*ze nicht . . . der dich *schlug*, gebrochen *ist*. *Denn* aus dem Samen der *Schlange* wird ein Basi*lisk* kommen, und seine *Brut* wird die *Vö*gel ver*schlingen*.

Rejoice thou not . . . [the rod of him] who *smote* thee is *broken*. *For* from the seed of the *serpent* shall come forth a basi*lisk*, and that which is *born* of it shall *devour* the *birds*.

Obviously the first stroke here merely signifies the start of another speech by Jochanaan, but after that the associations seem to be ones of generalised horror rather than specific references to the Divine. The specificity returns when the prophet appears on stage ('dem Erwählten des *Herrn*', Fig. 83/10; '*Gott*', Fig. 85; 'die Stimme des *Herrn*, meines *Gott*es', Fig. 97/7, etc., including a noteworthy 'Such' *ihn*!', Fig. 131/3). But the damage has been done. Towards the end of his dialogue with Salome, the tamtam is reduced to accompanying his curses ('Sei ver*flucht*', Fig. 137/6, the first of six such outbursts), and during the following interlude it becomes just one more percussion instrument adding its din to the general mêlée. In the Herod scene it accompanies the Tetrarch's delusions about the 'beating of vast wings' (Fig. 166/2, and again at 169), but by now we can no longer be sure whether the reference is to God or to Jochanaan himself: the tamtam was, after all, responsible for the 'bathroom acoustic' that muffled his first utterances. Jochanaan's offstage voice recalls the 'divine' association (Figs. 207, 220), but now along with worms (Fig. 226/5). Herod's renewed delusion of vast wings diffuses the association again, and as he cries 'er ist *heiss*' (Fig. 237) the tamtam player is instructed to rub the instrument with a triangle stick, an effect perhaps suggested by *Das Rheingold*. Despite some final desultory efforts to recapture the 'divine' association (Fig. 282), the tamtam remains firmly in the secular domain for the rest of the opera. It is treated as a mere percussion instrument throughout Salome's monologue (apart from her 'Deine Stimme war ein *Weih*rauchgefäss' – 'Thy voice was a censer' – Fig. 337/4), reinforcing without being tied to any specific association; and it sounds twice, *fortissimo*, during the orchestral postlude. What has begun with fixed textual, or dramatic, associations has ended up as a purely musical device.

On the other hand there are the various semiquaver motives that run through the first part of Scene 4 (from Fig. 155 to Fig. 172), or what I have called 'the Herod scene'. As befits his scattered personality, Herod himself has no strongly characterised *themes* (compare the sustained melodies given to Salome or the Baptist). It is only at the end of the work that his authority asserts itself: as the 'death sentence' motive rings out for the last time, signalling

Salome's demise, Herod shows himself a true 'survivor' (and the fact that the opera ends in C minor, the key associated with the 'death sentence', rather than Salome's C sharp proves that Strauss had a clear understanding of this). For the rest of the work he has to make do with a series of semiquaver motives: the whole-tone scale at Fig. 155, a chromatic pattern elaborating a C major triad two bars after 156, and an atonal configuration (reminiscent of *Wozzeck*) beginning on the last crotchet of 160. It is not even clear that these motives are associated specifically with Herod (some commentators associate the second one with Herodias rather than Herod himself). For much of the scene they have a purely musical function, acting as accompanimental figures and occasionally turning into ostinati.[35] The passage beginning at Fig. 160 is perhaps most remarkable: for thirty bars or so the 'atonal' configuration is subjected to numerous varied, pseudo-tonal harmonisations (this is the moment when Herod slips in Narraboth's blood and questions the guards about their captain's fate) before finally turning into the *moto perpetuo* that evokes the wind. It seems pointless to try to assign any specific meaning to such figures (later they turn into the triplets accompanying Herod's songs).[36] Rather, they take on meanings according to the context: at one moment they suggest the wind, at another Herod's panic, and so on.

These two examples show the continuum of music and meaning at work: each begins at one end and moves towards the other. Most of the leitmotives in *Salome* fall between the two extremes. Some do indeed maintain clear-cut associations throughout: the motive of the cistern (first heard five bars after Fig. 45), for example, or the complex of motives associated with the Jews (Fig. 4).[37] There are also important musical motives which have no discernible dramatic connotation (such as the tuba figure from the two bars before Fig. 273, which returns at 290 and obsessively at 295ff.) and which for this reason are often omitted from leitmotivic accounts of the opera. In between comes an idea such as Jochanaan's first theme (definitive statement Fig. 66).[38] This begins with a clear – perhaps too clear! – signification, which it gradually loses in the course of the Jochanaan–Salome dialogue (passages such as Figs. 81ff. show it turning into an ostinato or generalised accompanimental figure of the type associated with Herod, and since this is one of the most ubiquitous themes in the opera it is often recalled, as at Figs. 216–19, for the sake of purely musical development, in this case to pad out one of Jochanaan's interminable offstage tirades); but the original meaning survives, at some abstract level or other, so that when one of the original, diatonic versions of the theme is invoked at Fig. 341, during Salome's monologue ('der seinen Gott schauen wollte' – '[he] who would see his God'), Jochanaan himself seems to be restored to life.

At this point a certain amount of generalisation may be in order. Leitmotives in *Salome* are most clearly associated with persons, rather than with objects, events or abstract concepts (the cistern is an exception).[39] This is already obvious from a comparison of the various leitmotivic accounts of the opera, which are unanimous in their labellings only where the main characters are concerned. (Labels such as 'Salome's dawning sexuality', however, are to be distrusted.) Even here there is minor, and sometimes amusing, disagreement. Gilman calls the Prophet's first theme 'Jochanaan' and his second (the theme based on fourths) 'Prophecy', while Roese has these labels the other way round. In general Gilman's labels tend towards the abstract: they include 'Yearning', 'Anger' and 'Fear', this last referring to what Roese calls the 'Herod scale', or the whole-tone figure already mentioned.[40] So far as I know there is no authority whatever for such labellings. Yet Strauss himself was inclined to label motives in this way, as has already been shown, and certainly the emphasis on personal motifs (as opposed to Wagner's more wide-ranging concerns) tends to suggest a rather simplistic conception of leitmotive technique.

This is confirmed by the actual musical processes involved. Although it is true, as Dahlhaus says of Wagner, that 'unchanged recurrence is the exception rather than the rule' – indeed there is probably *less* exact restatement in Strauss than in the earlier composer, since variation, as a metaphor for organic growth, had now become an article of aesthetic faith, one to which, incidentally, his contemporaries Mahler and Schoenberg also subscribed – certain elements do remain surprisingly static. Take the Page's immortal one-liner, 'Schreckliches kann geschehen' ('Something terrible may happen'). This is heard three times, at Fig. 8, Fig. 11[41] and Fig. 28/3. On its first appearance the phrase descends from e^2 to a^1 sharp, outlining a diminished fifth and supported by a II–V^7 progression (not resolved) in B minor. On its second appearance the phrase begins a third higher, on g^2, and falls through diminished-seventh harmony to e^1; it is now supported by a diminished-seventh chord (on B flat), and the dotted-crotchet-and-quaver rhythm of the fourth and fifth notes has been compressed into a dotted quaver and a semiquaver.

On its final appearance (the text now is 'Schreckliches *wird* geschehen' – 'something terrible *will* happen') the pitches of the second version are retained, as is the diminished-seventh chord that supports it; but the chord is underpinned by an E flat, which gives the music a new direction, and the vocal rhythm is that of the first version. In other words, the vocal pitches are the same in versions 2 and 3 (though some of them are present in version 1); the vocal rhythm is the same in versions 1 and 3; and the chord changes each time. The metre is different each time, too, passing from a $\frac{3}{4}$ bar followed by a $\frac{4}{4}$ bar in version 1, through straight $\frac{3}{4}$ in 2, to a *combination* of duple and triple ($\frac{2}{2}$ in the voice, $\frac{3}{4}$ in the orchestra – a common 'conversational' device in Strauss) in 3. The orchestration, however, remains dominated by oboes, cor anglais and heckelphone: on their own in version 1, reinforced by flutes and bassoons in 2, and further reinforced by clarinets and trombones in 3. So on the level of pitch, metre, vocal rhythm and orchestration – not to mention text – each version retains certain characteristics of the preceding ones (and thus remains immediately recognisable as a *variant* of something already heard before), while at the same time varying others (and thus achieving an effect of progressive intensification in line with the dramatic situation).

Strauss's technique here is best understood in the light of the following statement by Schoenberg:

Motif is a unit which contains one of more features of interval and rhythm. Its presence is manifested in its constant use throughout a piece. Its usage consists of frequent repetitions, some of them unchanged, most of them varied . . . Not all the features are to be retained in a variation; but some, guaranteeing coherence, will always be present. Sometimes remotely related derivatives of a motif might become independent and then be employed like a motif. *Variation* is that kind of repetition which changes some of the features of a unit, motif, phrase, segment, section, or a larger part, but preserves others. To change everything would prevent there being any repetition at all, and thus might cause incoherence.

These text-book definitions[42] in fact constitute an accurate description of Strauss's method. He varies one aspect of a motive, and then another, but rarely more than one at a time. In this way it always remains recognisable while being able to express any facet of the dramatic situation (in Dahlhaus's words, 'each impression throws one particular feature of a situation, one trait of a character or one element of an idea into musical relief').

This point can be illustrated with reference to three of the principal motives, those of Narraboth, Salome and Jochanaan. Here the information is conveyed most efficiently in tabular form: not only is a table more economical with space than a verbal description would be, but it actually conveys more clearly the relationship of the various statements to each other. First the statements of Narraboth's motive, listed with reference to pitch level (octave transpositions are regarded as equivalent to the original pitch), intervals, metre, rhythm and timbre (it is taken for granted that the motive will be reharmonised). Where an element changes *in relation to the first statement* it is marked with a '●'. Scene divisions are indicated by lines:

Table 1: *Narraboth*

Fig./bar	Pitch	Intervals	Metre	Rhythm	Timbre
0/6					
1/1	●				●
19/4		●		●	●
34/5	●		●	●	●
49/13			●	●	●
52/1			●	●	●
54/5			●	●	●
56/3		●	●	●	●
56/7			●	●	●
57/5	●		●	●	●
76/4				●	●
78/3	●			●	●
80/4			●	●	●
86/3	●			●	●
90/5	●			●	●
123/1ff. (see below)	●			●	●
125/3					●
163/1				●	●
'Dance' M/10[43]			●	●	●

Here it is possible to list almost all the statements, since there are only a small number of them (Narraboth's part is confined to the first third or so of the opera). Such a chart is necessarily crude, since it is unable to *qualify* differences: for example, *all* variations in timbre are shown, whether the change is from cellos (in the first statement) to violas or from cellos to horns.[44] Nevertheless it tells us quite a lot. It is axiomatic, for instance, that orchestration should be changed: every line has a '●'. The next most common element to be varied is rhythm: there are '●'s in every line but two. (Particularly interesting is the diminution at Fig. 19/4, as Narraboth comes under stress for the first time: here he sees Salome approach.) The next most common is metre. (The entries at Figs. 34/5, 49/13 and 52/1 show the motive in $\frac{2}{2}$ being squashed against the $\frac{3}{4}$ of the rest of the orchestra.) More interesting, however, because less common, is the variation in pitch. The transpositions at Figs. 1/1 and 78/3 can be discounted because each is part of a sequence. Otherwise the motive is virtually pitch-specific, that is, it almost invariably unfolds a triad of F. The only significant exceptions are the entries beginning at Fig. 86/3. These occur towards the end of Scene 3, at the point where Narraboth starts to despair (Salome is throwing herself at Jochanaan before his eyes). The statement at Fig. 123 launches a contrapuntal stretto made up of overlapping entries of the Narraboth motive (not shown on the chart), Salome's first motive and her 'Ich will deinen Mund küssen'. Here the Narraboth motive is heard in several different transpositions as the character tears himself apart. Then, *for its very last statement during his lifetime* (Fig. 125/3: see Ex. 5 below), the motive reverts to its original pitch, a rhetorical gesture comparable to the recollection of the opening bars of *Tristan* as Wagner's hero dies. Narraboth kills himself at Fig. 126/2. Thereafter his motive is heard only twice: as Herod recalls him near the beginning of Scene 4, and during Salome's dance. Both times it is at its original pitch.

These remarks provide a perspective for considering the whole of Narraboth's role. Looking at the chart above we notice that it divides into three cycles, each corresponding to one of the opera's first three scenes. Three times the character comes under stress: as he sees Salome approach, as she persuades him against his will to release Jochanaan from the cistern, and as he watches the woman he loves trying to seduce another man. These three cycles form an emotional *crescendo* culminating in his death. Similarly Strauss's restatements of his basic motive go through a *crescendo* of change, one element changing after another but always in a progressive, disciplined way. Yet even after the motive has relinquished its original pitch, only to return to it as Narraboth dies, we may still feel it has not changed much. Narraboth is, after all, a one-dimensional character, his dramatic interest confined to his love for Salome just as his motive rewrites the opening cello phrase of *Tristan*.

Salome's second theme (the A major one accompanying her entrance) is ubiquitous and impossible to reproduce concisely in chart form. Nevertheless a selection of some of its more interesting variants, all taken from the first three scenes, reveals the following:

Table 2: *Salome*

Fig./bar	Pitch	Intervals	Metre	Rhythm	Timbre
8/8	●		●	●	●
20/5					
30/1	●			●	
31/2	●				●
69/1			●		●
87/1	●	●	●		●
102/1	●			●	●
112/1		●	●	●	●

Here the statement at Fig. 20/5, the moment of her entrance, is taken as definitive, and all the other statements measured against it: this is not only because this particular form is identified with the first physical appearance of the character on stage but also because this Salome motive, too, is pitch-specific, occurring more often in an A major context than in any other.[45] The version at Fig. 8/8 (when the First Soldier asks whom the Tetrarch is staring at) has therefore to be regarded as an anticipation, outlining a C sharp major triad rather than an A major one, in $\frac{3}{2}$ rather than $\frac{3}{4}$ and assigned to cellos and basses pizzicato rather than upper strings. The version at Fig. 30 is interesting because it is given, unusually, to the voice ('Ja, wie die Schönheit [einer Jungfrau]'). The statement at Fig. 69 has the motive in semiquaver sextuplets against a $\frac{4}{4}$ background; this is the moment when Salome, after having heard Jochanaan deliver himself of his first sally against Herod onstage, asks naively 'Von wem spricht er?', her vocal phrase itself presenting the same pitches as the orchestral motive, though in a different order. Figure 87 introduces a whole-tone version on the timpani ('Tochter Sodoms'), while Fig. 102 combines the motive heterophonically with itself (original form in flutes, crotchet variant in violins), first in D flat and then in its familiar A (Fig. 103/5). Finally the version at Fig. 112, one of the few to alter the opening interval, manages nevertheless to preserve a semblance of A major within a highly dissonant context. Even this selective gathering of statements conveys something of the *progressive* character of Strauss's variations: like Narraboth, Salome is apt to bend under pressure, though the prevalence of A major perhaps suggests the steely side that will emerge in her dealings with Herod.

For a character who does *not* bend under pressure, see Jochanaan, whose second theme maintains its intervals and rhythmic profile through endless changes of orchestration. His first theme, however, is more flexible:

Table 3: *Jochanaan*

Fig./bar	Pitch	Intervals	Metre	Rhythm	Timbre
12/1	●				●
14/7	●				●
60/13	●				
66/1					
89/1		●			●
128/1	●	●			●
207/1	●				
283/1	●	●	●		●
303/1	●	●			
308/5	●	●	●		
329/5	●	●		●	●
341/1	●	●			●

Again, this is selective, perhaps too much so to be of use. Nevertheless some points can be made. The 'definitive' statement this time is the one at Fig. 66, not only because it accompanies the character's first entrance but because it is the nearest thing he gets to a *theme* (with a balanced, periodic structure). Also, and above all, because this statement is given to the horns. For Jochanaan's first theme is instrument-specific, that is, closely identified with a specific timbre (that the horns are often doubled by other instruments accounts for the large number of '●'s in the 'timbre' column).[46] Unlike the other motives we have considered, it is not pitch-specific. There are only two blanks in the 'pitch' column. And the other columns show that it is much more likely to vary in its intervals than, say, the Narraboth motive, while at the same time its metre and rhythm remain relatively unchanged. The latter are its defining features, in other words, along with the horn sound.

The first three statements must therefore be regarded as anticipations, which become more like the 'definitive' version as they approach it (the very first statement, for example, is given to cellos, the next to strings and horns; it is only at the third attempt that the 'pure horn tone' emerges). After its 'definitive' statement the theme is developed extensively – we are now in the middle of the Jochanaan–Salome dialogue – but at Fig. 74 (not shown on the chart) it returns in its definitive form. This statement serves to round off the section. Figure 89 presents the theme in a new guise, with an expanded interval ('und suche des Menschen Sohn!'); this is the form that will be heard at 341, when the Prophet is 'restored to life'. At Fig. 128, shortly after Narraboth's suicide, it moves to trumpets and oboes, again with an expanded interval, as Jochanaan begins finally to lose patience. In the ensuing interlude it reverts to something like its original form, in which it returns several times (though transposed) in the first half of Scene 4 (Figs. 207ff.). These are the long stretches in which Jochanaan, now back in the cistern, resumes the prophesying strains of his first utterances. At Fig. 283 his theme is taken over by Herod in $\frac{7}{4}$ ('Er ist ein heil'ger Mann'); and it is Herod, too, after the ring of death has been drawn from him, who is responsible for the amazing stretched-out version at Fig. 303. Now as chromatic as formerly it was diatonic, and rhythmically distorted where formerly it was simple to the point of banality, the theme pervades Herod's and Salome's final speeches as if haunting them from beyond the grave (Figs. 308/5, 329/5). 'Aber du bist tot', she crows in the second of these; but he lives again now that he has seen his God. Again the sense of progression, from the first clear-cut statements to the final distortions (cancelled only by the very last statement of all, Fig. 341), is plain.

This 'progressive' aspect is one of the most distinctive characteristics of Strauss's leitmotive technique, and one which links it, historically, with the constant variation of Mahler and Schoenberg (not to mention the 'developing variation' of Brahms) while setting it off a little from the leitmotive technique of Wagner. A sense of progression would not be possible without a definitive statement, at or near the beginning, against which subsequent statements could be measured. My charts are of course predicated on this idea. And yet this cuts directly across the 'relativist' concept of a leitmotive postulated by Dahlhaus. To recall: 'It is seldom wise to take the earliest form in which a theme or motif appears as necessarily its primary form, from which all subsequent forms derive as secondary variations. Rather, they are all different impressions of the same material, and all principally equal in status . . . ' This is the most contentious aspect of his description. The idea of a perfectly relativist universe, in which all the different forms of a leitmotive circle around an imaginary centre without any one of them being more important than the others, may be attractive in theory, but it is too abstract to serve as a model of how the music actually works (let alone how we hear it: in practice, of course, we can *only* experience a leitmotive in relation to its previous forms). It certainly does not apply to Strauss. I doubt that it even applies to Wagner, except for the Wagner of *Götterdämmerung* and *Parsifal*. What is the first appearance of the Valhalla theme in Scene 2 of *Das Rheingold* if not a 'definitive statement'?

Nevertheless a contextual approach to the leitmotive, such as Dahlhaus himself adopts in his commentaries on Wagner, is essential if we are to get beyond surface detail. Strauss's 'progressive' conception of the leitmotive, with its dependence upon an initial statement, may well be tied in with the 'simplistic' view outlined earlier in the chapter. If a composer conceives of his themes as embodying clear-cut dramatic ideas, and indeed labels them as such in his sketches, it is likely that the initial version will prove a *starting-point* for the later ones. The result is naturally a sense of progression from one version to another. This can also be tied in with Strauss's idea of musical inspiration.[47]

My final example is designed to show that an awareness of a motive's 'definitive' version is essential for an understanding of what happens to it subsequently. The motive chosen this time is Salome's first one, which sounds as the curtain rises.[48] Again, the motive is so ubiquitous that every statement cannot be discussed. I shall concentrate on those that maintain the original pitch level. First, the initial statement itself, which is shown in Ex. 2. This outlines a descending triad, with the G sharp acting as $\hat{5}$ of C sharp minor. After a transposed version in which G natural functions as $\hat{2}$ in F (Fig. 2/8), the motive returns at its original pitch level, though an octave lower and in diminution, to accompany the Page's 'Du siehst sie immer an' ('You are always looking at her', Fig. 7/2); now, however, G sharp, enharmonically reinterpreted as A flat,[49] functions as $\hat{3}$ of F minor (see Ex. 3). As we would expect, there are

Example 2

Example 3

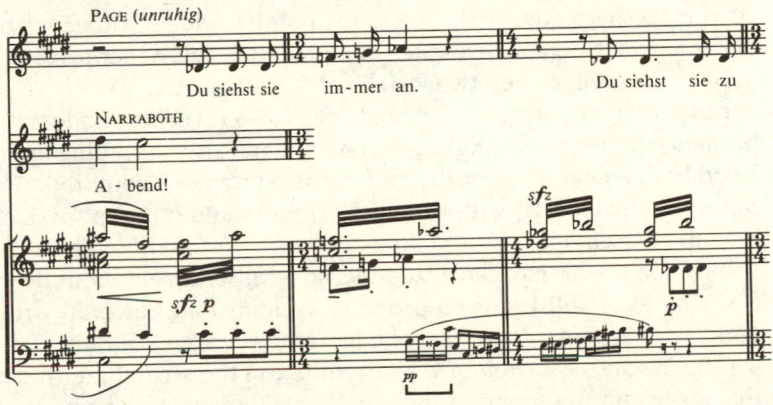

many statements of this motive (often with fascinating rhythmic variations) in Scene 2. From these I single out the one at Fig. 29/10, where it is harmonised in D flat to accompany Salome's reference to the moon.[50] It returns again at pitch at Fig. 37/7, now supported by a *Tristan* chord (Narraboth is speaking), and again at 44/3 (plain C sharp minor as Salome asserts herself).

Scene 3 sees Salome's motive combined with those of Jochanaan as well as with Narraboth's. At Fig. 77/5 the *Tristan* chord returns, supporting a spiky ostinato derived from the first three notes of her motive; but now the motive is no longer at its original pitch. This is restored at Fig. 79/2 (D flat major again, since she has just compared Jochanaan to the moon). Still more imaginative is the version at Fig. 83, where the motive is heard at pitch but in an A major context

Example 4

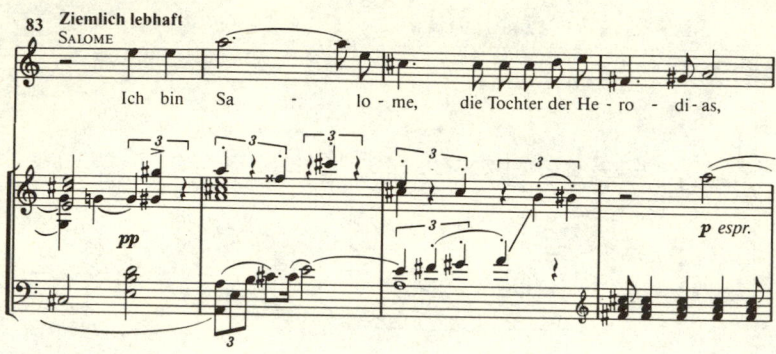

(that is, G sharp now = $\hat{7}$). This is the point at which Salome introduces herself by name, evoking simultaneously two of her principal motives as well as her two principal keys (see Ex. 4). There is another original-pitch reference at Fig. 109/3 ('Tochter Sodoms'), but much more interesting is the contrapuntal stretto leading up to Narraboth's death, when the motive is combined (admittedly at different pitch levels) with that of Narraboth and other motives of Salome herself (see Ex. 5). Strauss's *grandes combinaisons de thèmes* sometimes have an academic, self-conscious air about them (as if he were still trying to prove to Brahms that he could write good counterpoint),[51] but this one has real weight.

The massive assertion of C sharp minor in the second interlude, the opera's turning-point, brings another statement of the motive at its original pitch, this time the famous one in the contrabassoon, with its new, whole-tone continuation (Fig. 151/6).[52] The most interesting transformations in the scene that follows, notably those at Fig. 175 (Strauss's heckelphone proving indispensable) and in the 'Dance' (D/2–3), are not at the original pitch. But at the opera's climax Strauss rises to the occasion with a version that absolutely demands to be related back to the initial statement. The 'bitonal' racket that greets the appearance of the head (Fig. 314) boils down to a C sharp minor statement of the motive jammed against a diminished-seventh chord in C, the whole underpinned by a C bass pedal. G sharp is reinterpreted again as A flat, but now as flat $\hat{6}$ within the new 'tonality', an astonishing rereading. The C sharp minor triad can also be understood as a minor Neapolitan ($\flat$II) of C, one of the most intense relationships in classical harmony (the first

Example 5

Example 6

movement of Schubert's *Death and the Maiden* Quartet provides a
rare example). But in fact the 'tonic' C sharp resolves upwards, as
an appoggiatura, to D (Fig. 314/2), confirming the underlying
diminished harmonisation. And a few bars later the whole passage
is to 'resolve' to C sharp minor, with the horns braying out Salome's
motive, now consonant with the harmony (see Ex. 6). The motive
has remained at pitch throughout. But by 'harmonising' it first in C

and then in C sharp (the two most important keys in the opera),[53] Strauss has stood the rules of harmony on their head: instead of the dissonant melody notes resolving into the harmony, the harmony has swung round to the melody. Salome achieves her ends by sheer persistence; it is only by understanding the history of her motive, with its almost obsessive adherence to a particular pitch level, that we can feel the full force of the climax.

IV

Moments like these open up large issues of representation in Strauss's opera: the leitmotive is, after all, a means of representation. Strauss was what the Germans call an *Ausdrucksmusiker*: that is, he 'subscribed vigorously to an aesthetic oriented toward feeling and expression as opposed to an aesthetic oriented toward formal concerns'.[54] This is clear from his Foreword to Berlioz's orchestration treatise, with its emphasis on 'great, poetic ideas', and from many anecdotes. Alfred Kalisch quotes a 'well-known saying' attributed to Strauss: 'There is no such thing as Abstract Music; there is good music and bad music. If it is good, it means something; and then it is Programme Music.'[55] This attitude even influenced his conducting: Strauss told Klemperer in 1928 that he was unable to conduct a Beethoven symphony unless he had a programme in mind, a remark which amazed the younger man.[56]

In *Salome* this attitude is reflected first and foremost in the innumerable examples of pictorial description (or 'onomatopoeia', as Robin Holloway calls it). Everyone has his or her favourites: the notorious solo double bass, the tambourine that sounds at every reference to a dance, the astonishing succession of images that bursts forth after Herod's final capitulation (Fig. 300).[57] One of my own is the music accompanying the following exchange:

HEROD: . . . wie ein betrunkenes Weib, das durch Wolken taumelt . . .
HERODIAS: Nein, der Mond ist wie der Mond, das ist alles. Wir wollen hineingehn.

HEROD: [The moon] reels through the clouds like a drunken woman . . .
HERODIAS: No; the moon is like the moon, that is all. Let us go within . . .

The lurching figure in the lower strings, suggesting Herod's 'drunken woman', and the prosaic nature of his wife's response (see Ex. 7) create musical images that are unforgettable.

And yet . . . In a famous letter to Romain Rolland, concerning the programme of the *Symphonia Domestica*, Strauss wrote:

In my opinion . . . a poetic programme is nothing but a pretext for the purely musical expression and development of my emotions, and not a simple *musical description* [his emphasis] of concrete everyday facts. For that would be quite contrary to the spirit of music. But so that music should not lose itself in pure abstractions and drift in limitless directions, it needs to be held within bounds which determine a certain form, and it is the programme which fixes these bounds. And an analytic programme of this kind should be nothing more than a starting-point. Those who are interested in it can use it. Those who really know how to listen to music doubtless have no need for it.[58]

There are echoes here of Schopenhauer; the reference to 'the spirit of music', especially, recalls Schopenhauer's remarks on Beethoven in *The World as Will and Idea*.[59] According to the philosopher, music expresses the 'innermost essence of things', which mere words cannot reach. He was extremely hostile to programme music (by which he could only have meant music before Beethoven, since his book was first published in 1818). Schoenberg reformulated these remarks nearly a hundred years later in his essay 'The Relationship to the Text'. In a vocal or programmatic work the music represents the 'real' language, the text a translation; the music must not, therefore, rely on the text for its coherence.[60] This attitude has become almost axiomatic for music analysis.

Its implication for Strauss is that analysis based on the text, 'musical imagery', etc. is of limited value in itself. In seeking to understand a passage like Ex. 7, we need also to consider its 'purely musical' features: the rhythmic structure, the juxtaposition of whole-tone and diatonic elements, the use of B sharp/C as a pivot and the relation of this pitch to the large-scale tonal design – as well as the place of the passage in the opera as a whole (a variation of it occurs immediately before the 'Dance', for example). This would take us far beyond the scope of the present chapter.

The matter is complicated by the fact that in Strauss criticism, as in music criticism in general, representation has become confused with realism. As Dahlhaus points out, the composer's earliest critics – including Rolland himself – interpreted passages of musical illustration as being 'realistic', using the word in an approbatory sense.[61] Ernest Newman, writing in 1910, equated realism with progress.[62] Strauss himself seemed to be influenced by such thinking when, having reached a bad patch in the composition of *Die ägyptische Helena*, he wrote to Hofmannsthal that he wished to avoid 'the so-

Example 7

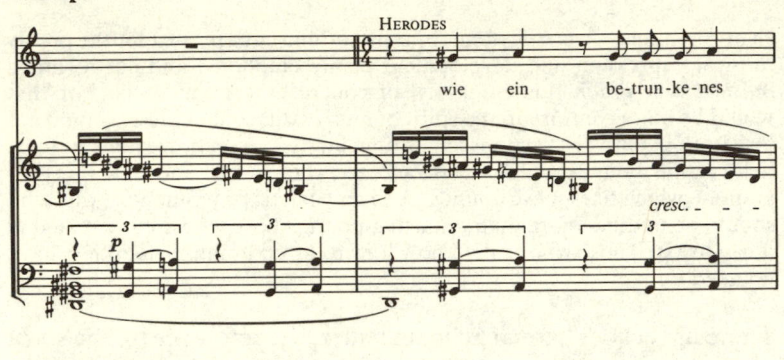

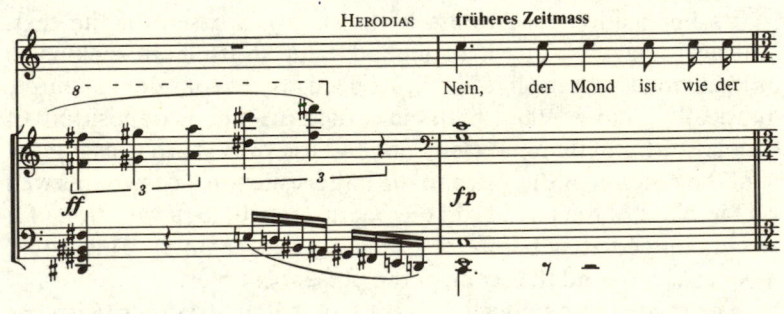

called realism of *Salome*.[63] But the illustrative passages in *Salome* are no more realistic than the bleating of the sheep in *Don Quixote* or the carping of the critics in *Ein Heldenleben*.[64] They are more properly understood within the context of Symbolism, in which Wilde's play has its roots,[65] or even within that of literary aestheticism. Ellmann writes in his Wilde biography: 'Pater declared that, life being a drift of momentary acts, we must cultivate each moment to the full, seeking "not the fruit of experience, but experience itself." Dorian Gray quotes this without acknowledgement.'[66] Surely Strauss was an adherent of the same philosophy (though he would never have articulated it as such). The illustrative textures in *Salome*, constantly changing in response to the text, are his means of 'cultivating each moment to the full'.[67] Perhaps this is how we should understand his subsequent career. The stylistic discontinuities in *Elektra*, the 'retreat' to a simpler harmonic language in *Der Rosenkavalier*, the various types of neo-classicism in the later works – these are all no more than a logical extension of the aestheticist tendencies in *Salome*, in other words, a variety of different ways of satisfying a musical appetite that wants to experience everything.

V

To speak of an unbroken history of music drama in terms of a specific operatic genre founded by Wagner, a history that reaches from Strauss's *Salome* (1905) and *Elektra* (1908), Schoenberg's *Erwartung* (1909) and *Moses und Aron* (1930–2), Berg's *Wozzeck* (1925) and *Lulu* (1937) to Bernd Alois Zimmermann's *Die Soldaten* (1965) is not misguided, despite the differences in musical language between the various works.

Dahlhaus's bland statement[68] provokes disagreement; it is all the more provocative in that he argues elsewhere that music drama is 'not really a genre' at all (rather, each work of Wagner's represents 'an individual recourse').[69] To answer platitude with platitude, the truth probably lies somewhere between the two extremes. If one looks at any individual work in enough detail, one will end up by arguing its genre out of existence. On the other hand there can be no genre that consists entirely of exceptions. *Salome* is a music drama in all the accepted senses of the term. But if the statement is to carry conviction, we must get beyond the level of platitude and ask in what ways the work (as opposed to the leitmotive technique) *differs* from Wagner.

Above all, in its pace. *Salome* is a one-acter, a form of stage work that Wagner never tried (if we discount *Das Rheingold*, with its four scenes rolled into one, and the early, 'Bayreuth' version of *Der fliegende Holländer*). The entire action is compressed into an hour and three quarters, roughly the time taken up by the first act of *Parsifal*, the last of *Die Meistersinger* or the Prologue and first act of *Götterdämmerung*. Yet we have only to think of these 'precedents' to realise how utterly different they are in pace, character and dramatic timing. The epic sweep of Wagner, his ability to suggest a lifetime in an afternoon, is utterly foreign to Strauss. *Salome* zips by (the same is true of *Elektra*, though not of Strauss's earlier experiment in this form, *Feuersnot*), glorying in its 'aestheticist' contrasts, its abrupt changes from one style to another: its actual pace, the rate at which things happen, is closer to Berg or Janáček. The only act of Wagner's remotely comparable in character and dramatic timing is the second of *Götterdämmerung*. Like *Salome* it has a built-in symphonic reprise (with Siegfried's and Brünnhilde's oaths recalled in the final trio, just as Salome's music is summed up in her final monologue); usually recapitulatory functions in Wagner are divided across the various acts, but here the compression that is necessary in order to achieve such an effect within a single span results in a dynamism more commonly associated with Strauss (not for nothing did he call *Salome* 'a scherzo with a fatal conclusion'). Indeed the 'continuous crescendo' characteristic of *Elektra* – it is less strongly felt in *Salome* – may well have had its origins here.

The dynamism of *Salome* is also a function of Strauss's 'progressive' conception of the leitmotive, which (to widen the discussion still further) derives from the 'narrative' type of thematic transformation developed in earlier, purely orchestral works such as *Don Juan*, *Till Eulenspiegel* and, above all, *Don Quixote*. In works such as these a theme becomes a means of 'telling a story', a peg on which to hang a series of discrete programmatic events; and as the theme is transformed under the pressure of the moment (that is, of the context), it acquires a 'history' and thus the potential for summing up an entire human life. In this respect, and in this respect only, Strauss's operas may legitimately be compared to symphonic poems.

The other major distinguishing feature of Strauss's music dramas, as opposed to Wagner's, is the quality (in both senses)[70] of the musical ideas. *Salome* particularly contains ideas Wagner would never have thought of (but then he never had any need of them): not only the exoticisms, but also and above all the utterly distinctive material associated with Herod (even if he has no distinctive *themes*). This is partly a matter of orchestral sound, partly a matter of the whole-tone and other non-diatonic configurations that were not a regular part of Wagner's vocabulary. But in addition to these, the sudden departures, changes of subject, wanderings of attention on Herod's part – in their musical realisation also a matter of pace – create an atmosphere not unlike that of *Wozzeck*, as has often been remarked. 'Expressionism' is only just around the corner. And even the melodic shortwindedness hints at (non-Wagnerian) things to come. Towards the end of his life, many operas later, Strauss was to badger his librettist for 'closed forms' and rhyming couplets.[71] So, by a commodius vicus of recirculation, *Die Liebe der Danae* joins up with *Arabella*, *Ariadne* and *Der Rosenkavalier* to find its unlikeliest source: not in Mozart, nor in the number operas of any other composer, but in music drama.

6 Tonal and dramatic structure

TETHYS CARPENTER

I

Strauss's choice of subject for *Salome* represents a departure from the preoccupations of his earlier works. At the time of its composition, his success as a composer rested principally on his body of tone poems from *Aus Italien* (1886) to *Ein Heldenleben* (finished in 1899). These appear to continue in the Lisztian tradition, making use of thematic transformation in their delineation of a programme and employing a Wagnerian musical idiom. It is evident that this, at least, was Strauss's starting-point. But by the late 1890s Strauss was tending to deal with either massively grandiose conceptions or series of very literal pictorial or characteristic episodes both of which stretched the boundaries of a purely musical form to the limits; *Symphonia Domestica* (1903), with its strict adherence to a somewhat absurd story-line, is often thought to mark a serious decline. When Strauss remarked in 1905, 'In my opinion . . . a poetic programme is nothing but a pretext for the purely musical expression and development of my emotions, and not a simple *musical description* of concrete everyday facts',[1] he was summing up not only its strength, as he imagined, in terms of freedom but also its weakness in terms of structure: unless bound by purely musical laws, a piece that is not literal must be in danger of complete formlessness.

Initially Strauss adopted the musical laws of sonata, rondo and variation forms and tied the surface together thematically. But one senses an increasing rift between this surface, however well organised, and the conventional background, particularly in terms of key, because, curiously, his themes, unlike those of Liszt, are rarely transformed in a tonal sense (*Zarathustra* is possibly an exception); rather, they are manipulated rhythmically. Nor do they imply any particular tonal context or resolution; tonal form itself seems to

88

have implied no particular tonal principle to Strauss. Instead, he employed both a brilliantly illustrative and developmental leitmotive technique, supported by local harmonic innovation, and, most importantly, very sophisticated orchestration. Indeed, orchestral sonority almost appears to have become a function of structure. But the later, expanded tone poems frequently sound, on the large scale, overworked and incoherent, in spite of the fact that they are obviously more descriptive than he might, theoretically, have wished.

To Strauss, Wilde's play must have seemed the perfect opportunity to avoid such formal problems: it has a highly overcharged and exotic story, shocking enough positively to demand the sort of 'modern' tonal and orchestral effects for which he was already well known; it has a text (if *Salomé* 'cries out for music',[2] most of the tone poems had cried out for words); and, best of all, this text is perfectly structured. He must also have been attracted by its voguish orientalism; by its strong female lead and its simple but dramatic oppositions; by its psychological undercurrents, which might be effectively portrayed by means of leitmotives; and by the textual leitmotives already mentioned,[3] descriptive and suggestive allusions which could be ideally reflected in the orchestra. *Guntram* and *Feuersnot*, his first attempts at opera, contained little of this: he found them hard going and their appeal was limited.

Strauss's first task was to cut the play. As Roland Tenschert has shown, he removed almost half of it, including references to some of Wilde's most powerful 'motifs',[4] in particular the moon, who watches over the play, changing her face in a reflection of the action; Strauss's moon is hardly more than a conversational gambit. In general his omissions consist of fairly inessential exchanges (especially theological) and characters (a Nubian, the guests), and the result is, with the odd exception, greatly to tauten the dramatic structure without fundamentally altering its basis.

The concision of Strauss's libretto seems to have been designed to emphasise Wilde's most formal, rather than his most 'musical', devices; he would appear to have been concerned to maximise its structural rigidity. Two features are of special importance: the clear use of symmetry and the grouping of events on all different levels in threes (see Table 1).

In each scene these groupings are slightly differently arranged, but the overall episodic and symmetrical nature is remarkable. The first scene functions as an atmospheric introduction to the whole, an

Table 1

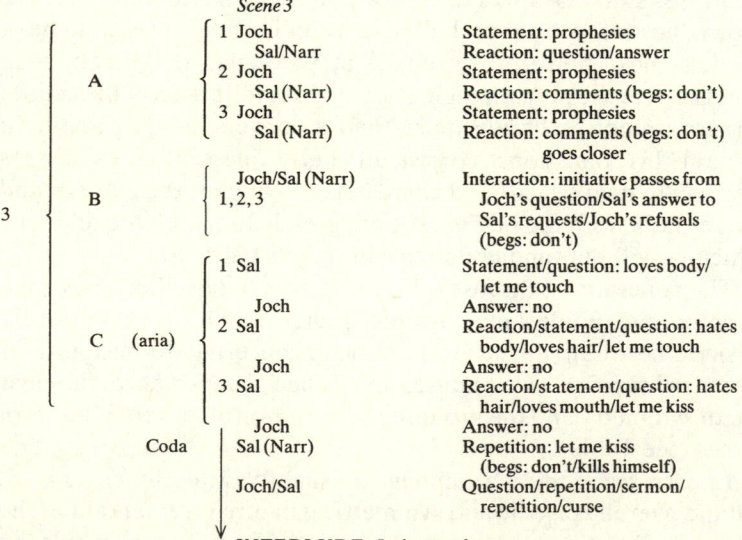

			Scene 1	
1		a	Narraboth/Page	Comments: Salome/moon
		b	Soldier 1/Soldier 2	: Jews
	A	a	Narr/P	: Sal/warning
		b	Sol 1/Sol 2	: Herod
		a	Narr/P	: Sal/warning
	B		Jochanaan	Statement: Prophesies
		b	Sol 2/Sol 1	Reaction: comments
	A	b1	Cappadocian/Sol 1	: questions/answers
		a	Narr/P	Comments: Sal/warning
			Scene 2: Salome appears	
2		Intro	Sal(P)	Comments: Sal (warning) moon
		a	Joch	Statement: prophesies
	A	b	Sal/Sol 2 (Narr)	Reaction: questions/answers
			Sal/Sol 2 (Slave)	
			Sal (Narr)/Sol 1	
	B	a	Joch	Statement: prophesies
		b	Sal/Sol 2	Reaction: wants/refuses
			Sal	Comments: cistern
			Sal/Sol 1	: wants/refuses
	C	(aria) 1	(P)Sal	Persuasion: (warning) seduces
			Narr	: refuses
		2	Sal	: seduces
			Narr	: refuses
		3	Sal	: seduces
			Narr	: agrees

. . . . INTERLUDE: Jochanaan appears . . . .

			Scene 3	
3		1	Joch	Statement: prophesies
			Sal/Narr	Reaction: question/answer
	A	2	Joch	Statement: prophesies
			Sal (Narr)	Reaction: comments (begs: don't)
		3	Joch	Statement: prophesies
			Sal (Narr)	Reaction: comments (begs: don't) goes closer
	B	1, 2, 3	Joch/Sal (Narr)	Interaction: initiative passes from Joch's question/Sal's answer to Sal's requests/Joch's refusals (begs: don't)
	C	(aria) 1	Sal	Statement/question: loves body/ let me touch
			Joch	Answer: no
		2	Sal	Reaction/statement/question: hates body/loves hair/ let me touch
			Joch	Answer: no
		3	Sal	Reaction/statement/question: hates hair/loves mouth/let me kiss
			Joch	Answer: no
	Coda		Sal (Narr)	Repetition: let me kiss (begs: don't/kills himself)
			Joch/Sal	Question/repetition/sermon/ repetition/curse

. . . . INTERLUDE: Jochanaan leaves . . . .

Table 1 (*cont.*)

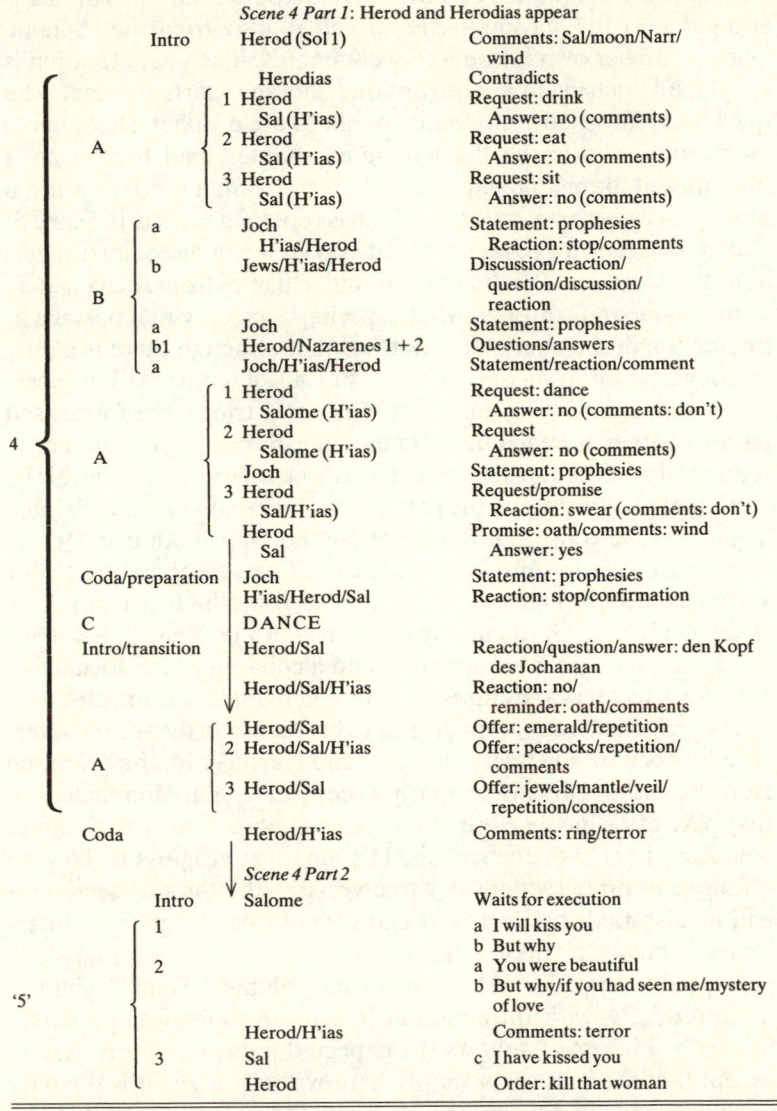

		Scene 4 Part 1: Herod and Herodias appear	
	Intro	Herod (Sol 1)	Comments: Sal/moon/Narr/ wind
		Herodias	Contradicts
A	1	Herod	Request: drink
		Sal (H'ias)	Answer: no (comments)
	2	Herod	Request: eat
		Sal (H'ias)	Answer: no (comments)
	3	Herod	Request: sit
		Sal (H'ias)	Answer: no (comments)
B	a	Joch	Statement: prophesies
		H'ias/Herod	Reaction: stop/comments
	b	Jews/H'ias/Herod	Discussion/reaction/ question/discussion/ reaction
	a	Joch	Statement: prophesies
	b1	Herod/Nazarenes 1 + 2	Questions/answers
	a	Joch/H'ias/Herod	Statement/reaction/comment
A	1	Herod	Request: dance
		Salome (H'ias)	Answer: no (comments: don't)
	2	Herod	Request
		Salome (H'ias)	Answer: no (comments)
		Joch	Statement: prophesies
	3	Herod	Request/promise
		Sal/H'ias)	Reaction: swear (comments: don't)
		Herod	Promise: oath/comments: wind
		Sal	Answer: yes
Coda/preparation		Joch	Statement: prophesies
		H'ias/Herod/Sal	Reaction: stop/confirmation
C		DANCE	
Intro/transition		Herod/Sal	Reaction/question/answer: den Kopf des Jochanaan
		Herod/Sal/H'ias	Reaction: no/ reminder: oath/comments
A	1	Herod/Sal	Offer: emerald/repetition
	2	Herod/Sal/H'ias	Offer: peacocks/repetition/ comments
	3	Herod/Sal	Offer: jewels/mantle/veil/ repetition/concession
Coda		Herod/H'ias	Comments: ring/terror
		Scene 4 Part 2	
	Intro	Salome	Waits for execution
	1		a I will kiss you
			b But why
	2		a You were beautiful
			b But why/if you had seen me/mystery of love
		Herod/H'ias	Comments: terror
	3	Sal	c I have kissed you
		Herod	Order: kill that woman

The left brace groups the rows labelled **4** and **'5'**.

ABA structure where the A sections comment and B presents Jochanaan. Narraboth's ecstatic 'Ja, sie kommt auf uns zu!' leads straight into the second scene, which is also tripartite. Salome begins with her own introductory comments. Then her attention is caught by Jochanaan's interruption, and she starts to react: she questions Narraboth; she wants to talk to the prophet; she seduces Narraboth, who in the third verse capitulates, and Jochanaan is brought out during the interlude. Here the format is ABC (aria), a more processive arrangement, which is repeated exactly in Scene 3. But in this scene the tendency to set everything in threes is stronger, as is the symmetry: the dramatic initiative passes from Jochanaan in A to Salome in C through what is perhaps the only real passage of interaction in the opera. It is notable that although there is plenty of conversation in *Salome* – it is, after all, a 'conversation piece' – this almost invariably takes the form of a trio in the formalised pattern statement/reaction/comment, question/answer/comment or request/answer/comment, each heard three times. In the central (B) section of the third scene the pattern briefly breaks down as Salome begins to take control of the situation and Narraboth becomes an irrelevance. Even this is built around her three requests for Jochanaan to speak to her; in the outer sections the structure is very clear. Unlike her third entreaty to Narraboth in Scene 2, Salome's third entreaty here is not granted, and a coda, in which Jochanaan questions, lectures and curses her to her demented refrain, ensues.

As Jochanaan retreats in disgust to his cistern in the second interlude the focus of the opera changes, and Herod (with the charming Herodias, whose duty is primarily to contradict him) dominates the first part of Scene 4. Here is charted his obsession with Salome, balancing hers with Jochanaan. His amatory progress is likewise arranged in three sections of three verses – the three A sections – and he also finds that his final extravagant plea is ignored. Interspersed between these stanzas are the religious discussions prompted by the voice of Jochanaan and Salome's 'Dance', giving a large ABACA with Introduction (again atmospheric) and Coda. Salome's 'Liebestod' follows the expected pattern in three verses, except that she must now supply her own responses; it is the only extended solo in the opera. Her concluding phrase, 'Ich habe deinen Mund geküsst, Jochanaan', needs, for the first time, no response; Herod supplies one, violently rounding off the symmetry.

This compelling balancing of every statement with a counterstatement or refrain – within such a systematised structure – is perhaps what Strauss found especially fascinating about the play. Wilde must surely have been referring to this when he commented that *Salomé* contained 'refrains whose recurring *motifs* [Wilde's emphasis] make it so like a piece of music and bind it together as a ballad'.[5] This observation generally prompts an examination of Strauss's leitmotive technique,[6] which is certainly complex. However, as he had discovered to his cost in the tone poems, referential motivic working does not necessarily provide a satisfactory musical framework. (He was, in any case, quite fluent enough at this not to require help from Wilde.) It was, rather, far more important that the play – besides making greater use of textual motives – actually implied a definite type of musical structure. This was precisely what Strauss needed in the background to 'bind together' the very various and often opposing strands of his musical surface. His cuts render the libretto still more carefully structured: there is as little descriptive material as possible, and those 'external' sections which do remain (such as the Jews' dispute) seem to owe their existence simply to the necessity for formal symmetry. It is also significant that when there is too much going on in a section of text Strauss overlays the parts, or even, in his setting, speeds up the tempo: each dramatic unit is approximately the same length.

II

The extent to which this 'formalising' procedure is immediately noticeable is difficult to say, for although one clearly sees and hears successive alternations of ensembles and styles, Strauss's musical language is, of course, extremely powerful and sounds continuous. In *Salome* the normal leitmotivic texture is strikingly enhanced by the range of his methods of characterisation. It is evident that as well as leitmotives each character or group of characters also has its own key areas. One or two of these are stable and simply used.

The Jews are mentioned and sing only in D minor, while D major, used by Jochanaan at the end of his first prophetic utterance in Scene 3 (Fig. 68) and to close his sermon (Fig. 135/9), illuminates divine revelation. As Herod blasphemously offers Salome the Veil of the Sanctuary (Fig. 297/5) we hear the Jews' D minor motive followed by a blaze of quickly fading D major, instantly recognisable. And when, in the second verse of her final aria (Fig. 338/7), Salome slides into D major as she recalls Jochanaan's strange-sounding music (here his theme in fourths), she might almost have begun to understand it. The other, subsidiary religious figures have no tonal independence, merely echoing Jochanaan (Figs. 14–19, 209–14), and this is generally true of Narraboth, who is obsessed with Salome, and the Page, although they have their own motives which do recur at pitch.[7] Only Narraboth's death succeeds in diverting the orchestra away from Salome (Fig. 126/2).

Herodias, by the end of the opera, seems to have adopted E major, and to good effect (Fig. 351/2), but she is so thoroughly inflexible a character that she can impose her peculiarly flat and strident diatonicism equally well in any key, usually one at some distance from that of its immediate context and often with bitonal effect: she functions by opposing her surroundings, and her bitonality is a symptom of her contrariness. This is partly illustrated by the orchestration, and the tonality of Herod, likewise, is closely bound up with Strauss's other means of characterisation. He appears at the beginning of the fourth scene to a background of C major, but this is so overlaid by the cacophony of the Jews and then by his own slithering whole-tone scales (Fig. 155) that he is depicted more by the sonority of his accompaniment than by its tonality which, though static, is deliberately weak. It is only when Herod's anxiety at his surroundings ceases and he focuses on Salome (Fig. 172) that he is able to pull himself into a series of bright and stable keys – none of which is, in fact, his own. Throughout the scene he continues to appropriate keys apparently at random or to reflect those of Jochanaan or Salome. His reception of her dance and his rapturous interruption of her request (Fig. 250) are good examples of this, yet how easily he reverts to his nervous ambiguity when he finds out what she wants. It is only when he gives in to her demand and moves onto a dark C minor (Figs. 298, 351) that he acquires any sort of resolve of his own: his last command is entirely decisive.

The difficulty here is that neither C minor nor C major is exclusively Herod's key, although he is rarely referred to in any other (see, for instance, how the First Soldier's phrase 'der Tetrarch hat es verboten' veers into C minor at Fig. 19). Rather, Strauss is using C both as a descriptive key, in its specific colourings (such as the blurred C minor which comes to be associated with death), and as a more abstract symbol, on which may be built all sorts of sonorities, of everything that opposes or conflicts with Salome.

As one would expect, Jochanaan's music also centres on C, usually settling into A flat or E flat major; when he proclaims his faith all three keys are clear and uncomplicated, unlike Herod's (Figs. 11; 30/9; 130; 210). E flat, differently orchestrated, is also the key of the cistern (Fig. 45/5). However, as the second and third scenes progress, his condemnations of Herodias and his furious repulsions of Salome's advances become less and less referential as he loses control of the situation and is sucked progressively further towards her tonal orbit: eventually his curse pivots him abruptly into C sharp minor as he abandons the attempt to reform her and returns to his prison. This sort of transferable tonality has a powerful dramatic effect; as an extension of Wagner's technique, Strauss's use of tonal leitmotives, though not altogether consistent, often makes it possible to tell at once who is dominating the action even when the surface may be busy with more immediate matters.

Salome's music has as its centre C sharp; again this has various functions. The opera begins in C sharp minor with Salome's motive, but when Salome herself appears she does so in A major, and the second scene begins and ends in this key. Here is Strauss's first attempt at a 'progressive' tonality, for Salome's character develops from naivety through frustrated desire to satisfaction of that desire, mirrored by A major, C sharp minor and C sharp major; as the central protagonist of the opera she not only inspires but also motivates the dramatic progress. This is not to say that she is not initially influenced by her surroundings: as she sees and speaks to Jochanaan for the first time in Scene 3, she not only sings in his keys (Fig. 91, taking up the B major of his Fig. 66) but borrows his motives (Fig. 78/6) and hangs on to his pronouncements (Fig. 89: 'Wer ist das, des Menschen Sohn?'; compare Herod's suspicious 'Was soll das heissen, der Erlöser der Welt?', three bars before Fig. 209).

It is worth noting here, incidentally, that all of the servants' and soldiers' music is distinguished by a lack not simply of tonal but also of thematic independence: they slavishly repeat the material used by the questioner (Figs. 35, 69, 80) or invert it, particularly when talking to each other (Figs. 8–9). It has to be said, however, that Strauss was rather fond of this sort of device. It is disconcerting to find it where it is not expected, as at Fig. 39, where Jochanaan inexplicably – and in the 'wrong' key – transposes a soldier's reply.

Salome, in any case, is not disposed, after the transitional 3B section, to imitate anyone. Even in her more innocent early guise it is quite apparent that she is deeply – tonally – self-centred. When she is not talking about herself directly, she absorbs everything that interests her into her own sphere, including the moon (C sharp →

A major, Figs. 29–30), Narraboth, whom she serenades in A minor, and Jochanaan (see Ex. 1).

Example 1

The use of the minor mode as she seduces Narraboth is interesting; the suppression of her C sharp recurs in the outer (A minor) sections of the 'Dance', in which Salome is again acting insincerely (and where it must also represent her apparent subservience to Herod's C major). When she gets what she wants from Narraboth (Fig. 59), it reappears. But in her 'innocent' A major she is mostly quite straightforward, introducing herself to Jochanaan with clear confidence (Fig. 83).[8]

It is Jochanaan who jolts that confidence. By the end of Scene 3, during which she has surged impetuously into sharper keys and been repulsed, her longing and desperation have thrown her quite off-centre; but then in the ensuing interlude C sharp minor is unmistakably confirmed by Strauss's graphic use of leitmotives as the key of her new, mad resolution. When, having endured Herod's attentions all the way through the first part of Scene 4, she is finally given the object for which she has schemed, C sharp suddenly emerges as the tonic of her monologue. At first this is her spiteful C sharp minor as she gloats over her revenge, but as she recalls Jochanaan's beauty and her desire for it she softens into C sharp major, in which key, having at last kissed his mouth, she finishes.

It would appear from this that, because of the formal symmetry of the libretto, Strauss has provided himself with both a superb descriptive technique and the perfect means of controlling the tonal structure. Indeed, his underlying plan is remarkably symmetrical,

Example 2

Jochanaan/cistern	E♭	E	Salome/Herodias
Jochanaan/Herod	C	C♯	Salome
Jochanaan	A♭	A	Salome

as Ex. 2 shows. Jochanaan's A flat and E flat balance around his central C, Salome's A and E around her C sharp. By Salome's final 'transfiguration' at the end of the opera, C natural and C sharp – eventually C minor and C sharp major – are juxtaposed without preparation, clarifying the widely differing tonal events earlier in the opera into their fundamental opposition.[9] However, although this opposition and the progress towards its clarification is evident at the background of Strauss's setting, it is not, for several reasons, some of which are implicit in his musical material and others in the background itself, in fact an entirely satisfactory solution to the problem of large-scale tonal coherence.

As is apparent from a more detailed graphing of *Salome*'s key structure, there are certain areas which seem to bear no relation to either referential centre (see Ex. 3: this should be read in conjunction with Table 1). Jochanaan's keys are particularly flexible. Often they appear irrelevant, such as the B flat major at Fig. 207, but can be seen to be part of some larger scheme (here a falling progression in thirds – see also Fig. 39). The most extended non-referential area is the B major of Scene 3, which is maintained, complete with perfect cadences, until at least the end of the first verse of Salome's paean of adoration (3C: cadence on V at Fig. 95). The orchestral interlude preceding this has clearly taken the key from A major to Jochanaan's C major, where his theme in fourths is heard, managing actually to sound powerful rather than cloying. The end of this theme has as its distinctive feature a modulation down a semitone, which naturally takes the key to B (see Ex. 4). This is heard as temporary, but Strauss decided to retain it as a tonic. His reason, no doubt, was to give a strong internal symmetry to the tripartite form of the scene, but of all his 'non-structural' tonalities this B major is the most curious, especially as he also uses the theme as a means of structural modulation, first between Fig. 68 and Fig. 69, where Salome, still in A major, ignores the anticipated C sharp, then at Fig. 78, as she echoes his theme and the C sharp/D flat recalls the moon, and finally with most beautiful effect at Fig. 339.

On a local level, types of modulation themselves are used as a

Example 3

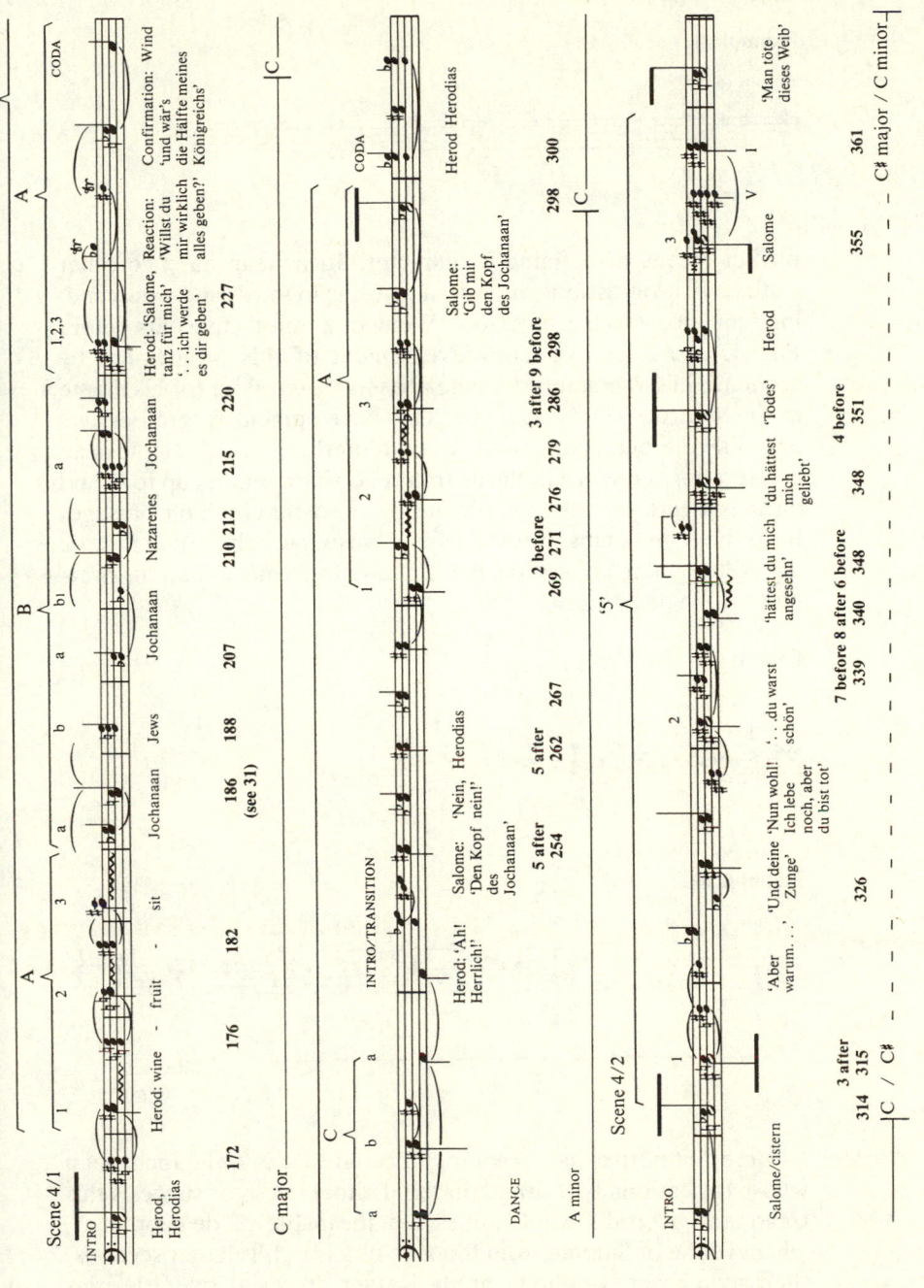

Example 4

5 before 66

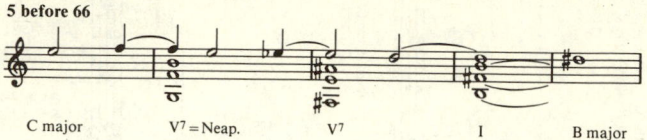

C major   V⁷ = Neap.   V⁷   I   B major

further means of defining a character. Jochanaan has two other
distinctive progressions: his initial pivoting in thirds and a descending sequence which grows from 'Wenn er kommt' (five bars before
Fig. 15) (see Ex. 5). The development of this progression by
sequence in the first interlude neatly sets a precedent for his theme
at the start of Scene 3 (Ex. 6). This development is 'progressive'
and, like the main part of the second interlude, which employs an
accelerating sequence in thirds from I (C sharp minor) up to V and
back, is pseudo-symphonic, reminding one of innumerable passages
from the tone poems: it is the sort of writing which earned Strauss
the still popular accusation that *Salome* is no more than an over-
blown tone poem itself.

Example 5

5 before 15   15

A♭   A   B♭

Example 6

Here leitmotive has become procedure; it is only Jochanaan
whose (intentionally?) stilted material either needs or suggests this
treatment. Herod's whole tones are incapable of development;
whenever he or Salome, who tends to lyricism, fills larger sections,
their style is not symphonic at all. Rather, they sing operatic arias

with tonally stable verses not necessarily linked by logical key progression and where the orchestral texture, though it may still sound dominant, is functionally accompanimental: their leitmotives at such points are vocal and the harmonic procedure is consequently non-developmental.

Strauss does not always need a leitmotive to inspire an unexpected change of key: the beseeching codettas to the three verses of Salome's 'Jochanaan! Ich bin verliebt in deinen Leib' (Fig. 91/2) and the musing 'und das Geheimnis der Liebe' (Fig. 349) are exceptionally lovely – but they are also inconsequential. One sometimes gets the impression that although Strauss had an extraordinary ear for a 'telling' modulation or sonority (especially when prompted by the female voice) his sense of key across a wider space was limited; there is a peculiar dissociation between immediate effect and assumed continuity, or between one type of continuity and another.

Nevertheless, he was evidently concerned to unify as well as colour the work by means of harmony. The section at Fig. 349, continuing ' . . . ist grösser als das Geheimnis des Todes', comes to a halt on a form of what might be called the '*Salome* chord'. Variants of this dissonant chord occur throughout the opera. In this particular vertical arrangement it seems to signify death, either named or implied (see Ex. 7).

Example 7

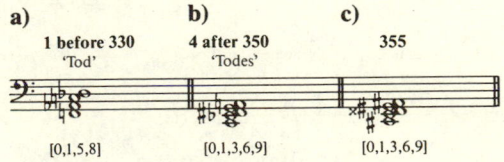

Note: Numbers in brackets denote pitch-class sets and are derived by collapsing the relevant sonority into the smallest space (which will always be less than an octave) and counting the lowest pitch as 0, the pitch a semitone higher as 1, and so on up to 11. Sometimes the sonority has also to be inverted.

Salome's transposition of this chord to C sharp as she considers the taste of Jochanaan's lips (Ex. 7c) is especially gruesome, as she has not yet realised that it must now refer to her. But in fact it has referred to her from the very first bars of the opera, for the sonority is a (varied) verticalisation of her opening motive (Ex. 8). Strauss clearly intended to use this as a generator of some of the most crucial motives and harmonies right across the work, and certainly many do echo its sonority (see Ex. 9). Salome's contradictions (3C) are likewise given this sort of dissonance, while Jochanaan's horror at being addressed by Salome at all takes his 'Zurück, Tochter Babylons!' right into the whole-tone insanity that dominates Scene 4 (see Ex. 10).

Example 8

Example 9

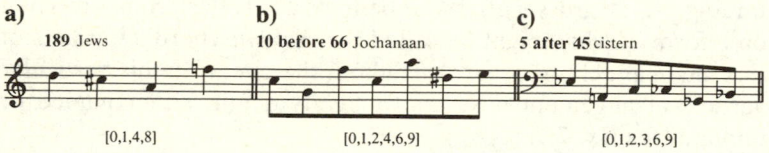

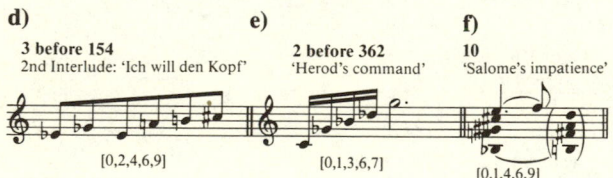

Example 10

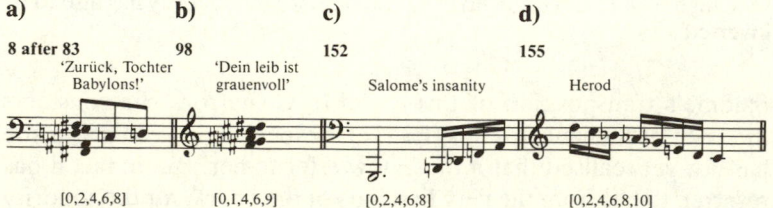

Strauss's use of this chord/motive can be interpreted in two different ways: as a chord and as an opposition. The first, assuming it to be a sonority in its own right, like the *Tristan* chord, from whose implications the opera evolves, is both fascinating and frustrating. Salome's motive (Ex. 8) is obviously not an open-ended statement but a closed juxtaposition of the two chromatic notes A natural and F double sharp within two C sharp minor triads. When this is verticalised it still sounds like a fundamentally stable superimposition, especially as it is generally heard in root position, and it fails, for this reason, to affect the harmony of the surrounding music; in fact, given the consistency of its instrumentation and its association, transposed, with C minor (Fig. 350/4), it appears to be a colouristic device. Perhaps Strauss saw it as an 'oriental' harmony, although if so it is odd that it actually illustrates the traditionally 'bad' or frightening elements in the libretto, much as a diminished seventh would have done a hundred years earlier (and does here, too, in the Page's motive, 'Schreckliches kann geschehen'), and not exoticism, which is given static diatonic harmony and an ornamental, chromatically inflected melody – like, to come full circle, the Salome motive that is the basis of this chord. Its origin as a quasi-oriental decoration – and its complete inadequacy as a functional harmony – become evident when it reverts to C sharp minor for the final verse of Salome's monologue (Fig. 355). Here Strauss plainly intended to clarify not only the background opposition of C and C sharp but also the dissonant notes of his *Salome* chord. To do so, he had to transform the A natural and F double sharp from decorative dissonances into some part of a directed tonal progression which would lead directly back to C sharp major, a difficult objective since both are naturally foreign to the key. In fact ♮6 had become ♯6 as soon as the motive was verticalised, a move which produced a more comprehensible chord and allowed him more scope; to make the most of this he placed the chord at Fig. 355 in combination with the semitone trill that had accompanied Salome from the moment the idea of revenge struck her – 'Willst du mir wirklich alles geben, was ich von dir begehre?' (Fig. 227/4) – at the a^2/b^2 flat level which signalled her 'visionäre Haltung an der Cisterne' at the end of the 'Dance', using it to emphasise both pitches at once and each in turn. Salome sings her motive (with A naturals) over the chord (with A sharps) and is pivoted briefly past B flat minor into F major and then F sharp major. As she repeats 'Was tut's?' the A natural emerges in an inner part as the tonic of a fourth key in counterpoint to F sharp; the harmony at this point is understood as $IV_{\natural 3}^{7}$, moving to V_{4}^{6} of C sharp major. But his real objective, the resolution of all the dissonant notes – without weakening the newly-established tonic – Strauss could only achieve by setting $A^{\natural 7}$, $\natural VI^{7}$, under $IV^{\sharp 3}$ and thus creating that famous double cadence.[10] It is a strange solution, for not only does the ear inevitably pick out the A natural/A sharp clash, giving the impression that the whole passage is principally a working out of the trill, but he can in effect only resolve his superimposed dissonant chord by a further very obvious superimposition[11] (see Ex. 11).

Example 11

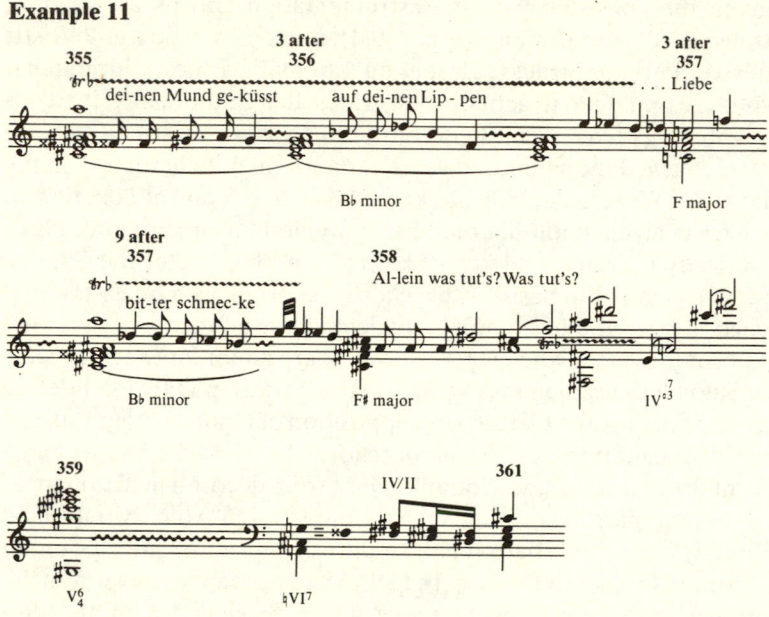

This has several implications. The very fact that Strauss felt it necessary to resolve the *Salome* chord does seem to negate any 'advance' into atonality as structural basis and defines his allegiance to tonality; maybe if those scandalised by this dissonance had considered its function they would have realised that they had no reason to be alarmed by Strauss's modernism. None the less, the contrast with the diatonicism of large chunks of *Salome* – fully exploited for dramatic purposes – initially makes his use of dissonance more, not less, shocking, and confuses one's critical faculties. On the other hand, this is not a *real* tonal resolution, nor is it a transformation:

here is implied a very much more disturbing confusion of the function of tonality itself.

Returning to the original motive and to its alternative interpretation, it can be seen to have provided Strauss not only with a chord but also with a specific means of highlighting the dramatic contrast between Salome and Jochanaan. Its most characteristic interval, when heard as a horizontal variant, is the tritone. In its initial form this is hardly accentuated (Ex. 12a); but when the cistern theme in E flat minor appears, the tritone, now transposed to E flat/A, is very prominent (Ex. 12b), and it recurs in Jochanaan's theme at the start of Scene 3. Here the pitch level has been retained, but is hidden in a tonal context where the E flat/D sharp resolves up to E natural, the third of C major (Ex. 12c). Then, as Salome broods over the cistern at the end of the second interlude, a grotesque caricature of this theme is heard on the E flat clarinet (a crib from Berlioz?), inverting the interval (Ex. 12d) and exploding, as she decides how to deal with him ('Ich will den Kopf des Jochanaan'), into a direct juxtaposition of E flat minor and A major, the opposite poles of each other's tonalities (Ex. 12e).

Example 12

This motive is used as an accompaniment to Salome's 'Dance', the two keys now inverted in A minor (Ex. 13a). Then, when she finds she must fight for her prize, it emerges with increasing intensity, not always, at first, at pitch, and in alternation with her throwaway arpeggio (Fig. 254/5), until, as she listens to Jochanaan's execution, it dominates both vocal line and harmony, finally simplified into her scream where A major and E flat minor are heard together (Fig. 313, Ex. 13b). As Herod echoes this (Figs. 351–5,

Ex. 13c) its relationship with the *Salome* chord on C is made clear: although the motive in itself is obviously meant to be descriptive of both Salome's and Jochanaan's tonalities (and is sometimes used to link them – see upbeat to Fig. 348), and although one assumes because the intention it conveys is Salome's that she controls it, in fact her A natural is now understood as part of the darkened C minor which heralds death (Ex. 13d) and only dissolves into the tonic triad as she herself is crushed. Thus Salome's triumph in C sharp major at her kiss and her valiant attempt to resolve the *Salome* chord seem to be poignant mistakes, for her A major has been destined from the moment she formulated her desire – and perhaps from even before that – to lead, with Jochanaan's E flat minor, to the downfall of them both.

Example 13

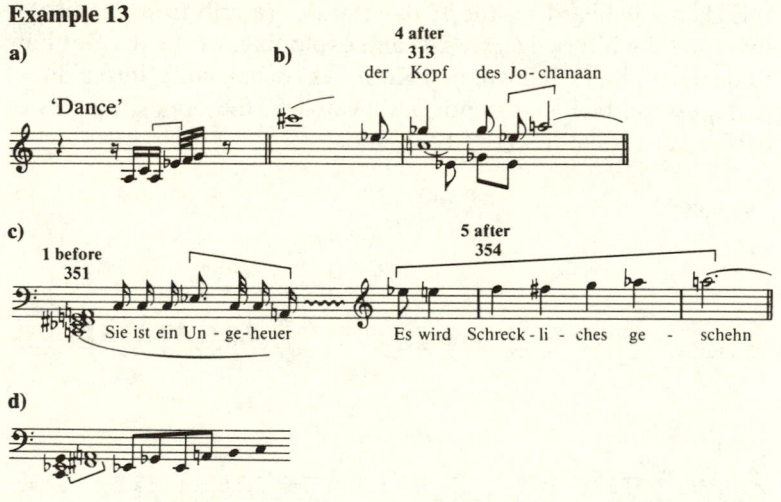

III

'Ich will den Kopf', by allowing Strauss to convey a sense of tonal distance or polarisation, which in turn articulates the C/C sharp duality, enables him to depict this powerful cross-over of dramatic undercurrents from one side to the other (see Ex. 2). It is the only motive that is capable of doing so; it certainly provides the principal musical 'action' of the opera. However, in itself the tritone remains neutral, whether as an 'oriental' raised fourth or as a tonal polarity, and it is not actually *resolved*; the disjunct statements of the motive with the *Salome* chord and the C minor of Fig. 362 can only be assumed to connect, without even the benefit of a bogus cadence.

This lack of real resolution into either C or C sharp at the end of the opera is extremely effective as a dramatic device, but frustrating musically, both because the dissonances are abandoned locally and because their context has been so very diatonic: they imply a Tristanesque tonal apotheosis. However, it becomes increasingly clear that Strauss had managed somehow to miss the point of *Tristan*'s tonality in spite of his sophisticated adoption of its harmonic and instrumental style, just as, in the tone poems, he had missed the point of the sonata principle while filling its outlines: his 'transfigurations' – especially, as it happens, that of *Tod und Verklärung* – are achieved not through tonal resolution but by a kind of dynamic and textural *crescendo* which accumulates momentum quite irrespective of key. For Strauss the idea of transfiguration seems to have been something of an abstract concept; indeed, tonal form itself almost appears to have been an abstraction, in which conventional tonal expectations may have no particular relevance, even though the ear may be misled for long stretches into believing that they do. It is a curious feature of his music that the more conventional a passage may sound, the more superficial, structurally, it is likely to be (the B major stretch in *Salome* Scene 3), and the larger a work, the more disparate and irreconcilable these passages will become. The later tone poems suffer from this. At the same time, on an immediate level tonality itself often appears to have become an expressive device, shades of consonance and stability colouring the musical surface, which changes instantly to suit dramatic effect. On the whole his music becomes less tonal in direct proportion to the increase in violence (the 'anachronistic' style of *Der Rosenkavalier* was therefore the inevitable result of its libretto). This is true even when he *is* clearly composing in a particular key.

By employing a systematically organised tonal background in *Salome*, Strauss may have hoped to get round these problems, but actually he compounds them, for his background is bitonal and C and C sharp must, for dramatic reasons, be deliberately opposed. Because the opposition is insoluble, he is unable to create either a self-contained tonal structure – with resolution – or any real sense of dramatic progression: to the end Salome and Herod retain their separate identities, having merely subsumed that of Jochanaan. It seems paradoxical that it was precisely Strauss's adherence, tonally, to the most formalised features of Wilde's play that ultimately limited *Salome* as a musical form: 'ballad' treatment is fundamentally unsuited for opera in the Wagnerian style, unavoidably producing a series of non-processive tableaux. Strauss's later operas, from *Elektra* to *Capriccio*, were to propose a series of fascinatingly varied solutions to these problems.

7 Salome's final monologue

CRAIG AYREY

I

Conventionally, *Salome* has been described as 'a study in obsession', and the final monologue as a 'perverted *Liebestod*'.[1] But the critic should be wary of moving too easily from obsession to perversion as the central fact in an interpretation of the scena, for such an interpretation is not decisively supported either by Strauss's setting of the play or by the Symbolist complexity of Wilde's drama. My critical commentary on the monologue projects an individual interpretative trajectory, informed by the Symbolist intention and method of Wilde's play and Strauss's compositional response to it.[2]

To accept an interpretation of Salome as perverse is to accept the traditional view of the monologue as the apotheosis of passion consummated in necrophilia. It is, in fact, tempting to trace a progression of increasing 'perversity', from Narraboth's 'unnatural' passion for Salome, unnatural because it crosses class boundaries (Scenes 1–3), through Herod's 'unnatural' passion for her, unnatural because it violates familial relationships (Scene 4), to Salome's 'unnatural' passion for Jochanaan, unnatural because it transcends moral constraints (Scenes 3–4).

Such a unilateral view of this sequence of events can only be sustained if Salome is regarded as perverse. What she first and primarily desires is not Jochanaan's dead body but his living flesh. That she cannot have it is beyond her control, since Jochanaan refuses to look at her. Metaphorically this represents his refusal to recognise her as a person; instead he regards her at one remove – simply as the daughter of Herodias, whom he despises – and vilifies Salome as a 'daughter of Sodom'[3] (Fig. 87). In fact, Salome is the only character in the drama who attempts fully to engage with Jochanaan. The others are in awe of or afraid of him (Narraboth, Herod), distrust him (Herodias) or question his authenticity (the Jews). Salome

109

Plate 5: A scene from the English National Opera production of *Salome*, the London Coliseum, 1981, with Josephine Barstow (Salome); producer, Joachim Herz; designer, Rudolf Heinrich

alone is prepared to accept him as a human being – first as a man ('I am amorous of thy body', 'I will kiss thy mouth'), then sceptically as a prophet ('Thy voice was a censer', ' . . . thou hast seen thy God, Jochanaan'). She is reviled, however, not only by Herod, but also by Jochanaan, who fails to recognise that as Princess of Judaea she assumes a right to have what she wants, and that this desire is sincere (just as Herod fails to recognise the rights Salome claims through allegiance to her mother and her royal blood). But unconventionally, even existentially, Salome demands to be known for herself, not only as her mother's daughter, and it is this that precipitates her response to a situation in which her desires are frustrated. As Princess of Judaea she has rights, as a woman she has desires, and as a person she is at least due the respect of these being recognised. Because Jochanaan will not accept these aspects of her being, she takes the only course open to her and demands his head; although his eyes are closed to her in death as they were metaphorically in life, this is now a physical, not a willed, blindness, so that in the monologue she can bring him symbolically to recognise her as an individual.

These dramatic issues are not confined to the monologue itself. Beginning at Fig. 314, it recapitulates the dramatic issues, leitmotives and symbolic keys of the opera as a whole. Both the opera and the monologue are informed by the tension between Salome's desire to possess Jochanaan and her inability to achieve that desire. The monologue itself is constructed on the progression of her intention towards actualisation, culminating in the central, but not centrally-placed, action of the drama: the kissing of Jochanaan's severed head. The weight of the dramatic action is therefore located at the end of the opera, so that the monologue functions both as climax and as resolution of the drama.

The elements of this dual function are both dramatic and musical. Convinced by the cogency of thematic recapitulation in the monologue, Newman decided that:

The more one studies the score the more one is inclined to believe that the final scena was conceived first. Strauss, I imagine, would already have in his mind most of the main motifs of the work, but, as yet, principally as constituents of this superb piece of writing, which is, in essence, a closely and organically knit symphonic poem with a vocal solo. The latter allocations of the motifs to this or that passage in the earlier part of the opera were seemingly a matter with him of the suggestion of the moment . . . [4]

Kennedy, similarly impressed, describes the scena as 'the most fluently organic section of the score, erotic, seductive and genuinely tragic, words and music more closely interlocked than in some earlier parts of the opera'.[5]

Placing the climax and resolution of a drama at the end is not original, but it conforms to the structure of Wilde's play and makes special demands on the musical structure of the work. Since Salome's obsession with Jochanaan surfaces almost from the outset, this predominant theme is amplified by episodes in which the fulfilment of her desire in the monologue is frustrated (as in her adoration of Jochanaan in Scene 3, Figs. 76–139), diverted by incidental events (the disputation of the Jews, Scene 4, Figs. 188–207) or fleshed out by sub-plots (Herod's attempt to seduce her, Scene 4, Figs. 172–84). These additional episodes enlarge the dimensions of a full understanding of Salome as character and as victim of social circumstance.[6]

The large-scale dramatic structure is matched and supported by Strauss's harmonic practice, which perpetually postpones or avoids large-scale tonal resolution by means of harmonic ambiguity. Above this stratum of harmonic and tonal tension, however, there is a strikingly schematic opposition of keys[7] and an expressive leitmotive technique,[8] so that (as Newman suggests) the monologue gathers together most of the dimensions of the musical drama. Both strata are demanded by the recurrence of imagery and dramatic situation which functions as the symbol and representation of Salome's (perhaps neurotic) repetition of psychosexual obsessions. Two systems of musical organisation are therefore employed in the opera: in general terms, harmonic tension represents the larger emotional progress and vacillations of the drama, while thematic, tonal and formal recurrence articulates elements of character and plot. None of this mitigates the inexorable dramatic progress of the work: Strauss's technique does not conceal but elucidates, translating the complexity of Wilde's (verbal) dramatic structure – often simplified by Strauss's cuts in the play – into complexity of musical structure, in which leitmotives, tonality, key and even individual chords are the vehicles of symbolic reference.

II

All these characteristics are present in the final monologue in highly concentrated form. Within this relatively small dimension, the organicism of the scena is determined by the structure of the text, which facilitates a clear and logical musical structure. But although the leitmotives register changing relationships of character, they are surface phenomena. Deeper correspondences of dramatic idea and musical structure are present in the manipulation of shifting tonalities. For this reason, key relationships (there is no global tonal organisation)[9] are both the immediate and the large-scale agents of harmonic coherence.

Table 1 summarises the dramatic and tonal structure of the monologue. The ten sections (A–J) follow the structure of the text. Having had Jochanaan's head delivered to her, Salome initiates dramatic tension by declaring her intention to kiss his mouth; the act itself is normally postponed until the short, two-bar interlude between sections H and I, though this is not indicated in the score. The double symbolism of the mouth, as the desired part of Jochanaan's body and as the origin of his condemnation of her in Scene 3, is completed in section B ('And thy tongue, it says nothing now . . . Thou didst speak evil words against me'). Before this, Salome has turned her attention to Jochanaan's refusal to look at her, even in death. These two themes – the potential kiss and the refusal to see her as a person independent of her mother, Herodias, who is the primary object of Jochanaan's loathing (see Scene 3, from Fig. 69/5 to Fig. 76) – are the cornerstones of the monologue. Salome returns twice again to these topics, in the same order, in sections D and E, and F and G, respectively, finally reverting to the theme of desire when the kiss is eventually bestowed in section I. Two sections intervene: one contemplating death (section C), the other an exchange between Herod and Herodias (section H). In the last section, J, Salome herself is put to death.

The larger structure is summarised in Table 2. Corresponding to this is a system of symbolic keys (see Table 1, right-hand column). Section A is dominated by the key of C sharp minor, sections D and F by the key of C sharp major, confirming the dramatic structure shown in Table 2. The change from minor to major, however, parallels the change in Salome's perception of Jochanaan, from her initial insistence that he is alive (section B: 'Wherefore dost thou not look at me, Jochanaan?') to her acknowledgement in section C, in C *minor*, that he is dead, a change which culminates in the C sharp *major* of the later sections D and I, in which Salome's desire is first potentially and then actually achieved, now that the impediment of Jochanaan's living resistance to her has been removed. Sections A–C, then, are psychologically progressive: Salome speaks as if

Table 1: *Large-scale chord progressions and key structure*

Section	Text	Chord progression	Key
A [314]	Ah! Thou wouldst not suffer me to kiss thy mouth, Jochanaan!	⌈ C/G	C ⌉
	Well, I will kiss it now. I will bite it with my teeth [. . .]	⌊ c♯	c♯ ⌋
	Yes, I will kiss it now, kiss thy mouth, Jochanaan.	⌈ c♯	
	I said it. [. . .]	⎨ A⁷——→	
	Ah! Ah! I will kiss it now.	(a♭⁷) – D⁷	
B [323]	But wherefore dost thou not look at me, Jochanaan?		
	Thine eyes that were so terrible [. . .]	⌈ g♯	g♯ (= v of c♯)
	Open thine eyes! Lift up thine eyelids, Jochanaan!	⌊ (g – B♭⁷)	
	Wherefore dost thou not look at me?		
	Art thou afraid of me, Jochanaan, that thou wilt not look at me?	A♭⁷ (= G♯⁷)	
	And thy tongue, it says nothing now [. . .]	c♯	c♯ ⌉
	Thou didst speak evil words against me,	⌈ (b – E⁷)	
	me, Salome, daughter of Herodias, Princess of Judaea.	⌊ b♭	
C [329/3]	Well, I still live, but thou art dead, and thy head,	C – c	c ⌋
	thy head belongs to me. [. . .]	V → a♭	
	I can throw it to the dogs [. . .] That which the dogs leave [. . .]	⌈ C/c	c
D [332/2]	Ah! Ah! Jochanaan! Jochanaan! Thou wert beautiful.	⌊ C♯: V⁹ – I	C♯
	Thy body was a column of ivory set on a silver socket.	V⁷	
	It was a garden full of doves and of silver lilies.	I	
	There was nothing in the world so white as thy body.		
	There was nothing in the world so black as thy hair.	ii	
	In the whole world there was nothing so red as thy mouth.	V⁷	
	Thy voice was a censer [. . .] and when I looked on thee	A	A
	I heard a strange music.	⎨ A	
E [339/6]	Ah! Wherefore didst thou not look at me, Jochanaan?	⎨ C♯ – C⁷	C♯
	Thou didst put upon thine eyes the covering of him	a	a
	who would see his God.		
	Well, thou hast seen thy god, Jochanaan,	g	
	but me, me, thou didst never see.	C	C
	If thou hadst seen me thou wouldst have loved me.	(c♯°⁷) B♭⁷	
F [343/3]	I am athirst for thy beauty;	A♭⁷ (= G♯⁷)	
	I am hungry for thy body [. . .]	⎨ C♯	C♯
	What shall I do now, Jochanaan?	A⁷	
	Neither the floods nor the great waters can quench my passion.	E⁷	

G [347]	Ah! Wherefore didst thou not look at me? If thou hadst looked at me thou wouldst have loved me. […] And the mystery of love is greater than the mystery of death.	[f] C♯ G – (c♯ – e♭ – c°⁷)	C♯
H [350/5]	HEROD (to Herodias): She is monstrous, thy daughter. […] HERODIAS: I approve of what my daughter has done. And I will stay here now. HEROD (rising): Ah! There speaks the incestuous wife! Come! I will not stay here. Come, I tell thee. Surely some terrible thing will befall. Let us hide ourselves in the palace […]	c°⁷ E D♭ c°⁷	chromatic progressions
Ia [355/7]	SALOME (faintly): Ah! I have kissed thy mouth, Jochanaan. Ah! I have kissed thy mouth. There was a bitter taste on thy lips. Was it the taste of blood? No! But perchance it is the taste of love. They say that love hath a bitter taste. But what of that? What of that?	$\dfrac{e}{c\sharp/F\times}$ $(F-e)\ \dfrac{e}{c\sharp/F\times}$	F♯
Ib [359]	I have kissed thy mouth, Jochanaan. I have kissed thy mouth. (A ray of moonlight falls on Salome and illuminates her.)	F♯ C♯: V⁶₄ – I V⁴₃ – I I – ♮VI⁷ – I	C♯
J [361/5]	HEROD (turning round): Kill that woman! (The soldiers rush forward and crush Salome beneath their shields.)	d – B c – a♭ – c	c

Key:
1 Capital letters indicate major keys. Lower-case letters indicate minor keys. For example, C♯ = C♯ major, c♯ = c♯ minor.
2 Superscript numbers indicate dominant-seventh type chords (for example, A♭⁷). A symbol such as c°⁷ indicates a diminished-seventh chord.
3 Letters enclosed in brackets ( ) indicate intermediate chords or keys with dramatic or symbolic significance.
4 Letters connected by a square bracket ([ ) indicate chords or keys a semitone apart; those connected by a curly bracket ({) are a major or minor third apart.

Table 2: *Large-scale structure of the monologue*

Topic:	Physical desire	Demand for recognition	Death	Herod/Herodias
Section:	A [314]	B [323]	C [329/3]	
	D [332/2]	E [339/6]		
	F [343/3]	G [347]		H [350/5]
	I [355/7]		J [361/5]	
Predominant key:	c♯/C♯	c♯/C♯	c/C	c°7/E/D♭

Jochanaan were still alive in A and B, recognises his death in section C ('Well, Jochanaan, I still live, but thou art dead') and then imagines that she now possesses him ('thy head belongs to me').

Section C is therefore a turning-point in the drama. It is grounded in C major/minor, the keys of violence and death which are opposed to the C sharp major/minor world of desire. However, the strategic subtlety of Strauss's symbolic key organisation here should not be missed: the modulation to A flat minor at the words 'thy head belongs to me' suggests the theme of desire, as A flat minor is the enharmonic dominant minor of C sharp (i.e. A flat minor = G sharp minor). Throughout the monologue the chords of $A\flat^7$ and A flat minor have a global rather than a local relation to the text, in that they refer either specifically or obliquely to the C sharp major/minor symbolisation of Salome's desire. A clear example is the progression in the orchestral postlude, immediately following the prolonged C sharp major area in section Ib ('I have kissed thy mouth, Jochanaan') and Herod's final order ('Kill that woman') in J: the progression here is C minor–A flat minor–C minor, in which the central chord, as enharmonic minor dominant of C sharp major, makes oblique symbolic reference to the preceding section.

The C sharp major sections, D, F and I, have distinctive structures. Sections D and Ib are extended prolongations of C sharp major; section F is more complex, but the symbolic function of key is clear. Section D celebrates the beauty of Jochanaan and refers directly to the textual, motivic and tonal structure of the parallel passage in Scene 3 (Figs. 91–6). Ending this section is a move to A major, at the words 'Thy voice was a censer . . . and when I looked on thee I heard a strange music' (the D $^6_4$ chord at Fig. 338/7 must be understood as a prolongation of A). The change of key refers to Jochanaan's status as an outsider; to the key of Salome's 'Dance', grounded in A minor as a symbol of her exoticism; and to the trill on the note a^2 that sounds throughout section Ia and complicates the harmonic structure of the subsection. Section D therefore juxtaposes two aspects of character: Salome's adoration of Jochanaan as a man and her socially 'perverted' obsession with an outsider. This juxtaposition foreshadows the amorality of her final act.

Within the C sharp major region, the V^7 ($G\sharp^7$) is related enharmonically to the A flat minor seventh of section A (at the words 'Ah! Ah! I will kiss [Jochanaan's mouth] now' (Fig. 321/4) and the same chord in section B which leads directly into a reference to Jochanaan's tongue ('And thy tongue, it says nothing now'). The obsession with the mouth climaxes in section Ib, where the final affirmation ('I have kissed thy mouth, Jochanaan, I have kissed thy mouth') takes place over an extended perfect cadence (V_4^6–V^7–I). This confirms and closes the larger symbolic meaning of C sharp major/minor, since both the dominant seventh and the dominant minor of the key (in whatever tonal context), as well as the key itself, are associated primarily with Jochanaan's mouth. That this was the source of vilification earlier in the opera establishes a correlation between the acts of recognition (avoided by Jochanaan), kissing and sexual ecstasy, a correlation expressed through the relationship of the dominants and tonics of C sharp. It connects, for example, the G sharp minor in section B (at 'Thine eyes that were so terrible . . . are shut now') to the $A\flat^7$ in the same section (at 'Art thou afraid of me, Jochanaan, that thou wilt not look at me?'). This example reveals a symbolic function of key only implicit earlier: the major/minor relation of the same chord or key is an inflection, or mirror image, of a similar dramatic situation. Just as the transition from C sharp minor to C sharp major charts a process of recognition, so the transition from G sharp minor to $A\flat^7$ reveals a progression from Jochanaan's ability to inspire fear to Salome's perception of herself as being in control, in that she now imagines Jochanaan as afraid. Enharmonic relations in the monologue are unusual, in that they do not maintain their identity within a tonal context but form relations with one another, as agents of textual symbolism.

In opposition to the affirmative and fulfilling domain of C sharp major/minor, the C major/minor area represents the negative aspects of power. Salome herself is both perpetrator and victim of these situations. She begins, in the first line of the monologue, with a negative statement in C major/minor. Similarly, section C opens with a negative affirmation (negative in this context) of life over death ('I still live, but thou art dead'), again in C major/minor, followed in the same key by the type of authoritarian statement typical of Herod but here adopted by Salome: 'I can throw [thy head] to the dogs'. Salome's death in the final section (J) reaffirms the dominance of C minor and therefore of the threatened, but prevailing, moral order. The ambivalence of Salome's character is revealed by her participation in both C sharp major and C minor areas. She is caught between two worlds: as Herodias' daughter and the step-daughter/niece of Herod, she has her origins in the moralistic and repressive world of orthodoxy, but she also represents sincerity and innocence. Her exercise of power in section C falls back on the models of her social environment.

Essentially, then, the semitone relationship of C sharp major/minor–C major/minor (indicated by square brackets on Table 1) symbolises opposed world views. Salome's sincere love for and obsession with Jochanaan is opposed to the ethics of her society, in which the Princess of Judaea is forbidden such passion, most of all for a figure like Jochanaan, who is variously described as an outsider, a holy man (even Herod concedes this) and a follower of Christ.

Complementary to this dichotomous world is a system of keys related to C sharp major/minor by thirds, symbolising changes of social or psychological perspective. Section D, as mentioned earlier, has a particularly clear progression from C sharp major to A major, indicative of a change in social perspective for both Jochanaan and Salome: the key of A, and its major-third relation to C sharp major, supply what is absent in the text of this particular scene – the various types of exoticism that the characters embody. A similar progression occurs in section E, from A minor ('Thou didst put upon thine eyes the covering of him who would see his God'), indicating Jochanaan's opposition to both the sensuality of Salome and the world of Herod's court, to the C major at Salome's words 'but me, me, thou didst never see', symbolising Jochanaan's non-recognition of Salome.

Three further instances of third-relation are significant. First, in section A the move from C sharp minor to A^7 (and then to D^7) expresses on a small scale the beginning of the dramatic progression from Salome's intention to kiss Jochanaan's mouth to the act itself. The seventh chords on 'I will kiss thy mouth' remain unresolved, maintaining tonal and dramatic tension. Moreover the A^7 chord appears later as $\natural VI^7$ of C sharp major in the context of the final C sharp major tonic cadence (section Ib): the importance of this is discussed below. Second, section G opens with a move from F minor to C sharp major, reinforcing the pairing of ideas first announced in section E: 'Ah! Wherefore didst thou not look at me?', in F minor, is followed immediately by the restatement in C sharp major of 'If thou hadst seen me thou wouldst have loved me'. Third, in the inserted section H, Herodias' approval of her daughter's deed, declaimed in E major, is preceded and followed by the third-related chords of C diminished seventh and D flat (= C sharp) major. The former supports Herod's view of Salome ('She is monstrous'), the latter his view of Herodias ('There speaks the incestuous wife'). The third relations here delineate different perceptions of Salome and Herodias, as seen through Herod's eyes, with Herodias' central statement in E major, around which the thirds are clustered, presenting the positive view of Salome in the mediant major (E major) of C sharp minor.

There is one further symbolic harmonic structure. In section B the progression G minor–B♭^{7} occurs at the line 'Open thine eyes! Lift up thine eyelids, Jochanaan! Wherefore dost thou not look at me?' B♭^{7} then reappears in section E at 'If thou hadst seen me thou wouldst have loved me'. This single chord is used to symbolise the failure of Jochanaan to recognise Salome as a person in her own right. The irony of course is that Jochanaan professes to have seen God (in the form of Christ) yet is blind to the personality of a fellow human being. Hence the ambivalence of tonal context for the B♭^{7} chord: in both sections B and E it exists within a complex C sharp major/minor context, in which it is enharmonically (♯)VI^7. Its diatonic form (A♯^{7}), however, will play a crucial role in the C sharp major of Section Ib.

III

The final phase of the monologue (from Fig. 354/10) recapitulates most of the dominant techniques of the scena, and of the opera itself. It comprises three sections, Ia, Ib and J (see Table 1), immediately following two bars of a^2/b^2 flat tremolo in the strings (*lento*) during which Salome kisses Jochanaan's mouth. Each section has a distinct dramatic structure: section Ia presents Salome's final meditation on the nature of love, Ib her exultation at having achieved her desire, and section J her death.

As earlier in the opera, these changes of mood, action and psychological perspective are registered in the musical setting by distinct harmonic and thematic structures, though the segment as a whole has a cumulative intensity which is released only by the final repeated C minor chord. The first section (Ia), beginning at 'Ah! I have kissed thy mouth, Jochanaan', is the most complex harmonically, exemplifying Strauss's use of polytonality to convey complexity of emotion and character.[10] Example 1 shows the opening of the section. Piccolo and oboe reiterate in E minor, over a trill on a^2 (flute, clarinet and violin 2), the theme symbolising Salome's enig-

Example 1

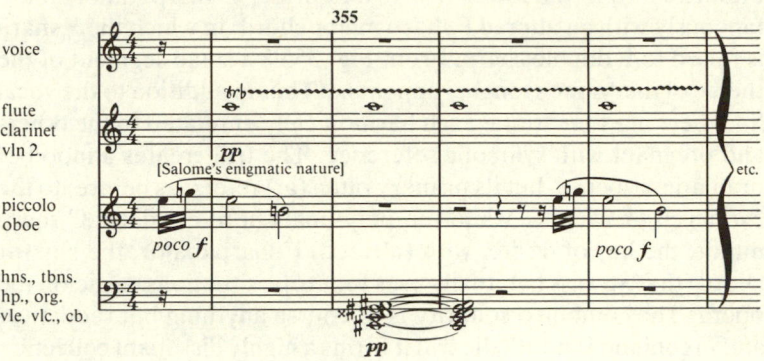

matic nature. Punctuating the statements of Salome's theme is a bitonal chord in the lower strings and brass, C sharp minor simultaneously with an altered F sharp major chord, in which the F sharp is raised to F double sharp. From Fig. 355/8 a small segment of the theme of the 'viper's tongue' appears.[11] Thus in addition to the vocal line there are four strata, each harmonically unrelated to the others and pregnant with symbolic reference. The trill creates a mood of dramatic suspense, but its primary pitch (a^2) refers, as before, to the exoticism of Salome, while the polytonal chord conflates C sharp minor, the key of desire, with (altered) F sharp major, the key (or chord) that Strauss habitually uses for erotic situations earlier in the opera. The combined sonority is of course anything but seductive, and in conjunction with the trill it forms a highly dissonant collection more menacing than erotic. By superimposing the chords and the pitch representing Salome's nature, Strauss symbolises the moral extremity of her action, while the dissonance of the sonority also foreshadows its consequences. The appearance of the 'viper's tongue' theme at the end of the opening vocal phrase appropriately reinforces the ambivalence of Salome's emotions in kissing Jochanaan's mouth. Earlier in the monologue (Figs. 326–7), the theme is used to underline Salome's description of Jochanaan's tongue as a scarlet viper spitting forth venom against her: here, though, she has silenced that tongue, so that the kiss once more symbolises the achievement of desire and the shift of the exercise of power from Jochanaan to Salome.

Following Salome's reflections on the nature of love ('There was a bitter taste on thy lips. Was it the taste of blood? No! But perchance it is the taste of love'), the 'desire' theme (see Ex. 2a) intervenes over an inverted F major chord (Fig. 357/3–6) and initiates a chromatic ascent to F sharp major/minor. The theme, stated three times in close imitation, produces an increase in tension that prepares for the intensity of the next section (Ib), which grounds Salome's final statement firmly in C sharp major. Section Ib is therefore one of the few moments of symbolic and tonal clarity in the opera. Example 2a shows the leitmotivic and harmonic structure of the section. In the first four bars of Fig. 359 the 'love' theme (strings) is combined with the 'desire' theme (voice, cellos and horns). But there are also brief appearances of the theme symbolising Salome's enigmatic nature (glockenspiel and triangle: Fig. 359/1–3). Her initial theme appears in the strings and trumpet (Fig. 359/2–3) as an intermediate melodic cadence. The varied repeat of the desire theme in the voice (forming a classical antecedent–consequent structure with the previous phrase) is presented in the first four bars of Fig. 360, where it is counterpointed against Jochanaan's 'prophet' theme in cellos and basses, leading to a perfect cadence in C sharp major. Jochanaan's theme is prolonged to cadence with the voice, so that the meaning of the text ('I have kissed thy mouth, Jochanaan'), in contrast to the ambivalence of section Ia, is extended through the leitmotivic structure to become an integrated symbol of the union of Salome and Jochanaan. Here Strauss achieves, by the simplest means, a union of opposites: Salome/Jochanaan, desire/revulsion, Salome's expression of love/ Jochanaan's physical inability to return it. A truncated version of the love theme appears in 360/5–361/4 but is soon transformed into a further, unorthodox cadence in C sharp major, containing what Schmidgall describes as 'that most sickening chord in all opera'.[12] A second reprise follows, in which chromatic alteration symbolises the consequences of Salome's final action.

Strauss's Symbolist treatment of the drama of *Salome* invests mutiple significance in the chord at Fig. 360/6 (marked with an asterisk in Ex. 2a). Schmidgall is not alone in citing the chord as one of the most extraordinary features of the score. It has been variously defined as: 'an orchestral upheaval that seems to rend the tonal tissue in twain . . . [but] the spasm is too intense to last more than a moment';[13] 'a shattering dissonance over which the musical world continues to dispute and comment more than half a century after it was written';[14] 'the epoch-making dissonance with which Strauss takes Salome . . . to the depth of degradation';[15] and 'the quintessence of Decadence: here is ecstasy falling in upon itself, crumbling into the abyss . . . '[16] Of these interpretations the last comes closest to realising the symbolic meaning of the chord, although what is absent even from that commentary is the perception that the chord is both the symbolic crux of the monologue and the climax of the musical drama.

The 'shock value' of the chord resides in its lack of conventional harmonic preparation and resolution. But it can be understood as having a more far-reaching significance if the components of its structure are related to the symbolic harmonic phenomena in the rest of the monologue. The reduction in Ex. 2b shows clearly the polytonal nature of the chord: A^7 in the lower parts is set against F sharp (becoming D sharp at the end of the bar) in the upper voices.[17] Even this simple description contains a Symbolist mean-

Example 2

a)

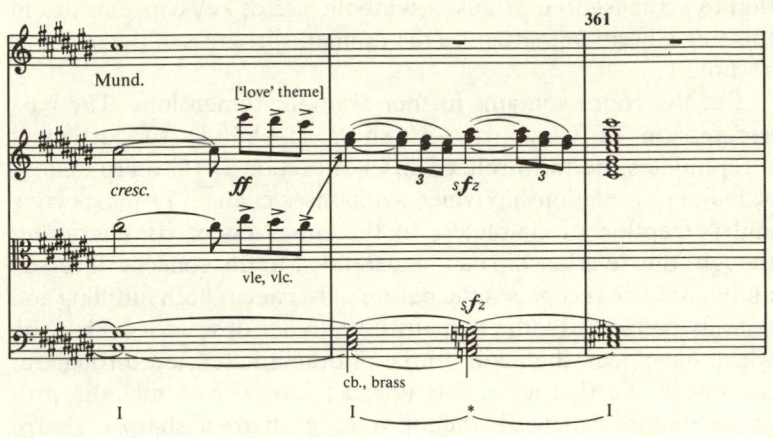

b)

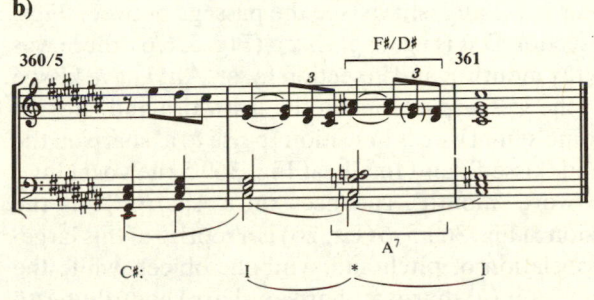

ing. The bass component (A^7) recalls the end of section A, in which the unresolved progression A^7–D^7 supports Salome's statement of her intention to kiss Jochanaan's mouth, while the single later appearance of A^7 in section F at the words 'What shall I do now, Jochanaan?' is also part of an unresolved progression (A^7–E^7: see Table 1). Thus A^7 symbolises potentiality and intention. The upper component of the chord, F sharp (the key and chord of eroticism), is used diatonically only in section Ia, at the words 'But what of that?', when Salome recoils from her preceding recollection that 'love hath a bitter taste'. There F sharp symbolises the beginning of Salome's intention to celebrate her love, to accept the eroticism of the act as fulfilment. The conjunction, then, of the two components of the chord encapsulates the progression in the drama from intention to actualisation: Strauss's symbolic use of key concentrates in this single harmonic structure the dramatic progress of the opera as a whole.

But the chord contains further symbolic dimensions. The bass progression of C sharp–A–C sharp (I–$\natural$VI^7–I) supporting it recapitulates the third-related keys of section D (C sharp major–A major), a relationship which symbolises changes of perspective and perception of character. In the chord under consideration, though, this relationship can be extended to the concept of recognition. Salome recognises the nature of her act as both fulfilling and morally dangerous – the two attitudes to her desire for Jochanaan which have been the main source of dramatic tension throughout the opera. Furthermore, the unusual larger-scale melodic progression of the cadence in the top voice, g^1 sharp–a^1 sharp–c^2 sharp, is symbolically referential. Within the monologue Salome's references to the kiss are normally associated with a strategic pitch. In section A the focus is a^1 flat/g^1 sharp (see the passage between Figs. 314 and 316); in section D it is again g^1 sharp (Fig. 336/6: 'there was nothing so red as thy mouth'); and in section Ia, at 'Ah! I have kissed thy mouth . . . ', the g^1 sharp occurs on the last word and later on 'kissed'. But Salome's final words in section Ib rise to a^1 sharp on the words 'mouth' and 'kissed'; and finally at Fig. 360/5 the vocal line, ending with the word 'mouth', cadences on c^2 sharp. Thus the melodic progression at Fig. 360/5–6 (Ex. 2b) is a reprise of this large-scale melodic association of pitch and symbolic object, while the ascending transposition (g^1 sharp–a^1 sharp–c^2 sharp) contributes to the increase in intensity towards the end of the monologue. The climactic chord and its cadential context therefore have multiple symbolic and formal functions, in recapitulating and summarising, within the space of two bars, the major concepts, larger-scale symbolic keys and principal melodic techniques of the monologue. Perhaps Newman was right to describe the chord as a 'spasm':[18] it is at once emotionally shattering and a compression of symbolic meanings which reveals quite blatantly the cogency of Strauss's musico-dramatic structure.

After this excess of dramatic effect the final section can only move rapidly to end the opera (see Ex. 3). Herod's order, 'Kill that woman!', retakes Salome's a^1 sharp, now spelt enharmonically as b^1 flat, on the word 'Kill' in a harmonic context in which it is almost agonisingly dissonant. Again Strauss employs the single pitch sym-

Example 3

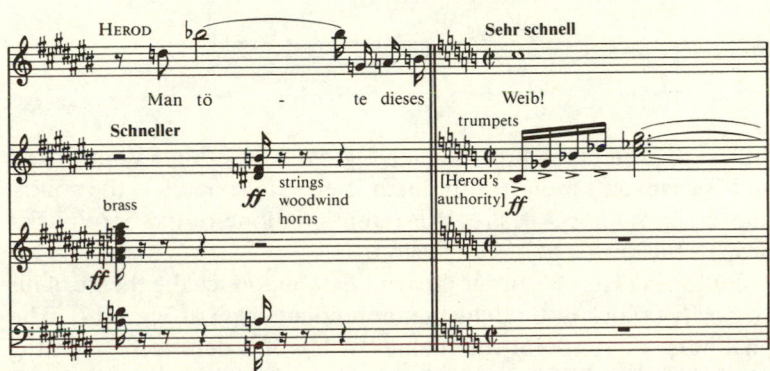

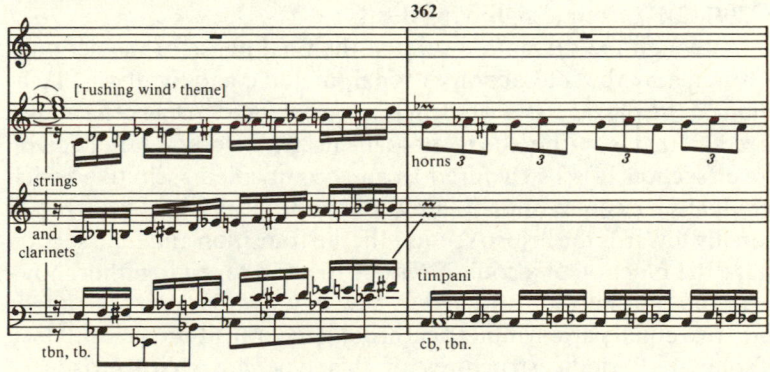

Example 3 (*cont.*)

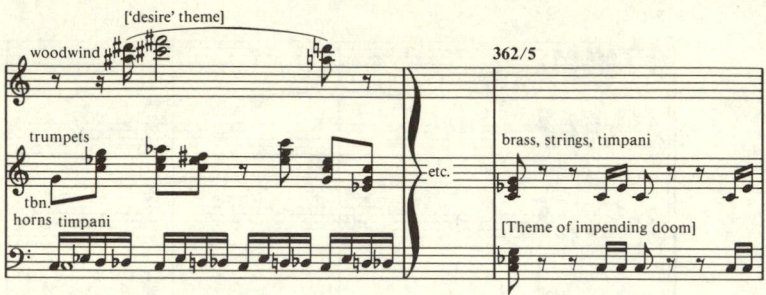

bolically, here extending its meaning by associating Salome's kiss and Jochanaan's mouth with death itself. Since death is the consequence of Salome's desire, the retention alone of a^1 sharp/b^1 flat propels the drama to its conclusion.

Following Herod's order the trumpets announce the theme of his authority (which also opens the monologue itself at Fig. 314). The final bars counterpoint the themes of Herod's delusion of rushing wind (Figs. 361/7–362/4) with a reprise of the penultimate notes of the desire theme (woodwinds, 362/2–4). The scene ends with the theme of impending doom (last heard immediately before section C (329/1–2)), this time signifying death.

Although the dramatic sweep of the final phase of the action is sustained by the interaction of tonal, melodic and Symbolist techniques, the passage as a whole has a formal logic. As a scena within a scena (that is, within the monologue itself), Salome's reflection on love (section Ia) is structured as an accompanied recitative which gradually becomes more ample enharmonically and progresses tonally towards the arioso section Ib; the transition and final section have the function of a coda. Sections Ib and J taken together, however, are formally constructed as a twenty-five-bar unit which falls into two equal parts symmetrical around the transition section[19] (see Table 3). Periodic structures of this type are characteristic of

Table 3: *Sections Ib and J*

Bars:	359/1–4		360/1–4	360/5–6–361/1	361/2–4	361/5–7	362/1–8
Key:	C♯			C♯ – A⁷ – C♯	C♯	c – a♭	c
Structure:	Salome's statement			tonic prolongation	transition	Herod	Coda
No. of bars:	4	+	4	3	3	3	4 + 4
		8	+	3	3	3 +	8
Proportions:		11		+	3	+	11

Strauss's style and function here as a firm foundation for the complexity of harmonic, leitmotivic and tonal relations and symbolism (in Exx. 2a and 3).

For all the violence and emotional intensity of the monologue, and of the opera as a whole, there is a sense of magisterial control: a control of dramatic and compositional resources which is achieved through the schematic organisation of leitmotive structures, symbolism and formal balance. The resemblance to Wagner's harmonic practice is superficial: Strauss achieves a greater degree of organicism in the monologue than Wagner normally needed to attempt. In fact, although remote in style, subject and aesthetic context, the monologue resembles the large dramatic scenas in the operas of his musical god, Mozart. And if it is true that much of Strauss's work might confirm his self-assessment as 'a first-class second-rate composer',[20] Salome's final monologue, at least, is an unequivocally first-rate composition.

CRITICISM

8 Critical reception

JOHN WILLIAMSON

I

Few operas have provoked more critical discord on their first appearance than *Salome*, and the controversy still persists. Yet even if *Salome* often seems to be as much a case as a work of art, its historical position is clear enough, as one of the earliest of the genre of *Literaturoper*. In accordance with Dahlhaus's maxim that the *Literaturoper* is in some sense a parasite on a work of literature,[1] views of *Salome* have always been tied to a large extent to Wilde's play and personality. This may surprise the English reader, to whom *Salomé* has tended to be the Cinderella of Wilde's plays in English-speaking performances. It is all the more remarkable, then, to encounter the view of Karl Kraus that *Salomé* was 'a masterpiece for which there is scarcely a parallel in world literature'.[2] Such an opinion, written in a period which also produced Hofmannsthal's portrait of 'Sebastian Melmoth' as tragic figure,[3] is a striking reminder of the importance of the author of, *inter alia*, 'The Soul of Man under Socialism' for a generation of European intellectuals of a stamp not commonly associated with the aesthetic climate of the nineties; it was no accident that the German translator of *Salomé* was the wife of the anarchist Gustav Landauer. Alongside extravagant praise of a kind that seems all the more surprising coming from so particular a critic as Kraus, however, there ran a contrary view which may be exemplified by Romain Rolland in a celebrated letter to Strauss:

In spite of the pretentious affectations of the style, there is an undeniable dramatic power in Wilde's poem; but it has a nauseous and sickly atmosphere about it: it exudes vice and literature. This isn't a question of middle-class morality, it's a question of health. The same passions can be healthy or unhealthy, according to the artists who experience them, and the personages by whom they are incarnated . . . Wilde's Salomé, and all those who surround her, except that poor creature Jokanaan, are unwholesome, unclean, hysterical or alcoholic beings, stinking of sophisticated and perfumed corruption. – In vain do you transfigure your subject, increase its vigour a hundredfold, and envelop it in a Shakespearean atmosphere – in vain do you ascribe moving accents to your Salomé: you transcend your subject, but you can't make one forget it.[4]

It is one of the central problems for critics of play and opera that, however much the writer may seek to place himself beyond the charge of 'middle-class morality', adjectives such as 'unwholesome' and 'sickly' are the common property of critics and middle-class moralists alike. Rolland amplified his criticism in more telling detail, measuring the distance between Strauss and 'the mirage of German decadent literature' in terms of the immortality of the former and the ephemerality of the latter. He turned to *King Lear* as a model of what Strauss should have been setting; the charge is clear: 'Oscar Wilde's *Salomé* was not worthy of you.' The reason, however, remains rooted in the belief that *Salomé* was intended at face value as a case-study in evil and perversion; for Rolland, as for so many otherwise intelligent critics, Wilde had never really left the dock. Even a student of Wilde who notes that *Salomé* 'is a play that aspires towards the condition of music', and that it was 'Wilde's most symbolic and least understood play', feels the need to portray the heroine as 'entirely evil because entirely uninhibited'.[5] There have been few writers with the insight of Richard Ellmann to probe the exact meaning of that symbolism. Strauss could hardly have approached the play with thoughts comparable to Ellmann's when he perceived the drama as a symbolic confrontation between an ascetic John (whose surname might have been Ruskin) and Wilde's other Oxford master, Walter Pater, advocate of a 'diseased contemplation of life' which might lead to the love of the 'literally disembodied'.[6] Ellmann, however, reminds the musician, most forcefully when he notes the possible future resonances of the play in the theatre of Yeats and Beckett, that the horrors of *Salomé* were in no sense offered as facile realism. Yet this is a lesson that has never been learned by more than a few critics of the opera.

The earliest critics made the most of their sense of outrage, and most of it led back to Wilde:

Certainly this poem is not lacking in more strongly artistic qualities; but the scene in which Salome kisses the severed head of John is for me the most nauseating that has been brought to the stage so far.[7]

Such reactions found a more ample setting in a booklet which Adam

Röder compiled from some essays originally published in the *Rheinische Kurier* on the occasion of *Salome*'s first performance in Wiesbaden. To Röder, the success of the opera could only be explained as a conspiracy between the composer and a knot of critics with the object of leading 'our people into error and darken[ing] the bright ideal of German art'.[8] Having established in a preliminary swipe at the composer that according to Strabo the name of the heroine was Salōme, not Sālome as in the opera, Röder got down to his real target. Wilde, as a homosexual, deserved pity, but when he presented his ideas 'within the confines of normal art, we must protest against that with all seriousness':

> We are no supporters of censorship. But if sadists, masochists, lesbians and homosexuals come and presume to tell us that their crazy world of spirit and feeling is to be interpreted as manifestations of art, then steps must be taken in the interests of *health*. Art has no interest in sanctifying bestialities which arise from sexual perversity. Only this cry matters: out with them![9]

Perhaps this is the true voice of middle-class morality. Röder may be taken as representative of that whole area of opinion from Archbishop Piffl of Vienna to J. Pierpont Morgan which laboured to keep *Salome* off the stages of the great metropolitan opera houses. At least the Kaiser's reported reaction, 'That's a nice snake I've reared in my bosom',[10] had the merit of brevity.

A consequence of the close relationship between play and opera was a rapid drawing of lines between the partisans of Wilde and Strauss. A cool appraisal was quickly to be found in Oscar Bie's *feuilleton* in Vienna's *Neue freie Presse* two days after the première:

> Musicians find Wilde so beautiful, musical and rich that they think he doesn't need or support this music. Literary people find Wilde a little shallow and wordy, and long for music.[11]

It is not difficult to find examples to sustain this viewpoint, but in practice Bie's classification is too glib. As has been seen, literary attitudes to the play were already divided. Musicians would react to the opera with equal acrimony.

A particularly interesting attitude is inevitably that of the translator, Hedwig Lachmann:

> You have worked a miracle in clothing in tones this entirely self-enclosed drama which certainly was unyielding material, and in creating from much that is unspoken a content which gave up its soul for your new creation. Individual scenes are of quite unprecedented dramatic power, for example that between Herod and Salome where she repeatedly rejects him with the

demand for the head of Jochanaan, and the end is a marvellously moving effect.[12]

The Styrian novelist and poet Peter Rosegger (who devoted an article in his periodical *Heimgarten* to the opera) expressed a similar point more trenchantly and with less respect for Wilde when he thanked the composer for 'having transfigured the hideous material so humanely by *this* music'.[13] But the wittiest arguments in favour of the opera came from Paul Marsop in an imaginary dialogue with an Italian Marchese:

'What do you think of Oscar Wilde?' I parried: 'Does Wilde rate as a poet in Italy?' The Marchese laughed knowingly. 'Oh no. Not even the Wilde of *Salomé*. He remains in every costume the formally polished charlatan. When he strikes the note of high song, he reminds me of Burne-Jones and other English Pre-Raphaelite painters who clothe themselves in the style of old Florence.' 'Quite correct; rather as when our root-bound North German Brahms wants to speak Schubertian or even Hungarian.'

The Marchese is puzzled that the Germans should have mistaken a play about a 'half-English, half-French *demi-vierge*' for a work of art. To which Marsop concedes that *Salomé* has been overrated because the Germans lost their own faculty for the lyric when they invented 'social lyrics, Eau de cologne and motor oil'. *Salomé* is 'good raw material for an opera'.[14]

Among music critics, Julius Korngold may be instanced as a partisan of the play who felt that Strauss had 'thrown off all seven veils'.[15] *Salomé* simply had no need of music. But in spite of all partisanship, a consensus quickly emerged that in some way Strauss had shifted the meaning of Wilde's play. Admittedly there were those like Friedrich Brandes who felt that Strauss and Wilde were blood-brothers simply by virtue of the fact that neither could ever be boring; they were too fond of striking attitudes.[16] If this was the simplest statement of the relationship between composer and play-wright, a more controversial line may be traced from those like Rosegger who thought that Strauss had transfigured the material. The poet Otto Julius Bierbaum (some of whose poems Strauss had set) noted that *Salome* was 'the strongest proof for genius's ability to make a virtue of its defects, to make beauty from its sickness', a viewpoint notably cloudier than that of Rosegger.[17] Use of terms like 'transfigured' is a short step from words like 'redeemed'. The transition was easily made, since critics everywhere fell over themselves in the rush to evaluate Strauss's relationship to the

Wagnerian music drama. Even in terms of orchestration, some critics felt that 'without Richard Wagner, no Richard Strauss';[18] Hermann Starcke set the tone in more general matters as well:

. . . we no longer see in Salome the inhuman woman, the beast in the beautiful body, as in Wilde's play; rather, in her musical glorification she seems to be brought humanly nearer to us as a superhuman figure transfigured in the madness of love's passion; she behaves thus under the force of a higher power, as though she could not do otherwise.[19]

By the time of the first London performance in 1910, even the critic of *The Times* had made the connection, that there was a close resemblance between Salome's final paroxysm and Isolde's 'Liebestod'.[20] A school of thought evolved that saw the essence of Strauss's transfiguration of the play in the 'redeeming' of Salome in a Wagnerian sense. This prompted some acid observations from Rudolf Louis in the *Süddeutsche Monatshefte* under the title 'Die erlöste Salome'. The view that Salome was redeemed struck Louis as remarkably unmodern; but then Salome's monstrous mother herself had ended up as the servant of the Holy Grail in Act III of *Parsifal*. Such harmless jokes served a useful purpose in puncturing a critical absurdity. The idea of the 'redeemed Salome' was the well-meaning critic's equivalent to the Kaiser's concluding star of Bethlehem at the first Berlin performance, or the bowdlerised lines concocted by Beecham and the Lord Chamberlain ('If you had looked upon me you would have blessed me').[21]

Louis had more serious objections, however, which went to the heart of the music. Strauss frequently discarded realism (which is presumed to be Wilde's intention) and composed conventionally 'beautiful' music, notably in the final scene; had Louis known Kerman's phrase, 'sugary orgasm', he would no doubt have used it.[22] It is at moments like these that Louis discerned kitsch of a type comparable, particularly at 'Er ist in einem Nachen', to the style of Wilhelm Kienzl in *Der Evangelimann* (1894); by coincidence, it was exactly the music of Jochanaan which Kienzl himself singled out for 'simple greatness and natural feeling':

With these tones Strauss himself, this most daring of all musical innovators, admits that the expression of the sublime is unattainable without simplicity.[23]

In fact, Louis concludes, Salome is none other than those old Straussian heroines, the helpmates of *Ein Heldenleben* and the *Symphonia Domestica*, in a new guise. He thus stated a particular instance of a general truth most trenchantly expressed by Max Reger:

I am not of the opinion that moral or religious feeling will be offended in any way by *Salome*. And whoever finally loses his religion through *Salome* already had none. Just as little do I regard *Salome* as a turning-point in modern music or the start of a new direction! Strauss is as much Strauss in the music for *Salome* as in his previous works![24]

As a pendant to the redemption of Salome, it may be noted that the Bayreuth circle had no time for the work and directed several blasts against 'the desecration of music as the depictor of perversity' (as Strauss described it to Schuch, adding that he felt 'colossally flattered');[25] the most striking came from Siegfried Wagner, who felt 'deeply sad that *Parsifal* will soon be available to theatres polluted by the dangerous works of Richard Strauss, to boards over which the loathsome Salome has passed . . . '[26]

II

The principal critical objections to *Salome* may be summed up by reference to Julius Korngold's review, constructed, like Marsop's essay, as a dialogue.[27] A partisan of the opera presents a naive case based principally on the work's claim to be innovative; a sceptic accepts as little of this as Reger or Louis. Overall the opera showed no stylistic advance on *Feuersnot*. Its style was based on 'the motivically depicting, realistically imitating symphonic poem', not on Wagnerian *melos*. Its motives were unoriginal. The orchestral brilliance served to conceal a 'cacophonous element' in the harmony. By retaining too many of Wilde's lines, Strauss slowed the dramatic exposition. The 'Dance' was too long. On the whole, the sceptic admired the numerous special effects, with the conspicuous exception of the 'moaning double bass string'. Many of these points recur in the earliest reviews, not always as unqualified reproach. Even critics who drew attention to the influence of Wagner admitted that in some way Strauss had modified the Bayreuth method. For most of them, this modification lay in the tendency they recognised from other works by Strauss, realistic illustration and depiction. Lawrence Gilman noted:

Its advance on Wagner, from the constructive point of view, lies in the greater fullness with which the orchestral commentary is elaborated and sustained. It has been aptly characterized as 'an orchestral tone-painting, accompanied by a dramatic action on the stage.' The instrumental commentary has, indeed, almost the substance and independence of purely symphonic writing. The Wagnerian system of typical themes is elaborately exploited, and is made to serve an illustrative and significant purpose that never flags in explicitness and detail.[28]

The charge of unoriginality of themes was not always a brutal dismissal. Admittedly there were critics like that of the *Berliner Tageblatt* who looked upon Strauss as original only in the exoticisms of the 'Dance' and elsewhere heard mainly echoes of past composers; the love theme (perhaps as at Fig. 335) reminded him of Loewe (perhaps 'Er küsste sie' from 'Tom der Reimer', which has the same melodic fall as the beginning of Strauss's theme).[29] A more judicious evaluation of the quality of Strauss's invention came from Fauré in *Le Figaro*:

The novelty which principally distinguishes the score of *Salome* is that M. Richard Strauss transports there the particular aesthetic which typifies his symphonic poems, that is the principle of the description and analysis of sonorities pushed to the extreme limits. *Salome* is a symphonic poem with additional voice parts.[30]

Although the themes were mediocre in quality, it was Strauss's ingenuity in developing them that represented the real triumph of the work. There were drawbacks for Fauré even here, however, since the constant search for novelty ended in 'a perpetual dazzle which tires not only the spirit but also – does this seem absurd? – the eyes'.

One block of material was singled out for special criticism. Although there were some like Kienzl who warmed to the portrayal of Jochanaan, the prophet has always been the least appreciated figure in the score. When Heinrich Schenker noted in 1927 that 'the Jochanaan motive [was] shallow as an operetta', he was merely recapitulating in brutal shorthand a feeling common to both admirers and detractors of the work.[31] Korngold's dismissive use of the epithet 'Mendelssohnian' for the prophet's utterances had by 1923 grown into a more general critique by Ernst Bloch:

. . . the resources used here are basically only muscular talents. A soul is lacking, however lyrical-erotic the prevalent mood throughout, for the pitiful, Mendelssohnian, Jokanaan motif already reveals the religious shallowness and lack of substance. In its deepest passages, Strauss' music wears at best the melancholy expression of a brilliant hollowness.[32]

Two years earlier, one of the composer's most articulate champions, Richard Specht, summed up the case against Jochanaan by suggesting that Wilde had 'already bathed Jochanaan in toilet essence' and that Strauss had completed the taming of the wild prophet into 'the tranquil quietism of a Vicar of Wakefield'.[33] Specht felt compelled to exempt one theme from this blanket condemnation, the theme in fourths from the opening of Scene 3, a figure already singled out for special praise in Schoenberg's *Harmonielehre* alongside 'certain quartal progressions in Mahler . . . the fourth chords of Debussy and Dukas . . . '[34] But such names and comparisons were not enough to save even this motive from the vitriol of Korngold's sceptic.

That it was the combination of themes and not their quality that characterised the score had important consequences, as almost everyone realised. To one critic, Strauss's method of combination seemed retrospective, producing voice leading that suggested 'the vocal style of the Netherlands in the Middle Ages'.[35] But most preferred to talk of cacophony, though they realised that this might be part of the illustrative aesthetic they discerned in the work:

Elsewhere is it because of the particularly brutal character of the subject, or only for innovation, that Strauss has introduced so many cruel dissonances which defy all explanation?[36]

Gilman was more confident as to Strauss's intention, believing that his 'harmonic *tour de force*' was in large part 'designed quite frankly and obviously as sheer noise, intentional cacophony'.[37] He was probably thinking of such episodes as the music of the squabbling Jews or the execution scene. At any rate there were plenty of effects for lovers of the new; Zemlinsky, Schoenberg and his pupils Berg and Webern, and the ever-curious Puccini (to whose *Tosca* the horrors of *Salome* were often compared) all must have heard sounds to stretch their ears at Graz in 1906 (as no doubt did Thomas Mann's Adrian Leverkühn, who, although unsympathetic to the work's aesthetic, felt obliged to rehear it *en route* to the fateful encounter with his Esmeralda in Pressburg). The analytical world has bent its mind ever since to the description of Fauré's unexplainable. As late as 1948, Schoenberg, though long past his infatuation with the music of Strauss, turned to *Salome* to illustrate the phenomenon of extended tonality.[38] Ernst Kurth had already begun to classify systematically harmonic phenomena from the opera. Examples of leading-note relationships among dissonant chords, *Klangfarbensymbole* and independence of line from harmony led Kurth to the conclusion that to enrol Strauss simply among the Impressionists or the Expressionists would be a drastic over-simplification.[39] Yet beneath the novel and dense surface of *Salome* there was undeniably a traditional and explainable core. Schenker realised it at once; there were no mysteries in the score for his dogmatic and well-rooted certitudes:

Strauss's music in its 'motives' (of one bar's length and even shorter!) is based again and again on the same trick, the trick of neighbouring-note tension, – in the broader dimension, therefore, of an unequalled triviality.[40]

Whereas Kurth never forgot that the harmonic innovations were the product of an instrumental polyphony, Schenker saw through the novelties to provide the technical data for aesthetic mud-slinging. The observation on neighbouring-note tension helps to clarify even the notorious dissonance just before Fig. 361 (see Chapter 7, Ex. 2b); the unexplainable becomes what Kerman calls the 'most banal sound in the whole opera'.[41]

One aspect of *Salome* did attract considerable unqualified admiration, especially from fellow composers: the orchestration. Dukas, according to Rolland, 'confessed on leaving after a performance of *Salome*, "that until then he thought he knew about orchestration, but he could certainly see now that he didn't"'.[42] As for Ravel:

Yesterday he heard *Salome*, which he considers a stupendous work, together with *Pelléas* the most outstanding work in European music for the last fifteen years. He is above all struck by the unparalleled richness of the rhythms and of the orchestration.[43]

Among his fellow composers, Strauss generally found favourable reactions; the more acid verdicts could in some cases be written off as the jealousy of a rival, as with d'Albert's remark, 'I find it hideous – but the work will certainly exert a strong sensual charm on sensitive virgins.'[44] Yet the appraisals of the composers still left room for interesting qualifications. It was part of the inanity with which sections of the press responded to *Salome* that composers were frequently asked to pass moral rather than musical judgment. The opinions of Reger, Busoni and Schillings were all solicited by a journal intent on establishing whether *Salome* could lead to the hearer losing his religion. Schillings took the request at face value; Reger smuggled an aesthetic response into his answer; but Busoni's answer alone addressed the work rather than the sensation:

. . . That in its harmonic and orchestral part it shows a score commanding the highest respect.

That the libretto is a theatrical poem of gifted ingenuity, and the natural final fruit of a long genealogy: the Bible – plastic art of the Renaissance – Gustave Flaubert.

In art everything changes step by step. With this *Salome* such a step may have been taken on the top of other manifestations which will hurry on to the ascent of a new and higher step. Every son has the stuff of his ancestors in him – by his side flourish a hundred other species.[45]

In spite of the cramped form in which they were expressed, Busoni's views could form the basis for a rational discussion of the work. Mahler was more confused. Neither he nor Alma had much good to say about the 'Dance', and Strauss's composition of it after the rest of the work struck Mahler as 'risky'.[46] However much Mahler worked on *Salome*'s behalf in Vienna, he always had difficulty sifting 'the chaff from the grain':[47]

Salome, then, yesterday. The impression it made was stronger than ever and I am firmly convinced that it is one of the greatest masterpieces of our time. I cannot make out the drift of it, and can only surmise that it is the voice of the 'earth-spirit' speaking from the heart of genius, a spirit which does not indeed make a dwelling-place for itself to suit human taste but in accordance with its own unfathomable needs.[48]

The question of human taste was a particular puzzle to Mahler, confronted by the evident success of the work with the public but 'convinced that not one in a hundred really understood the music':

We ourselves, even during the performance, had grave doubts about the whole theme and subject-matter, about the music for the dance, which we did not like, and about a great deal else, in spite of so much that showed the hand of a master – and yet the public without hesitation gave a verdict of success. Whose was the verdict and on what authority? Rosegger said the voice of the people was the voice of God, to which we replied by asking whether he meant the people here and now or the people as posterity.[49]

Strauss himself hoped for this much recognition from posterity:

Unsuspecting critics have called *Salome* and *Elektra* 'Symphonies with accompanying voice parts'. That these 'symphonies' convey the kernel of the dramatic content . . . will perhaps be completely understood by our successors.[50]

It is striking that it is a technical matter which Strauss raises, as striking as the fact that Mahler almost certainly felt happier with *Salome* as a musical masterpiece than as a work in the theatre. Most of the composers cited would probably have admitted to a fascination with

Salome as a 'technical fantasy', in Grieg's phrase,[51] without subscribing to its aesthetic aims. Admiration for *Salome* has in general proceeded along technical lines.

In part this was due to standard perceptions of Strauss's character and achievements. Hermann Bahr was convinced that *Salome* in no sense reflected 'an immediate inner relationship' on Strauss's part, rather the opera represented an act of arrogant will to shape alien material to the composer's own purpose; 'his German musician's sense' would not let him leave the material alone until it had somehow been forced into an appropriate musical form.[52] Later, Gerhart Hauptmann went further and saw in Strauss an art that 'remained true to the old health', regardless of the spiritual ailments of the Wilhelmine Empire and the war. Strauss spoke for the immediately visible, and even *Salome* avoided 'the sorrows and death of the Gospels'.[53] This essentially robust image of Strauss only partly explains his achievement in *Salome*, which can unquestionably bear interpretation of a more colourful nature:

A ballad. No drama. Entirely tableau, entirely colour, in magical impressionistic flow and gliding intermediate tones, glinting evilly like the jewels on Moreau's *Herodias*. Colour also in the rhythm, in the blurred simultaneous tonalities and tempi unconcerned with one another. A symphony in opal green, purple blue and gold-streaked scarlet red. No drama, for each character stands for itself, speaks for itself, lives for itself.[54]

Behind the unmistakable prose of Richard Specht, there lay a coherent viewpoint which took *Salome* for a *Tristan*-like *Nachtstück*, from which more 'normal' pieces might emerge, as *Die Meistersinger* followed *Tristan*. Although there were precedents for *Salome* in earlier works (for example, the Jews' music could be compared with the critics in *Ein Heldenleben*), it stood as a special case. There was no feeling of prose being sung; rather, the piece was a deliberate stylisation with no roots in realism. Even the concluding act of necrophilia was not to be seen as a deliberate portrayal of perversion; the true comparison was not with the sadism of *Tosca* but with the act of cannibalism at the end of Kleist's *Penthesilea*. The final apotheosis of Salome's music was no redemption, but 'the death of a soul'.

Although Specht provided the most sustained and passionately argued case for taking *Salome* as something more than a mere triumph of technique, he had to reckon with the undoubted fact that all overnight sensations are replaced. 'Wie schön war die Prinzessin Salome', was Korngold's first thought on hearing *Elektra*,[55] and the arrival of Strauss's next one-act opera provided *Salome* at once with a twin and a rival. The relative merits of the two works were inevitably debated at length. Even Specht, while granting that '*Salome* might be more inspired, newer and richer in daring', contrasted *Elektra*'s 'elemental soaring to the superhuman' with the 'small and distant' court of Herod.[56] It was hardly Hofmannsthal's intention to create one of a new pair of 'heavenly twins', and letters to Strauss and Kessler attempted to distinguish clearly between the 'purple and violet' of *Salome* and the 'black and bright' of *Elektra*.[57] Most tellingly, he noted that there was a crescendo to a climax of purification in *Elektra* which *Salome* lacked. Hofmannsthal never attempted to state what *Salome* meant to him as the collaboration developed; the libretto for *Elektra* was well in hand before he heard *Salome* or read the enthusiastic critique sent to him by his friend Eberhard von Bodenhausen.[58] Like Bodenhausen, however, he may have sensed in the music something that extended beyond the superficial resemblances to Wagner, a composer whom Hofmannsthal was to spend many years attempting to purge from Strauss's background and instincts. Late in the collaboration, he made the remarkable admission that *Salome* remained Strauss's 'most beautiful and distinctive work', subsequently qualifying that with the reminder that *Salome*, 'in all its splendid impetuous novelty, was the irresistible upsurge and triumph of a *new* composer'.[59]

III

In spite of the scandals, *Salome* was a triumph, and not merely in that it paid for the Villa at Garmisch, as Strauss joked.[60] With the passage of time, critics spoke less of scandal, and the innovations became part of the musical world. Even Schenker by 1927 noted that 'an artistic personality expresses itself in the work which today assuredly has no equal'.[61] With the onset of the Nazi period in Germany, there was some reappraisal, such as prompted Thomas Mann to comment on 'the superficiality, the outdatedness, and the ridiculous coldness of this showpiece':

It is distinctly pre-war in its middle-class aesthetics. Has not Richard Strauss, this naive product of the imperial era, become far more old-fashioned than I? As an artist should he not be far more 'impossible' in the Third Reich than I?[62]

But in spite of his Jewish collaborators, Strauss survived in the

Reich, so much so that he could afford to twit Hans Severus Ziegler, the organiser of exhibitions of 'degenerate music', with not including *Salome* and its 'four Jews who sang the purest atonality'.[63] By 1941, *Salome* could take on for Gerhart Hauptmann an afterglow of an altogether more nostalgic kind than Mann had imagined. In view of the possibility of 'the universal power of expression into the psychic' opened by the work,

One fills with pride at a departed epoch of art which, had it produced only this work, would be immortal, but was in other respects too a rich one.[64]

Such judgments bathe in memories of the excitement *Salome* generated on its appearance. Although the work continues to be a challenge to conductors, directors and sopranos alike, criticism has tended to plough the same furrows as were established amid the invective of the work's first thirty years. Joseph Kerman's attack in *Opera as Drama* remains rooted in the dichotomy of technical ingenuity and aesthetic irrelevance, committed to the notion that Strauss's illustrative gifts were dedicated to 'an abstract display of sexual perversion' yet complaining of lack of reality.[65] Beyond this lies the reading of Peter Conrad, who extends 'perversion' to encompass a technical commentary on the 'blatant and exotic' way in which Strauss composed the score; yet much of his critique remains perverse itself in its wilful bending of facts:

. . . in the case of Herod (as with Aegisth in *Elektra*) he expects the voice of a heroic tenor to controvert himself by portraying an effeminate, babbling coward. Siegfried is assigned music fit for Mime.[66]

Yet Mime is a tenor too; if musicians have committed aesthetic solecisms in their praise of technique, the literary critics have tended to set the facts on their head, as though, in this instance, the character tenor did not exist. Herod and Mime lie within the one *Fach*. Undeniably there is an element of coarsening in Strauss's use of Wilde, and perhaps, as both Conrad and Gary Schmidgall have suggested, this is partly the responsibility of the German language (though the naivety of this view is refuted by Schmidgall himself): 'Had a great and resourceful German poet such as Hoffmannsthal set Wilde's play, perhaps a far closer approximation of "Salomé's" feline grace and buoyancy might have been achieved'.[67] However this may be, at least one famous exponent of the part preferred to sing it in French.[68]

It is probably safe to say that critical appraisal of *Salome* has yet to reconcile the restless, innovative and often brutal technical triumph of the music with the aesthetic roots of the subject. Schmidgall's attempt to locate the former in the present century while relegating the latter to the nineteenth lends a certain historical perspective to the debate without really explaining why Strauss saw in the subject the type of opera that he wanted to write. One can agree with Specht's comparison of *Tristan* and *Salome* while entering the reservation that the one subject has a universality appropriate to myth that the other lacks or has lost. Perhaps this is why critical comment on *Salome* remains voluminous but fragmented. A rounded description has never been achieved by the commentaries of William Mann,[69] Norman Del Mar[70] and the like, for all their diligence in tracing motives. As for the sceptical view, Strauss can rest in the assurance that the worst has already been written, most trenchantly perhaps by that 'celebrated musician' who told Beecham that 'the overture appealed to him at once as a fine bit of writing as well as a perfect epitome of the whole work'.[71]

9 'Salome': art or kitsch?

ROBIN HOLLOWAY

> . . . people who are most strongly imbued with an instinctive taste for bad music and for melodies, however commonplace, which have something facile and caressing about them, succeed, by dint of education in symphonic culture, in mortifying that appetite. But once they have arrived at this point, when, dazzled – and rightly so – by the brilliant orchestral colouring of Richard Strauss, they see that musician adopt the most vulgar motifs with a self-indulgence worthy of Auber, what those people originally admired finds suddenly in so high an authority a justification which delights them, and they wallow without qualms and with a twofold gratitude, when they listen to *Salomé*, in what would have been impossible for them to admire in *Les Diamants de la Couronne*. Proust, *The Guermantes Way*[1]

> . . . there is not a character whose physical individuality, whose morality (or immorality), whose thoughts and acts are not minutely translated, almost to the point of naiveté. Atmosphere and colour are portrayed in their finest nuances, all by means of mediocre themes, it is true, but developed, worked, interwoven with such marvellous skill that their intrinsic interest is exceeded by the magic of an orchestral technique of real genius, until these themes – mediocre, as I said – end by acquiring character, power, almost emotion. Fauré, reviewing *Salome* in 1907[2]

> I really like this fellow Strauss, but *Salome* will do him a lot of damage. Kaiser Wilhelm II[3]

I

I am impatient both with the piety that can unquestioningly place Strauss among the great composers, and with the dismissive distaste that, pleased with its good taste, deprives itself by banishing him to 'whichever purgatory punishes triumphant banality'.[4] *Salome*, just because it is one of his strongest and most characteristic works, poses the problem at its centre. If it were classic art in whatever mode (*Orfeo*; *Figaro*; *Tristan*; *Ballo*; *Wozzeck*) or if it were masterly

145

kitsch (*Butterfly*; *Die tote Stadt*; *Troilus and Cressida*) the position would be unanxious; there would be no problem, and the various appetites would agree to differ. That it is at the very simplest a mixture of both is clear from Fauré's direct and Proust's oblique comments. A work that can at such voltage hold the mediocre in suspension with the inspired has a fascination of its own. It is precisely with such pieces, where just estimation is trickiest and it behoves the admirer equally with the carper to try to work out exactly what they mean, that new ways of seeing and understanding can come into being; new definitions of taste adjudicating more subtly, more in accordance with how a listener actually vibrates, than the blanket endorsement or discredit of good or bad.

Which, nonetheless, still makes the best starting-point for a preliminary survey. *Salome* does contain some unambiguously great music. *Pace* Fauré there is one superb theme whose beginning is worthy of Bruckner at his most primeval, though it always tails off into inconsequence: the motive in fourths (first appearance nine bars after Fig. 65; biggest statement six before 141) that suggests the spiritual stature of the Baptist and his irreducible integrity. From Fig. 298 into the final scene is perhaps the work's greatest stretch and certainly its most 'advanced' – even the meanest historicist view would have to acknowledge that this music is astonishing in every parameter: timbre, gesture, quality of emotion and, above all, harmony. The writing is cleaner here than earlier (even without considering for the moment the famous solo double-bass note); Strauss explores the excruciating sonorities that render Herod's frenzy and Salome's anticipation with an essentiality and intensiveness quite different from the often routine textures earlier on. The remarkable harmony as Herod sinks in despairing defeat – at Figs. 299 and 303–4 – is not lost on the Schoenberg of *Die glückliche Hand* or the Mahler of the Tenth Symphony. Between these two places the texture makes the starting-point for the Schoenberg of Op. 16, No. 4 and especially No. 1 – the low D-centred cluster (D in octaves on bassoons, horns and timps, B flat and C on trombones, G trilling with A flat on bass clarinet and two low clarinets, the whole reinforced by the whole-tone tattoo on the four drums) underpinning an all-hell of shrieks and yelps in high woodwinds, horns and strings. The creepy music of Salome's panting impatience, from Fig. 307 to 313/8 when the gigantic black arm brings up the head, curdles the blood as previous thunderings from Jochanaan fail to (it even succeeds in partially redeeming his *other* motive, the far-from-superb one, in the two bars before 309). And the music from Fig. 314, when the head is hers and she addresses it in ecstatic triumph, makes one of the greatest passages of orchestral exaltation in the repertoire. Not every note is audible in these wonderful pages, either before or after C sharp minor is decisively reached (see especially the celeste at this very moment – the three bars beginning two before Fig. 316 – vainly *undoubled* on the work's opening theme!); but the overall effect could have been achieved no other way. These millions of notes are not merely fun for the eyes; they make a teeming froth of multiform textural invention, equal or superior to contemporary parallels in Mahler, Schoenberg or Berg for which it is anyway the prototype, and far more intense than anything comparable in Scriabin, early Szymanowski, etc. The inspiration continues to burn hot and bright throughout most of the heroine's final scena (the four bars before Fig. 341 lapse into the Marschallin, and the twenty-odd bars that follow are distinctly weak; but by 344 Strauss is on course again). The passage from 348 to just after 350, and the extraordinary juxtaposition of murky bitterness as she broods on what she has tasted (Figs. 355–8) with (358–61) ecstatic abandonment to what she has done, sustain a pitch of intensity not unworthy of Wagner.

Nor are the manifest successes of Salome always a matter of exaltation and extremity. There are at least two devices where 'less is more' as surely as in the music of Webern or Stravinsky. The first is the brilliant use of woodwind trills (which Stravinsky surely remembered in the 'Rondes printanières' from the *Rite*). They begin to figure in the crucial moments where, before deigning to dance, Salome extorts from Herod the promise of whatever she will ask, and persist intermittently till the work's final climax.[5] At the opposite extreme is the famous high pitched solo double-bass note (well-taken by Webern both early and late) as Salome peers down into the cistern trying to make out what is going on after her desire has been granted. Notwithstanding the elaborate instructions for its execution (see full score p. 294: Strauss's punctiliousness of detail is worthy of Ligeti!) it is nonetheless a simple idea, whose result is the most unnerving, and understated, sound in the entire operatic repertory.

Turning to bad music, the choice is embarrassingly wide. A recurrent low-point is the unctuous strain that usually characterises Jochanaan, heard first at Fig. 66 and in its full flatulent flower from Fig. 132 to *c*. 134. But perhaps the worst single moment is the duet

for the two pious Nazarenes (Fig. 210 onwards), with its pat conclusion at Fig. 212, where in answer to Herod's question they sing
together ('Jawohl. Er erweckt die Toten') as if a Savoy refrain had
strayed into *The Martyr of Antioch*. Equally bad but very different
music is employed for Jochanaan to denounce the corruption of
Herod's court (from four before Fig. 70 to Fig. 76), to rave away at
Salome herself (*c*. Figs. 81–5) or to foretell (Figs. 220–2) the dread-
ful end of the world. Piling on the dissonances and the orchestral
frissons to make our flesh creep is as vain as the oleaginous appeal
to 'higher things'. Indeed they appear in close juxtaposition in the
first passage cited: at Fig. 73 the prophet exhorts Herodias to arise
from her incestuous bed ('Green Horror' music)[6] to heed the word
of the Lord at Fig. 74 (churchy strains) and repent her of her sins
(Fig. 75, back to the shivers and shakes). We know about Strauss's
difficulties with religious emotion that is not broadly pantheistic/
erotic from his reluctance to depict the 'goody-goody' hero of
Josephslegende;[7] it is no surprise that baleful imaginings from the
Apocalypse should   produce   an   equally   stock   response.
Onomatopoeia and mimicry just cannot render such things.

But give him a *wind* (Fig. 164; again at 167; a third gust at 168;
and finally up, away and over the top from 233 to 241) and his
virtuosity with straightforward orchestral depiction can flourish
unchecked by the creaking stilts of spiritual content. As we shudder
with Herod and with him grow hot and cold, the physical force of it
almost lifts us from our seats. This is neither good nor bad in itself,
it is merely breathtakingly *successful*. And within a few bars of the
last, extremest gust – bars in which Herod has exhaustedly asked
Salome for the last time to dance for him and she has, this time,
knowing his oath, agreed – the Baptist is at his pious exercise again
(Fig. 243).

Juxtapositions like this, of materials indifferent or even positively bad, can be the source of some of *Salome*'s most telling
moments. Thus to take two simple instances first, the 'Green
Horrors' of the prophet's warning of doom set off by extreme contrast Herod's lavish gesture, just as impoverished in musical substance, of Invitation to the Dance (three bars before Fig. 224); while
the chorus of Jews (from five before Fig. 189 to Fig. 207) with its
thousands of notes zipping past, composed by rote with unflagging
skill upon indifferent material, makes its full effect, as a well-aimed
comic scherzo, by placement against, at one end, the angry jitterings
of Herodias, Herod's waxing *voluptas* and Salome's indifference,

and, at the other, the bland duet of Nazarenes already singled out for its special awfulness.

But the crucial instance is of course the 'Dance of the Seven Veils'. Here there is an additional stratagem involved: cunning use of the audience's expectations. Both Herod's previous invitations – to the dance already mentioned (three bars before Fig. 224) and to 'trink Wein mit mir' (fourth bar of Fig. 172) – launch generously into a tune that never comes, foundering equally upon Salome's indifference and Herod's short concentration-span. Disappointment at such withholding as to seem like an incapacity for delivering the wished-for goods is amply assuaged when the 'Dance' at last comes (thus deftly aligning the audience at once with Herod's desires and Salome's knowledge that she possesses the means of steering them towards the realisation of her own). After its flurried introduction it is *all* tunes from beginning to end. All of them are 'vulgar' (Proust) or 'mediocre' (Fauré), if not frankly bad. But we know how strangely potent cheap music can be.[8] The bargain-basement orientalism at letter F is both blenchmaking and stirring; at letter V we continue to be stirred even when we realise we are being taken advantage of – the oriental knicknack is a palpable fake. Are we stirred against our better nature, or do we gratefully acquiesce in our true baseness? Strauss is very clever at raising such puritanical teeterings upon the verge of the ocean of kitsch. They should already have been banished by letters K to P, where we have perforce to give in, submitting to the experience for what it is worth, for what it has cost, realising that it couldn't and shouldn't be otherwise. This sense of the music's quality and character as inevitable enables it to survive the glimpse into the wrong chamber three bars before letter O (where a peruked bourgeois gentilhomme makes a tiny accidental appearance some seven years, or seventeen centuries, before his due time), because our goal, now so sure, is the thirty-two-bar slow-waltz tune that commences eight bars before letter Q, where all this 'genius for bad taste' is clinched with 'triumphant banality' indeed. Sustained, masterly, deeply-thrilling kitsch here comes into its own as the absolutely right level and intonation for this particular situation in this particular work. 'Good taste' would involve a loss of face, even a chickening out, and therefore be artistically fatal. This defence is not offered as a sop to the allure of a camp aesthetic whose ultimate wriggle says 'it's good *because* it's awful'.[9] Much more straightforward: if it weren't what it is it wouldn't come off; it succeeds within the same stylistic area as the 'wind', already discussed, that has Herod crying ice and fire in almost the same breath.

The fact that the 'Dance of the Seven Veils' is so maligned shows the difficulty of defining this area and evaluating it fairly. In one sense it *is* cheap, mediocre, vulgar music. But this is *Salome*, not *Les Diamants de la Couronne* (nor yet *Tristan*), and Strauss as always provides exactly what is needed. What do people *expect* otherwise, who complain of its tawdriness? What do they *want*? – the perfumed garden and calls-to-erection of the *Poème d'extase*, the ultra-elegance of amorous soft porn à la *Daphnis et Chloé*, the small print of sensuality refined and spiritualised à la *Jeux*? The *donnée* is Strauss, adapting as opera Wilde's play on Salome and the Baptist with the artistic aims and resources of a thoroughly up-to-date German master in the prime of life, *anno* 1905.

The questions raised here will have to be sorted out later. For the moment, before continuing the exploration of *Salome*, it is enough to see how quickly consideration of the work's purely musical character leads in to central questions about its composer in the large. The norm of the work, far more frequent than high exaltation, vigorous vulgarity or cunning mediation of different levels of badness, is the 'perpetual dazzle' of which Fauré's review goes on to speak, 'which tires not only the spirit but also – does this seem absurd? – the eyes'. And above all the critical faculty; for it is an essential part of Strauss's technique to produce such a copious and detailed rush of sound as not to grant time for its examination. Or even assimilation; there isn't time to stop and reflect – he has contrived that we cannot distinguish good from bad, tiring us into an unresisting acceptance of whatever happens next. The clearest examples are the orchestral interludes where Jochanaan is brought out of the cistern (Figs. 59–66) and, still more, when he is taken back down (from six bars before Fig. 141 to just after 151): astonishing in their audacity of raw excitement and extreme compositional crudeness, the protagonists' motives juxtaposed or superimposed any-old-how, jacked up and down in sequences, at once insouciant, importunate and mechanical – ice and fire at the turn of a knob, as if in a well-practised and knowing improvisation. Thus if we reflect; as we hear it at the speed with which it seems to come into being before our very eyes like a carpet unrolling before our feet, this music is, again, 'exactly what is needed' in these particular places; it is as totally efficacious as the ungraspable rushing of the Jews' chorus or the wind, or the readily-assimilable slow-waltz tune in the

'Dance'. Strauss's technique *holds* like good luck: his indifferent mastery is such that we are able, as we listen, to play off almost unwittingly the improvisatory scurry of the work's norm of texture against the underlying simplicity, definiteness and slow-motion of the structure as a whole.[10] Thus the drastic slowing-down for the final scene, so that it can actually be taken in at the same speed at which it comes out, both mitigates the audience's anxiety at not quite having caught the earlier events as they flashed by, and gives them the comfort, and the satisfaction, of having worked hard to earn such expansion, ease and warmth. All this being in perfect accord with the composer's saving his greatest inspiration for this final scene as if all the earlier stages were the improviser's warming-up, trying over his material, getting into gear, working up the heat that at last, extruding all this slag and fuss, leaves only the gold, red-hot and more or less pure.

II

The phrase 'exactly what's wanted' is a portmanteau enclosing a number of possibilities. They range from the most practical exigencies of the opera's stagecraft and timing (as it were Petipa's instructions to Tchaikovsky) to what will be required of the music by way of matching, interpreting, enhancing, transforming the original play (as it were Boito to Verdi); from the lively sense that this practical type of artist always shows for just what his performers will seize on (the Strauss of the *Ariadne* Prologue, at home backstage, intimate with his prima donna, his tenor, his soubrette) to the vital business of what the audience wants (the Strauss of the Producer in *Capriccio*, sticking to his philistine guns amidst the pretty salvoes of the poet, the composer, the elegant man of the world and his sensitive sister) – all its desires from the most elevated to the most debased, all its reactions whether communal or covert. What Strauss himself wants is seemingly lost in the gratification of accommodating all these prior commitments with the successful outcome of his endeavours. After 'exactly what's wanted' has been handed out all round, it might begin to be possible to see what *he* might want in composing *Salome* (apart, with hindsight, from the income that paid for his villa in Garmisch); and thence to define him a little more closely. He seems to set out only to give, not to get, satisfaction, as if irrespective of his own predilections, or indeed as if he had none. That this is not true is clear from the remark already quoted: 'If a thing bores me I find it difficult to set it to music.' Yet, in the epoch of unprecedented self-expression and larger-than-life artistic profile, in spite of such grandiosity of self-presentation as *Heldenleben* and *Domestica* (not to mention the potent sorcerer in *Feuersnot*), he is curiously absent from all his richest creations, as if *Salome* and *Elektra* were not so different from a *Taillefer* or a *Festliches Präludium*.

Stravinsky said that Strauss 'didn't give a damn';[11] Hans Keller that he had 'a hole in the heart'.[12] But these negatives fail to describe the kind of artist who is the opposite of self-expressive and passionately engaged in his every utterance; equally the opposite of the mediumistic, the chosen vessel through which a divine message passes. He could say, 'I want to put myself to music';[13] and he could say, 'I want to give music as a cow gives milk'.[14] He manages both: the apparent megalomania of the first actually comes out as a kind of young-bullish boastfulness and selfishness miles removed from typical late-Romantic *Angst* and introspection; while the self-effacement and homeliness of the second allows him to get inside a Juan or a Till, a young superman or deluded old Quixote, a lustrously indifferent Salome and her lust-besotted stepfather, or to depict from the outside himself routing his enemies and taking off to the mountains with his mate, or, a few years later, the selfsame couple plus infant son, rioting over the breakfast table in a positive bacchanal of bourgeois domesticity. Above all, these pieces are so entertaining! – hilarious and exhilarating, if not always intended in quite the same spirit as we now take them – and so greatly adding to the gaiety of nations as to make his desire later in life to be 'the Offenbach of the twentieth century' not such a *volte face* as it at first seems.[15]

Strauss is neutral. He is a kind of emporium, whose rich, well-stocked and widely diversified wares are all produced on the premises by reliable craftsmen. Whether humdrum or exalted, everything is a job of work, planned and executed with business-like efficiency. Strauss is protean in his own enterprise, being at once the craftsman who makes, the merchant who sells, and the middleman who ascertains (even creates) demand and links up the various separate departments. He is also the genial provider, the cornucopian source who fuels his company and keeps it fed. As with so many of the big nineteenth-century producers, it is as much a matter of machinery as of Art[16] (though something very similar in spirit is already present in descriptions of the workshops of the great painters and sculptors of the Renaissance). When everything functions with such manifest smoothness, copiousness and success, it seems not so much churlish as irrelevant to ask for something else, something 'more'. What would it be? No one with a sense of what's what in matters of style and artistic nature would demand sublimity, severity, spirituality, intellectual grappling, philosophical profundity from Strauss at his most characteristic and best – and therefore from *Salome*. We know where such qualities are located, and go there to find them. He gives us what he's got, gold and dross, poured out like milk.

How does 'exactly what's wanted' actually work in all its various meanings? The 'Dance' requires (say) at one point a long, slow thirty-two-bar waltz-period. The exigencies of the stage require (say) just such-and-such a length to raise Jochanaan from his cistern and get him back into it, or for the soldiers at the end to rush forward and crush Salome to death before the curtain falls. Herod and Herodias (say) require to be memorably and effectively characterised; and the wind that he feels and she does not will need to be rendered in music. The subject itself, and its time and setting, require the sheen of opulent near-Eastern depravity in which all its events are swathed. When we turn to the details of the text and its musical matching, such general needs become more precise and well-defined. In itself Wilde's play is a poor thing, the ingrown child of a whole line of literature evoking antiquity in its decadence. Closest behind it stands Flaubert's late *Hérodias*, of which Wilde's play is indeed a virtual plagiarisation, sensationalising its treatment of the same story and trifling with its underlying theme.

But it all suits Strauss down to the ground; it is the native soil of his most avid fecundity. The operatic *Salome* is a perfect match of genius and talent. Wilde's poetic language, at once hyped-up and debased, covers a void that cries out for Strauss's descriptive powers to fill. Such period-piece poetastery as '[The moon] is like a woman rising from a tomb' (from the first scene) or 'Thy hair is like clusters of black grapes' (etc. *ad nauseam*, in Salome's attempted seduction of the Baptist) releases true gorgeousness in the music. The bankrupt's largesse in the accumulation of treasures Herod offers her if she but desist from the only prize she really wants finds its perfect complement in Strauss's well-heeled literalism; the composer who prided himself on being able to distinguish in music between silver and silver-gilt is here given the richest opportunity in all his œuvre (until the late shower of gold in *Danae*) to exercise this freakish gift.

Plate 6: *Salome*, by Olivier Merson (reproduced by permission of the Mansell Collection)

Such pseudo-sublimity as 'The mystery of love is greater than the mystery of death' (from the final scene) becomes in this composer's hands, not profound for sure, but a genuine and expertly-posed shudder, rendered in the external manner which we have seen to be his way with everything, through which we, like the heroine, may kiss the dead lips of a severed head.

So Strauss can flesh out Wilde's flashy insubstantiality, provide gold and dross to redeem his paper money, animate his languid literariness. What he cannot do is ennoble or deepen the treatment of the subject itself. Something that might in more thoughtful hands be subtly disturbing and genuinely subversive remains decorative and, for all its apparatus of lust and violence, extraordinarily *comfy*. There is, moreover, a vein of opportunism in Strauss's appropriation of what for Wilde had been an *exercice de style*; the lurid treatment of a Gospel episode (however peripheral) would inevitably scandalise authority both ecclesiastic and civic, to the work's enormous initial advantage till, the honeymoon over, it settled down, like all erstwhile shockers that turn out to have staying-power, to become 'fun for all the family'. And thus, in the end if not at once, 'exactly what's wanted' by the audience too: a whipped-cream panto with strip-tease and an improving moral. In its day the combination was irresistible of outrageously advanced but fundamentally recognisable music with a quasi-sacred story which, pretending to treat the anyway thoroughly corny but tolerably serious theme of sensuality's head-on conflict with asceticism, was really all set to yield a below-the-belt thrill. What survives of it now for us who see so clearly how the machinery works, and why does the appeal remain so potent? Strauss's worldly wisdom concerning his audience's desires, how it goes about gratifying them, and how it squares the gratification with the demands of heavy-duty high culture, is as infallible for nowadays as for 1905. *Salome* neither invites nor needs tendentious new interpretation to remain perennially 'relevant'.

The word 'invites' opens up another large metaphor. If Strauss the artist can be compared to an emporium, *Salome* the art-work is something of a *grande horizontale*. This metaphor of the opera's meretriciousness, in thoroughly bad taste, is closer than any other to the way it remains so successfully and perennially enjoyable; it can be exploited for what it's worth and so far as it will go. Where low pleasures meet high culture we tend to be hypocritical and devious. We want a bit of a thrill, a touch of danger, a whiff of the exotic; but decent appearances must be kept up, and elevations and ticklings must be legitimised. We want to be excited and stirred but not disconcerted, disturbed, singed or seared. *Salome*, so well-made, efficient, comfortable and safe, is the perfect answer: a night on the side for the assiduous spouse of great art. An important element is the willingness and habituality of both parties-in-pleasure. Embarrassment and vacillation, whether over the function or the payment, have long since disappeared. The opera knows what it is for, does it well, enjoys it, flourishes on the proceeds; and there is general satisfaction all round.

Such directness about why Salome and her client have come together overlays another kind of knowingness, that what they are doing is wrong. This is not *sin*; it doesn't fan 'the fire i' th' blood', let alone open a peephole upon the sublime knowledge of evil of which Baudelaire speaks in his *Intimate Journals* in words which truly make us tremble.[17] That would not be *Salome*: it would be *Parsifal* Act II or *Lulu* Act III. The area of misbehaviour is, rather, the domain evoked by such clichés as 'naughty but nice' or 'a little of what you fancy does you good', a brief self-indulgence as we abandon for a moment 'the straight and narrow'. We know this and it is part of the attraction. We cannot live with Parsifal and Lulu all the time, any more than with Hänsel and Gretel, or with the in-laws and the next-doors. Our desire for a package-debauch is perfectly understood and used: our need to be thrilled and our willingness to spend to obtain it are in exact collusion with the work's very being. There is no evil in it, and its horrors are dangerous only so much and so little as Belgian chocolates are dangerous. Indulgence in *Salome* is more like the smoker's habitual ignoring of the government health warning than the bravado of 'unsafe sex'.

The metaphors of the emporium and of the 'good-time girl' both operate in a thoroughly bourgeois/consumer way to render the nexus between art-work and audience completely grateful. Bouvard and Pécuchet would purr over *Salome*. Conspicuously well-crafted, its materials ostentatiously the best that money can buy, with notes like sequins stitched on in their millions by expensive specialised labour, it is not cheap in any material sense. Nor is it mere entertainment. It has pretensions to serious presentation of deep matters – a thoroughly modern study of the psychopathology of crazed pubescent sexuality deflected from one aim to seize morbidly upon another, gaining its own way by flagrant will-power till suddenly and satisfactorily crushed like a poisonous snake; it is set in the East, with its well-known mysteriousness and ungoverned abandonment to unnatural appetites, where the air is heavy with perfume and blood; and to dangerously advanced music by a notorious modernist. Yet all these potentially explosive ingredients are defused and turn out to be *entertaining*, with no need to furrow the brow or search the soul: scratch the modernity and you have *Liebeslieder* waltzes, scratch the exoticism and it is 'made in Birmingham', scratch the psychological profundity and you get sensationalised stereotypes in a stock situation. Finally, Strauss draws no moral. *Salome*, contrary to the early reactions of outrage, is not immoral in the slightest. Nor is it 'improving': a moralist wants to teach, exhort, reform, change lives, and for such modes Strauss indeed 'doesn't give a damn'. In short the whole thing is pre-digested, processed and (so to speak) served up on a plate.

III

Commercial, meretricious and shallow! But, evidently, something that, like sugar, we want and even need. Generous indulgences are called for, rather than denunciation and contempt. We willingly bend our severe standards to admit such a grossly pleasurable intrusion into our ordinary lives. For *Salome* is powerfully enough itself to permit a grateful defence of its supremacy in a category where it is not necessary to reproach its composer or ourselves for confusing art and kitsch; where their mingling together produces not only the cheap thrill and the naughty chocolate but an emotion too – fugitive but genuine – the warmth of the work's response to what in us, its listeners, is always able, willing and indeed longing to be taken for a ride. Its peculiarly satisfying quality lies in the surprisingly substantial depth of feeling induced by the frankness of the reciprocal arrangement made so easily once our hypocritical, hyper-critical hang-ups are overcome. There is an aesthetic realm of rich cheapness, sufficient shallowness, genuine corn: the bargain-basement below the belt, the rag-and-bone shop of the heart, where such art as Strauss's comes into its own. *Salome* is surely its principal ornament; manifest high inspiration works with supreme technical accomplishment, in a spiritual void, to raise kitsch to *Kunst* by sheer genius. Its sense of its own success is so convincing that we have perforce to share it. We are not so much convinced as convicted, partners in a guiltless relinquishment of our supposed better nature, mown down like grass before such energy, inventiveness, headiness, an overall *Schwung* that not only mends the insouciance as to larger absences but melts away all qualms as to what is present, be it never so vulgar or mediocre. He knows how to get a stage to vibrate, a girl to sing, an orchestra to seethe, erupt and incandesce. He knows how to rouse his audience to a frenzy. Later, with the Marschallin, he begins to manipulate tears and heartstrings; in *Salome* he is still content if (as Bernstein says) 'there's not a dry seat in the house'. Nobler things had been done supremely well; this is Strauss's thing; it is new aesthetic territory even if he and his admirers after him persuade themselves into thinking that he is still in line with the great tradition. Only if we forget the damaging absurdity of taking *Salome* and *Die Frau ohne Schatten* to be Wagnerian, and *Der Rosenkavalier* and *Capriccio* to be Mozart-ian(!),[18] can Strauss come into his own, a category apart. His denigrators, equally, are missing something unique and extraordinarily interesting.

These genre-mistakes arise because Strauss, unlike the comparable Puccini, is complicated by cultural striving, a sort of do-gooding which remained a weak point all his life, from *Macbeth* to *Metamorphosen*, well before and after Hofmannsthal nagged and rebuked him into airy-fairy-land. Admiration for his serious aspiration has inevitably to place *Die Frau ohne Schatten* at the head of the operatic output and the *Alpine Symphony* at the summit of a series of increasingly profound symphonic poems (the succession regrettably lapsing with the *Domestica*). The 'earthy' riposte would urge the claims of *Don Juan* and *Till*, the most vital music in *Feuersnot*, *Der Rosenkavalier* without the massive longueurs, and *Intermezzo*. In fact at his best he exploits the comic and expressive potential of juxtaposing high and low.[19] Latent in *Till*, this becomes the actual substance of *Don Quixote*, and when after his Expressionist excursion Strauss discovers his native Bavarian rococo with Viennese trimmings, it lies at the core of his style. The *seria* of *Ariadne abbandonata* is not particularly inspired in itself; the *buffa* of Zerbinetta and her troupe seems rather middling once we spot its origin in that masterpiece of confectionery *Hänsel und Gretel* (whose première Strauss had conducted); the heroics and erotics of Bacchus are distinctly saggy. But the juxtapositions and tentative comings-together of these diversely undistinguished strains give *Ariadne auf Naxos* a unique flavour; thereafter the differences do not need such emphasis, and by the time of *Capriccio* their fusion is harmonious and total.[20]

The fascination, and the quality, lie in the mixture.[21] *Salome* is the best instance of this in his entire œuvre. Her sister *Elektra* over-does both the horrors (leaving the audience half-saying 'go on, do it again, do it more', and half-stunned into indifference) and the beauties (in the voluptuous hedonism, quite wrong for its context, of the Recognition Scene). Moreover in *Elektra* the true seriousness of the subject is traduced by Strauss's being his most natural self, so that in order to enjoy the high inspiration of its best music we have to divorce it from its relationship to the situation, and take it for itself alone.[22] *Salome* is not beset by such problems: high and low are tellingly juxtaposed or else rub down well together; the high scrapes the depths and the low is exalted to the heights (as it says in the Bible), with Strauss in the prime of his energies, superbly indif-ferent to good and bad, generously covering the trashiness of characters and situation with the fruit of his copious cornucopia.

Salome is of course a crucial work historically. Taken one way, it opens up important aspects of early Schoenberg and later Mahler; *Wozzeck* and *Lulu* are inconceivable without it. Taken another, it facilitates more colouristic sensationalism by smaller talents, from the relative distinction of *Die Gezeichneten* and *Eine florentinische Tragödie*, via *Violanta* and *Mona Lisa*, to the pure low-grade kitsch of the film scores of Hollywood's palmy days. But for Strauss him-self these 'German Green Horrors' are an excursion. Being a master of mimicry, costume-change and ruses, he is 'trying it on'. After *Salome*, and as *Elektra* is already under way, he is begging Hofmannsthal for further sensational subjects – 'a really wild Cesare Borgia or Savonarola would be the answer to my prayers'.[23] Fortunately he was diverted via the huge success of *Der Rosen-kavalier*, and its sense of stylistic homecoming, into more fruitful paths; so that, as we have seen, he can by 1916 claim that his princi-pal gift is for sentimentality and parody and that he feels called to be the modern Offenbach.[24] Surely this master of the quick change of mask is responsible for *Salome* too? Everything in it stems, as shown, from 'what is wanted'; which turns out to be, what to wear that will suit the occasion. Like his own *Till* he is seeing what he can get away with, how far he can exploit this particular vein. In the end his best-fitting fancy costumes are the 'rococo' (eighteenth-century in setting, with heavy admixture from the mid-nineteenth-century Viennese waltz, the whole as unmistakably of its epoch as the pastiche Mansart of the Edwardian Ritz Hotel) and the neo-Greek (somewhere between Schinkel, Böcklin and the 1936 Olympic

Stadium). And his easiest undress is the skat and slippers of the homely husband of Garmisch. Underneath Salome's seventh veil, or the bitchiness of Herodias, or the bittersweet of the Marschallin, or the hefty ordinariness of Barak's wife, lies Pauline.

IV

Strauss as we have seen him to be, Strauss *au naturel*, provides in setting this particular story at this particular time everything that might be expected; the work fulfils its promises to the utmost and, tenderly stripped of its illusory pretensions to depth or sublimity, stands naked before us as itself – 'ich bin Salome'. So the earlier comment that 'what he cannot do is ennoble or deepen the treatment of the subject itself', if uttered as a complaint, puts the emphasis wrong. Understanding Strauss aright, we should neither require this of him nor blame him that he does not do it. And the same goes for reproaches or denunciations of the sharply inconsistent calibre of his musical materials.[25] These are questions that simply did not occur to him. No artist would *choose* to be patchy or shallow; it is manifestly involuntary. Strauss, as properly seen, would no more labour for the purity of his gold (à la Webern) than he would be capable (à la Stravinsky) of ironic play with inverted commas around the debased coinage. *Salome*, unlike his more serious subjects, is enhanced by this rather than traduced.

He trusts himself totally, thoughtlessly, to what his fertility yields him. Such unabashed naiveté is surely vindicated, for greater discrimination in the part would have inhibited the whole; 'sentimental' self-consciousness would not have allowed *any* of this red-hot mix of gold and slag past the censor. The vindication lies in *Salome*'s serendipity; not only of incidental wonders all the way, but in the fact that the whole *kitsch suprême* lives in spite of every objection that can be raised. It's not 'good *because* it's awful': on the contrary, it is the best, by far, of its own kind.

Postlude: images of Salome

What's a nice girl like Imogen Millais-Scott doing in a place like this?

Miss Millais-Scott, twenty last week, descendant of the painter,[1] a Lamda gold medalist, an accomplished dancer and mezzo-soprano, plays the title role in Ken Russell's new film, *Salome's Last Dance*, which will startle all those over eighteen from July 1, when it opens at the Prince Charles (does he know?) Cinema in London's Leicester Place.

She plays a boy prostitute taking the title role in Oscar Wilde's play *Salomé*, staged by the inmates and customers of a homosexual brothel, with Bosie (Lord Alfred Douglas) as John the Baptist, for the entertainment of Wilde, whose play was banned from public theatres.

The idea of the play within the film is that Salome's disastrous passion for John, as recorded by Wilde, mimics Wilde's for Bosie – a fact Wilde discovers too late . . .

Imogen, a bubblingly gamine and thoughtful young woman of great individuality, brought up in bohemian circumstances by her painter mother Jean, disputed some interpretations of the film: 'To me, I was totally female all the way through. Some get muddled up because I have got a rather boyish figure, whereas normally Salome is rather curvaceous . . . It is a very moral story. Oscar gets arrested and I get done away with. Mrs Whitehouse should be very pleased with it.'[2]

Salome has come a long way since she danced for Herod in the gospels. No one would imagine that Wilde set out to provide an accurate historical record of his heroine's last hours, but even he might have blinked at some of her more recent transformations.

Britain saw two new productions of Strauss's opera in 1988 (the year in which this book was finished). The production at Covent Garden derived much publicity from the fact that the Salome, Maria Ewing, finished the 'Dance of the Seven Veils' totally naked, an effect common in contemporary German productions but not previously experienced in this country. The producer, Sir Peter Hall (who is also Miss Ewing's husband), defended his decision as follows:

We've tried to do the 'Dance'. It's completely danced, it's completely acted, it's completely done. It's very tough on Maria Ewing, because she has to do that after having been on the stage for an hour singing, and she's still got another twenty minutes of singing to do after it. But I don't think there's any escape. I've seen *Salome*s where somebody else comes on to do the 'Dance'. I've also seen *Salome*s where the ladies do an approximate shiver and shimmy and leave it to the imagination. But you *cannot* leave the 'Dance' to the imagination. The 'Dance' is very programmatic music; it's a bit like Schoenberg's 'Music Round the Golden Calf'. I mean, both these great intellectuals, Strauss and Schoenberg, are almost writing Hollywood music, scenario music, and a lot of musicians turn their noses up at the 'Dance' as inferior music. But as programme music it does its job dramatically, superbly, I think, if you actually do the 'Dance'. The 'Dance' is about her discovery of herself as well as her provocation of Herod.[3]

Hall is more perceptive than he knows: Strauss did actually write a scenario for the 'Dance',[4] and while the composer might not have approved of Miss Ewing's cavortings the idea that the 'Dance' 'is about [Salome's] discovery of herself' is certainly close to his intentions.

In the same week, Stephanie Sundine, performing in the Welsh National Opera production at Swansea, was taking great care to keep her clothes on. Her Salome was 'no knowledgeably sexy minx', wrote the *Observer* critic, Nicholas Kenyon, 'but a young, wilful, white-clad virgin coming to terms with the alarming discovery of her own sexuality'.[5] She performed the 'Dance' almost motionless. Tom Sutcliffe, reviewing this production in the *Guardian*, thought:

The dance of the seven veils is the hypnotism of a cobra waiting to strike. Rather than showing an opera-singer attempting to be a belly dancer, [André] Engel [the producer] forces the audience to concentrate on the battle of irreconcilable desires behind the dance. It is sex, but also it is power. The implications of this confrontation, which Engel presents with the stage empty apart from Herod and Salome, grow terrifyingly precipitous precisely because the movement is mainly in the music.[6]

This last remark recalls Strauss's own comment, after warning against 'the capers cut . . . by exotic variety stars indulging in snake-like movements and waving Jochanaan's head about in the air': 'The orchestra alone is quite adequate.'[7] The Swansea production, too, was faithful to Strauss in its fashion: here Salome 'discovered herself' by realising the true nature of her relationship with Herod.

The dichotomy between these two performances, both, in their different ways, true to the composer's intentions, suggests a further thought. A broad (and not entirely serious) distinction can be made between performers who emphasise the erotic aspects of the role and those who prefer a more restrained, 'classical' approach; or, between vamps and virgins. Queen of the virgins (though more of a Boadicea than a Bess) was surely Birgit Nilsson, whose voice cut through the dense orchestral textures like a laser; Herod must have quailed before her Viking gaze. Seductive, however, she was not. Virginal in a different sense was Hildegard Behrens, whose tremulous delivery projected the 'little girl' side of the character so successfully that the listener was almost made to feel like a paedophile. Coming to the vamps, the most persuasive I have seen was Teresa Stratas in the Unitel film of the work. This was a performance of quite extraordinary erotic power, giving new meaning to the final orchestral heavings in the central interlude (around Figs. 150–1). One could never believe in her as an adolescent for a minute, however. Perhaps the only singers who have coupled the vampish and the virginal aspects of the role with equal success were Ljuba Welisch (more convincing on record than in the flesh, by all accounts) and the less well-known Walburga Wegner (on the recording conducted by Rudolf Moralt).

The game can be extended to exponents of the role on film and in the theatre. Theda Bara, who played the role on film in 1918, was not known as the 'Vamp of Vamps' for nothing, while Alla Nazimova, financing her own film performance in 1922, was almost oriental in girlish stylisation. Rita Hayworth, who appeared in the Columbia Pictures version of 1953, turned the character into a sort of Joan of Arc, being made to dance not *for* John the Baptist's head but in order to *save* him.[8] Going right back to the turn of the century, we can sense from photographs of Maud Allan, whose 'Vision of Salome' (a ballet based on Flaubert, to music by Marcel Rémy) reached Vienna in 1904 and London in 1908, some of the erotic power that shocked and delighted her audiences.[9]

These contrasting approaches, astonishing though some of them might have seemed to Wilde, obviously derived from his own initial uncertainties about Salome's character. Should she be sensual, or should she be chaste? It was hard to tell.[10] Strauss solved the problem, after a fashion, by deleting two key sentences from Salome's opening speech. 'I know not what it means. In truth, yes, I know it', she says in the play, commenting on the way Herod looks at her.[11] Strauss thereby puts the focus on Salome's virginity, making her an altogether less self-aware person than she is in Wilde. But in solving one problem he creates another. While the orchestra heaves and gyrates around the characters onstage, what on earth is Salome to do? (She has to do *something*.) The orchestra may be 'quite adequate' for expressing the turmoil experienced by the characters, but its noise goes for nothing unless it is simultaneously interpreted by the performers we see. Strauss's words tell one story, the orchestra another. Salome cannot be both sensual and chaste.

The ambivalence built into Salome the character comes out, on a broader level, in *Salome* the work. *Salome* is most often criticised, nowadays, for the banality of the music given to Jochanaan, in other words the 'chaste' music. Yet it was the 'sensual' music of Salome and Herod, the 'progressive' aspect, that caused offence at some of the early performances. The fluctuating critical fortunes of the work – like Puccini, adored by the public, but somehow thought not quite respectable – are a function of changing views of music history. To a modernist like Adorno, *only* the 'progressive' side of the work, those aspects of it that anticipate Schoenberg, Berg and others (Messiaen sometimes sounds as if he has been listening to it), could be of any interest. What a performance Boulez could give of *Salome* (so far as I know, he has never conducted it) if only he could overcome his historicist scruples! Whereas, on the other hand, critics of a rather conservative cast such as Mann and Del Mar, who obviously love the work, tend to write as if they are ashamed of it: one senses that really they prefer the Jochanaan sections ('free from all those nasty modernisms'), however much they might complain about them.

Salome is such a rich work that it has something to offer (and to offend) everyone. Like the *Ring* it is full of characters one already knows; one can people it with one's friends. And like the other masterpieces of Wagner, Verdi and Puccini it will go on being performed whatever the critics write. A book like this cannot hope to say all there is to be said about it. It can only point to some of its ambiguities. Perhaps the greatest ambiguity of all is Strauss's personality. 'The most puzzling of composers – to say nothing of human beings', according to Robert Craft,[12] he resists categorisation just as *Salome* refuses to conform to moral or aesthetic expectations. Critics have been dubious of both. So far the public has shown that it knows better. But Salome has not yet danced her last dance.

Appendix A: Strauss's scenario for the 'Dance of the Seven Veils'

It is well known that Strauss composed the 'Dance of the Seven Veils' after he had finished the rest of the opera. The score bears the date 20 June 1905, but the 'Dance' was not written until August (when it was apparently sketched and orchestrated in a fortnight).[1] Alma Mahler commented on this state of affairs with caustic wit.[2]

Less well-known is the scenario that Strauss sketched out for the 'Dance', probably in the 1920s.[3] This was discovered by Willi Schuh and first published in a Swiss periodical;[4] it has since reappeared in a variety of places, but only once, to my knowledge, in English, and then in a book that is no longer in print. The translation is reproduced below:

Notes on Salome's 'Dance of the Seven Veils'[5]
Quite slow [*Ziemlich langsam*], $\frac{3}{4}$: begins with a swaying movement on the spot.
3rd crotchet after D, Salome takes off the first veil and adopts the pose shown in Moreau's picture of Salome printed on page 12 of *La Danse* by Vuillier [cf. Plate 2].[6]
3rd bar before E, 3rd crotchet: a few lively paces towards Herod. One bar before E, back again in three steps.
E: three-bar transition with swaying movements.
4th bar after E, a whirling movement; Salome turns rapidly round and round.
F: beginning of steady dance movement; at this point only the slightest suggestion.
H: Salome swiftly removes the second veil.
3rd bar after H a few (four) alluring steps.
Very measured [*sehr gemessen*]: three slow, menacing steps towards the cistern in which Jochanaan sits imprisoned.
Poco accelerando, A major: with a few alluring movements she again turns to Herod.
The earlier musical tempo is resumed [*Wieder im früheren Zeitmass*]: three bars before K, she recoils softly; the startled pose is relaxed in the next bar.
K: for four bars she remains where she is (with the swaying movement of the beginning).

Six bars after K (G sharp minor): very alluring, gentle movement.
M: Movement of passionate wooing towards Jochanaan.
Somewhat more lively [*Etwas lebhafter*]: two bars before N (F major): highly erect pose, much as in 'Idyll' (*La Danse*, page 17); more slowly [*wieder ruhiger*], again relaxing out of this pose.
Three bars before O transition to a light, graceful sidestepping movement.
– Second bar [after O], as indeed the third bar,[7] on the 3rd crotchet (dominant of A flat major) two short graceful, wooing gestures.
P: Salome tears off the third veil violently.
C sharp minor, 'the first tempo is resumed' [*Wieder erstes Zeitmass*]: start of a separate dance utilising poses such as (*La Danse* by G. Vuillier) page 11 Bacchante, page 2 Egyptian woman (!!!??),[8] page 59 *Danseuse à l'écharpe*, pages 224 & 225 *Japanese Dancers*, page 315 *Le Paradis de Mahomet*, page 319 *Fête de Nuit à Laghouat*, pages 321 & 322 *Bayadères*.
C sharp major: a much more lively display of all her feminine charms (!) before Herod.
From V onwards, a return to more disconnected movements and calmer poses.
6th bar after W: lively dance rhythm (round dance):
    exhaustion
    she summons new energy.
Y: tears off the 5th veil.
Furioso and conclusion as marked in the vocal score.

Richard Strauss

This document is of a fourfold interest. In the first place, it shows Strauss's willingness to involve himself in matters of design, costume and choreography, matters which are customarily left to the director. (So far as I know, Strauss's intentions as expressed in the scenario have never been realised on stage.) Ever the professional, Strauss wanted to have control over as many aspects of the production as possible, an attitude which derived from the Wagnerian concept of the *Gesamtkunstwerk*. The only 'stage directions' in the scenario that appear in the score are 'exhaustion [–] she summons new energy' (the wording is slightly different in the score). Curiously, there is no mention of her standing beside the cistern for a moment, 'in a visionary attitude', before she finally throws herself at Herod's feet.

Secondly, the scenario sheds light on Strauss's conception of Salome as a character. The actual movements he prescribes show clearly, as Schuh implies, that the dignity of the heroine, her regal aspect, was uppermost in his mind. It would be impossible to perform the part with the movements he wanted if the character were portrayed as the cheap seductress she is often made to appear: as Strauss later wrote: 'Anyone who has been in the east and has observed the decorum with which women there behave, will appreciate that Salome, being a chaste virgin and an oriental princess, must be played with the simplest and most restrained of gestures, unless her defeat by the miracle of a great world is to excite only disgust and terror instead of sympathy.'[9] Producers, please note!

Thirdly, Strauss's scenario (similar in some respects to his annotations on Lachmann's translation of Wilde's play)[10] confirms certain tonal associations already noted. For example, Salome's display of 'all her feminine charms' coincides with a tonicisation of C sharp major (eight bars before S). Salome has been associated with C sharp (major and minor) since the beginning,[11] and its return at this point could be said to represent a final crystallisation of the character. All that is lacking is a reference to the moon (D flat).[12]

Finally, the existence of the scenario provides an explanation for why the 'Dance' was composed last. Schuh suggests that the problem was primarily a musical one: Strauss needed to invent new, dance-like motives that would combine effectively with the motives he already had.[13] There may be some truth in this. But surely the problem was more fundamental. The 'Dance' was the one stretch in the libretto for which he had no text (even the interludes had a 'programmatic' basis). Strauss, who could hardly compose a note unless he had a programme before him, had to supply ten minutes of purely orchestral music without a word of Wilde to help him. No wonder the composition of the 'Dance' was delayed. It may be that he was unable to write the piece at all until he had visualised it in detail, in which case the scenario he sketched out in the 1920s was only the final version of something he had long had in his mind.

The only question is: what has happened to the fourth, sixth and seventh veils?[14]

Appendix B: From the diary of Luigi Dallapiccola

Berlin, 9 February 1930[1]

I was lucky to have been able to see *Salome* a few evenings ago,[2] an opera with which I was shamefully unacquainted. For Alexander von Zemlinsky directed, and this great artist (almost completely unknown in Italy) succeeded in making Strauss's dense score as transparent as that of *Così fan tutte*. From now on, if anyone tells me the score of *Salome* is muddled, I shall answer that the performance must have been inadequate.

The opera was finished twenty-five years ago. If it were merely a case of superficial 'modernity' – modernity seasoned with scandal at the première – probably no one would speak of it today. But *Salome* is much more than that. We hear it as an artistic success and, as such, part of our civilisation: an opera that has now become classical, clear.

There is one point, however – a page, to be exact – which disturbed me for hours on end, perplexed and even mortified me a little. I was in fact unable to identify the instrument (undoubtedly a *solo* instrument) that played two notes in the low register: two very sweet, intense tones of distinctive timbre – a long A, followed by an even longer D – intended to support for several bars the delicate body of high strings and a few wind instruments. It wasn't difficult to exclude the brass at the outset, but it seemed impossible to consider the low-pitched woodwinds or, finally, the strings, whose timbre would have been quite different. What then?

Promptly next morning I was the first customer in a music store. After making a very modest purchase of paper, I asked if I might glance at the score of *Salome*, and it wasn't difficult to find what I was looking for: p. 330. A miracle, without doubt, a stroke of genius. And, at the same time, an admirable lesson in 'economy' (a word that might at first sound strange if applied to Richard Strauss).

All differences granted, of course, it suddenly reminded me of Mozart's definitive lesson, when he reserved the entrance of the trombones for the last part of *Don Giovanni*.

With the gigantic orchestra at his disposal, Strauss had created in 329 pages many truly fascinating atmospheres and found instrumental mixtures quite unprecedented at the beginning of the twentieth century. Clearly, he desired to postpone until the last moment (the entire score consists of 352 pages) the presentation of an isolated timbre that one could never expect to hear, so unrelated does it seem to the commonly understood possibilities of the orchestra; a timbre that apparently comes to us from a distant, yet-to-be-discovered world.

Furthermore, the surprising colour seems to have been planned to strengthen the meaning of the words – fortunately quite audible in this passage! It occurs at the precise moment when Salome, bent over the decapitated head of Jochanaan, sings: 'und wenn ich dich ansah, hörte ich *geheimnisvolle Musik*' ['and when I looked on thee I heard *a strange music*' – emphasis added]. At the beginning of the bar in which the protagonist utters the adjective 'geheimnisvolle' enters the secret, mysterious instrument I couldn't identify: the organ, backstage, *pianissimo*.

March 1969

P.S.: A few years ago Italian Radio sponsored a series of discussions on a certain trend in contemporary music. During my exchange of views with Pietro Grossi,[3] I didn't fail to mention the passage that had prompted these thoughts thirty-nine years ago as a presentiment of electronic timbres.

Notes

Introduction

1 *Strauss' Salome: A Guide to the Opera* (London: John Lane, 1907).
2 *More Opera Nights* (London: Putnam, 1954), pp. 3–37.
3 William Mann, *Richard Strauss: A Critical Study of the Operas* (London: Cassell, 1964); Norman Del Mar, *Richard Strauss: A Critical Commentary on His Life and Works*, 3 vols. (London: Barrie and Jenkins, 1978).
4 'Richard Strauss: *Salome*', in *Literature as Opera* (New York: Oxford University Press, 1977).
5 'Opera, Dance and Painting', in *Romantic Opera and Literary Form* (Berkeley: University of California Press, 1977).
6 Anna Amalie Abert, *Richard Strauss: Die Opern* (Hanover: Friedrich, 1972 (the *Salome* chapter is translated in the notes to the EMI recording, EMI SLS 5139 (1978)); Alan Jefferson, *The Operas of Richard Strauss in Britain 1910–1963* (London: Putnam, 1963); Michael Kennedy, *Richard Strauss* (London: Dent, 1976); Romain Rolland, several publications, but see especially *Richard Strauss and Romain Rolland: Correspondence, Diary and Essays*, ed. and annotated with a preface by Rollo Myers (London: Calder and Boyars, 1968); Willi Schuh, many publications, but especially *Über Opern von Richard Strauss* (Zurich: Atlantis, 1947), *The Stage Works of Richard Strauss* (London: Boosey and Hawkes, 1954), *Straussiana aus vier Jahrzehnten* (Tutzing: Schneider, 1981); Richard Specht, *Richard Strauss und sein Werk*, 2 vols. (Leipzig, Vienna and Zurich: E. P. Tal & Co., 1921). especially Vol. 2; Roland Tenschert, *Dreimal sieben Variationen über das Thema Richard Strauss* (Vienna: Frick, 1944).
7 'Reminiscences of the First Performance of My Operas' (1942), in *Recollections and Reflections*, ed. Willi Schuh, trans. L. J. Lawrence (London: Boosey and Hawkes, 1953), pp. 150–4.
8 See below, pp. 31ff.
9 Richard Ellmann, 'The Fatality of Passion', Covent Garden programme note (London: Royal Opera House, Covent Garden, 1988), n.p.
10 'I never read Flaubert's *Tentation de St Antoine* without signing my name at the end of it.' Quoted in Ellmann, *Oscar Wilde* (London: Hamish Hamilton, 1987), p. 355.

170

11 'But, tell me now, is Flaubert still read? I regret to say we no longer speak: he, most foolishly, objects to the use of those few details I borrowed from him in my *Salome* . . . ' Quoted in John Espey, 'Resources for Wilde Studies at the Clark Library', in John Espey and Richard Ellmann, *Oscar Wilde: Two Approaches* (Los Angeles: William Andrews Clark Memorial Library (University of California), 1977), p. 21.

12 *Oscar Wilde*, p. 320.

13 See below, pp. 11–15.

14 Ellmann, *Oscar Wilde*, p. 323.

15 *Ibid.*, pp. 324–5.

16 See *The Annotated Oscar Wilde*, ed. with an introduction and annotations by H. Montgomery Hyde (London: Orbis, 1982), p. 305.

17 *De Profundis* (letter to Lord Alfred Douglas from Reading Gaol, January–March (1897), in *The Letters of Oscar Wilde*, ed. Rupert Hart-Davis (London: Hart-Davis, 1962), p. 432.

18 Douglas's name did not appear on the title-page as translator, only as dedicatee (*ibid.*, p. 344n.). But it has since been restored – the Penguin edition claims to publish the text 'in the translation of Lord Alfred Douglas' (Wilde, *'The Importance of Being Earnest' and Other Plays* (Harmondsworth: Penguin, 1954), p. 315) – even though Hyde, for one, insists that the translation is not Douglas's work (*The Annotated Oscar Wilde*, p. 305). Wilde later maintained that the translation was by a friend of Ernest Dowson: *The Letters of Oscar Wilde*, p. 834.

19 Not only *Salomé* was successful; other works of Wilde enjoyed the same favour, with *A Florentine Tragedy* and *The Birthday of the Infanta* providing the basis for important stage works by Alexander Zemlinsky (who set them both) and Franz Schreker.

20 'Reminiscences of the First Performance of My Operas', p. 150.

21 See Edda Fuhrich-Leisler and Gisela Prossnitz, catalogue to Max Reinhardt Exhibition (Vienna, July–August 1983), p. 15.

22 Sally McMullen, 'Sense and Sensuality: Max Reinhardt's Early Productions', in *Max Reinhardt: The Oxford Symposium*, ed. Margaret Jacobs and John Warren (Oxford: John Warren, 1986), p. 21; see also Margaret Shewring and Ronnie Mulryne, 'Max Reinhardt's *Salome*', Welsh National Opera programme book (Cardiff: Welsh National Opera, 1988), p. 22.

23 On Lachmann, see Schmidgall, *Literature as Opera*, p. 405, n. 5.

24 See Max Steinitzer, *Richard Strauss* (Berlin: Schuster and Loeffler, 1911), p. 257n.

25 *Richard Strauss: Partitur eines Lebens* (Darmstadt: Deutsche Buch-Gemeinschaft, 1965), p. 111.

26 *More Opera Nights*, p. 4. See also below, p. 111.

27 See *Die Skizzenbücher von Richard Strauss aus dem Richard-Strauss-Archiv in Garmisch* (Tutzing: Schneider, 1977), pp. 21–6, and Appendix A below.

28 *Skizzenbücher*, p. 25.

29 *Richard Strauss*, pp. 42–3.

30 See his remarks on Schuch's preparation of *Elektra* in *Recollections and*

Reflections, pp. 155–6. For their correspondence over *Salome* see Friedrich von Schuch, *Richard Strauss, Ernst von Schuch und Dresdens Oper*, 2nd edn (Leipzig: Verlag der Kunst, 1953), pp. 64–77.

31 'Reminiscences of the First Performance of My Operas', pp. 150–1.

32 See the reviews quoted in Schuch, *Richard Strauss, Ernst von Schuch und Dresdens Oper*, pp. 72–4.

33 See Steinitzer, *Richard Strauss*, p. 89n.

34 *Gustav Mahler–Richard Strauss: Correspondence 1888–1911*, ed. with notes and an essay by Herta Blaukopf, trans. Edmund Jephcott (London: Faber, 1984), pp. 150–1. Strauss continued to conduct, of course, but only on his terms.

35 'Reminiscences of the First Performance of My Operas', p. 152.

36 Quoted and translated in Kurt Blaukopf, *Mahler: A Documentary Study* (London: Thames and Hudson, 1976), pp. 241–2.

37 See *ibid.*, pp. 242–3. The entire correspondence is given in *Gustav Mahler–Richard Strauss: Correspondence 1888–1911*, pp. 85ff.

The knife was given a different twist in 1939, when certain Austrian performances of *Salome* were banned by the Nazis. As Strauss wrote to his nephew Rudolf Moralt (himself a distinguished conductor of the work):

> It's very funny that *Salome* is supposed to be a Jewish ballad. The Führer and Reichskanzler himself told my son at Bayreuth that *Salome* was one of his first operatic experiences and that he had cadged the money from his relations in order to travel to the first performance in Graz [May 1906]. His very words!!
>
> > Letter of 8 August 1939, quoted in Kurt Wilhelm, *Richard Strauss persönlich: Eine Bildbiographie* (Munich: Kindler, 1984), p. 124 (my translation).

38 'The Newman–Shaw Controversy Concerning Strauss', *The Nation*, reprinted in *Testament of Music* (London: Putnam, 1963), p. 129. Luckily he had got over this attitude by the time he wrote *More Opera Nights*.

39 *Richard Strauss*, p. 60.

40 *Richard Strauss*, pp. 273, 282.

41 *In Search of Wagner*, trans. Rodney Livingstone (London: New Left Books, 1981), p. 54.

42 'Richard Strauss', *Perspectives of New Music*, Vol. 4, No. 1 (Fall–Winter 1965), p. 22.

43 *Ibid.*, p. 14.

44 A notable exception is Stephan Kohler, who kindly sent me a copy of his article on *Salome* (for reference, see Bibliography) during the preparation of this book.

45 In *Between Romanticism and Modernism*, trans. Mary Whittall (Berkeley: University of California Press, 1980).

46 Quoted in H. H. Stuckenschmidt, *Arnold Schoenberg: His Life, World and Work*, trans. Humphrey Searle (London: John Calder, 1977), p. 544.

47 See Willi Reich, *Schoenberg: A Critical Biography*, trans. Leo Black (London: Longman, 1971), p. 25, and below, p. 184, n. 48. Strauss

apparently returned the compliment by using Schoenberg's *Harmonie-lehre* to teach his grandson! See Stuckenschmidt, *Arnold Schoenberg: His Life, World and Work*, p. 74.
48 *Romantic Opera and Literary Form*, p. 144.
49 Wilde himself could not decide whether to accent the word or not. See *The Letters of Oscar Wilde*, p. 306n.

1 Salome in literary tradition

1 [This chapter reprints extracts from Mario Praz, *The Romantic Agony*, trans. Angus Davidson (London: Oxford University Press, 1970). The work first appeared in English in 1933. Reprinted are sections 2 and 4 of Chapter 5, 'Byzantium', with part of the last sentence of section 3 ('. . . Moreau was a forerunner of Maeterlinck') added for transition. The epigraph – a passage from Huysmans *not* quoted by Praz – is my addition. All quotations are given in English. (The English edition of the book is inconsistent in this respect: Heine is translated, but not the French authors.) Published translations are used wherever possible; others are by Michael Gordon. Ed.]

2 J.-K. Huysmans, *A rebours*. [Translated by Robert Baldick as *Against Nature* (Harmondsworth: Penguin, 1959), p. 65.]

3 *A rebours*, Chapter 5. [*Against Nature*, p. 63.]

4 [*L'Apparition* is now in the Louvre, Paris.]

5 [*Against Nature*, pp. 63–4.]

6 *Œuvres complètes* (Paris: Imprimerie Nationale, 1902), pp. 50–1. [Translated by Kitty Mrosovsky as *The Temptation of St Anthony* (Harmondsworth: Penguin), pp. 101–2.

7 [*Against Nature*, p. 64.]

8 [*The Temptation of St Anthony*, p. 84.] Nevertheless Huysmans says in *La Cathédrale* (p. 331) that the Queen of Sheba

could only be incorporated in the *Tentation de Saint Antoine* as a puerile and colourless creature, a puppet which hops about, lisping; in the end only the painter of Salome, Gustave Moreau, could render that virginal, lustful woman as a casuist and coquette.

9 [*Against Nature*, pp. 65–6.]

10 [*Ibid.*, p. 66.]

11 [*Ibid.*, p. 68.]

12 [*Ibid.*, p. 69.]

13 *Salomé* was translated into English by Lord Alfred Douglas [but see above, p. 171, n. 18] and published with illustrations by Beardsley in 1894, at the Bodley Head. The influence on *Salomé* of Maeterlinck's plays was remarked by M. Arnauld in 'L'Œuvre d'O. Wilde', in *La Grande Revue*, 10 May 1897, and was the subject of particular study in E. Bendz, 'A propos de la *Salomé* d'Oscar Wilde', in *Englische Studien*, Vol. 51 (1917–18), pp. 48–70. There is also a dissertation on the subject (Munich, 1913) by F. K. Brass, 'O. Wildes Salome: Eine kritische Quellenstudie'.

14 [Translated by Robert Baldick as *Herodias*, in Flaubert, *Three Tales* (Harmondsworth: Penguin, 1961), p. 122.]

15 [Translated by 'Lord Alfred Douglas', in Oscar Wilde, '*The Importance of Being Earnest' and Other Plays* (Harmondsworth: Penguin, 1954), p. 342.]

16 Bendz says: 'It was Salomé's love that was Wilde's original idea. That was his masterstroke.'

17 On the tradition followed by Heine cf. Reimarus, *Stoffgeschichte der Salome-Dichtungen* (Leipzig: Wigand, 1913), pp. 46ff., 101–5.

18 Quoted from *Atta Troll and Other Poems by Heinrich Heine*, translated by T. S. Egan (London: Chapman and Hall, 1876).

19 In his picture entitled *Capital Execution under the Moorish Kings*, Regnault treated the blood of the victims in the same spirit in which he had treated the jewels in *Salomé*, like the 'hail of rubies' to which a seventeenth-century poet had compared the blood of a chastised courtesan. See [*The Romantic Agony*,] Chapter 1, p. 37.

20 [Wilde, '*The Importance of Being Earnest' and Other Plays*, p. 342.]

21 Note that the way in which the name is written is that of Flaubert. In fact, Laforgue's *Salomé* (which the author had conceived as early as 1882) is partly a parody of Flaubert's story. See F. Ruchon, *Jules Laforgue* (Geneva: Editions Albert Ciana, 1924), p. 110. But the figure of Salome is barely seen in Flaubert and he gives it the suggestion of an artless urchin, so that it could scarcely account for Laforgue's fantasy.

22 In 1894 a drama by Antoine Sabatier was performed, *Le Baiser de Jean*, in which Salome is presented in the same way as in Wilde as a hysterical woman, with demoniacal and macabre traits, mad with sadistic love. Salome has inspired also the Russian poet Alexander Blok (the second poem on 'Venice', in his *Italian Poems*, 1909) and the Portuguese Eugenio de Castro (*Salomé e outros poemas*, 1896), the author of *Belkiss* [*rainha de Saba, d'Axum e do Hymiar* (1894)] . . . [See also Praz's 1950 addition, p. 428, n. 114:] Among Italian paintings inspired by Salome attention may be drawn to a particularly morbid one by Francesco del Cairo at the Turin Picture Gallery, in which Salome appears as if swooning before the Baptist's head. If we follow the subject down to modern times, we should find a similarly deliquescent expression on the face of Gustav Klimt's Judith (*Judith and Holophernes* . . .). [Strauss admired Klimt. 'In the world of this painter of fantasy', he remarked, he had found 'much of my own music, especially *Salome*'. Quoted in Gary Schmidgall, *Literature as Opera* (New York: Oxford University Press, 1977), p. 286.]

2 Overtures to Wilde's *Salomé*

1 [This chapter reprints, with minimal editorial interference, Richard Ellmann, 'Overtures to Wilde's *Salomé*', *Tri-Quarterly*, Vol. 5, No. 1 (Spring 1969), pp. 45–64. Ellmann's essay originated as a commemorative address given at the School of Letters of the University of Indiana, where it was published as *School of Letters: Twentieth Anniversary*

1948–1968 (Bloomington: Indiana University, 1968); he later used some of its material in a Covent Garden programme note, 'The Fatality of Passion' (London: Royal Opera House, Covent Garden, 1988). See also Ellmann's *Oscar Wilde* (London: Hamish Hamilton, 1987), especially pp. 45–50, 322–6. Ed.]

2 Mario Praz, *The Romantic Agony*, trans. Angus Davidson (London: Oxford University Press, 1970), p. 201.

3 Unpublished letter, Mallarmé to Wilde, March 1893.

4 'J'ai laissé le nom d'Hérodiade pour bien la différencier de la Salomé je dirai moderne . . . ' Draft of a preface to 'Hérodiade', in Stéphane Mallarmé, *Les Noces d'Hérodiade* (Paris: Gallimard, 1959), p. 51. [See also Ellmann, *Oscar Wilde*, p. 320.]

5 See Yeats's comments on *A Full Moon in March* and *The King of the Great Clock Tower*.

6 [Herod Antipas (Matthew 4: 14), Herod the Great (Matthew 2: 1), and Herod Agrippa I (Acts 12: 19). See below, p. 179, n. 3.]

7 Praz, *The Romantic Agony*, p. 313. [See above, pp. 16–18.]

8 This edition was anonymous.

9 Heywood's *Salome* was one of several books discussed in Wilde's review, 'The Poet's Corner', *Pall Mall Gazette*, Vol. 47, No. 7128 (20 January 1888), p. 3.

10 According to E. Gomez Carrillo, a young Guatemalan writer who saw much of Wilde during the composition of the play, other details changed considerably in the planning, but the climax was always the same. Gomez Carrillo, *En Plena Bohemia*, in *Collected Works* (Madrid, n.d. [1919?]), Vol. 16, pp. 170ff.

11 *The Letters of Oscar Wilde*, ed. Rupert Hart-Davis (London: Hart-Davis, 1962), p. 469.

12 Vincent O'Sullivan, *Aspects of Wilde* (London: Constable, 1936), p. 139.

13 *The Letters of Oscar Wilde*, p. 471.

14 Yeats, *Autobiography* (New York, 1965), p. 87.

15 *The Letters of Oscar Wilde*, p. 471. At the Lord Queensberry trial Wilde spoke of Pater as 'the only critic of the century whose opinion I set high . . . '

16 John Ruskin, *Sesame and Lilies* (London, 1900), p. 203.

17 Pater, on the other hand, much preferred the activities of what he called in italics the palaestra.

18 Based on newspaper clippings of Wilde's American tour, 1881–2.

19 *The Letters of Oscar Wilde*, p. 218.

20 *Ibid.*, p. 61.

21 Derrick Leon, *Ruskin, The Great Victorian* (London: Routledge and Kegan Paul, 1949), p. 152.

22 In *The Critic as Artist*.

23 *Sesame and Lilies*, p. xxxiii.

24 Ruskin, *The Stones of Venice* (New York, n.d.), Vol. 1, p. 150.

25 *Ibid.*, p. 8.

26 *Ibid.*, pp. 38–9.

27 *Ibid.*, Vol. 3, p. 165.

28 Wallace K. Ferguson, *The Renaissance in Historical Thought* (Cambridge, Mass.: Houghton Mifflin, 1948), pp. 142–4.
29 Entry for 30 November 1880 in *The Diaries of John Ruskin*, ed. Joan Evans and John Howard Whitehouse (Oxford: Clarendon, 1959), Vol. 3, p. 995. Ruskin's earlier dedicatory tablet had been taken down because the well became polluted.
30 Ruskin, *The Crown of Wild Olive* (1866) in *The Works of John Ruskin*, ed. E. T. Cook and Alexander Wedderburn (London: Allen, 1903), Vol. 18, p. 443.
31 *Fors Clavigera* 79 (July 1877), in *Works*, Vol. 29, p. 161.
32 Ruskin, *Diary*, Vol. 2, p. 537, and Notes on the Turin Gallery. Quoted by R. H. Wilenski, *John Ruskin* (London: Faber and Faber, 1933), pp. 231–2.
33 Wilenski, *John Ruskin*, p. 69.
34 *Diary*, Vol. 2, pp. 720, 737.
35 Walter Pater, *The Renaissance*, ed. Kenneth Clark (Meridian, 1961), p. 214.
36 'It is so with the so-called *Saint John the Baptist* of the Louvre – one of the few naked figures Leonardo painted – whose delicate brown flesh and woman's hair no one would go out into the wilderness to seek, and whose treacherous smile would have us understand something far beyond the outward gesture or circumstances.' *Ibid.*, p. 118.
37 See *The Letters of Oscar Wilde*, p. 756.
38 Pater, *Renaissance*, p. 108.
39 *Ibid.*, p. 116.
40 *The Stones of Venice*, Vol. 3, p. 8.
41 Pater, *Renaissance*, p. 47.
42 *The Stones of Venice*, Vol. 3, p. 109.
43 *Ibid.*, p. 110.
44 Later 'sunlit'.
45 Pater, *Renaissance*, p. 211.
46 Wilde, letter to the Editor of the *St James's Gazette*, 26 June 1890, in *The Letters of Oscar Wilde*, p. 259.
47 *Ibid.*
48 *Ibid.*, p. 476.
49 [Fig. 109 of Strauss's opera.]
50 Jean Paul Raymond and Charles Ricketts, *Oscar Wilde: Recollections* (London: Nonesuch Press, 1932), p. 51.
51 Gomez Carrillo says that the play was originally to be entitled 'La Décapitation de Salomé', thus slighting St John by precisely equating the two deaths. *En Plena Bohemia*, p. 214.
52 [Strauss cut this epigram in his setting.]
53 Unpublished letter in the Houghton Library, Harvard.
54 *The Letters of Oscar Wilde*, p. 31.
55 *Ibid.*, p. 185.
56 *Ibid.*, p. 475.
57 *Ibid.*, p. 185.
58 See Proust, *Correspondance avec sa mère*, ed. Philip Kolb (Paris: Plon, 1953), p. 279.

3 Strauss as librettist

1 This chapter is a translation of 'Richard Strauss' Opernfassung der deutschen Übersetzung von Oscar Wildes "Salome"', *Richard Strauss Jahrbuch (1959–60)*, ed. Willi Schuh (Bonn: Boosey and Hawkes, 1960), pp. 99–106. The translation is by Alfred Clayton. All the notes to this chapter are editorial unless otherwise stated.

2 The composer's son. The 'libretto' is now in the possession of Alice Strauss, Franz's widow.

3 That is, Strauss used the first edition.

4 The appearance of the name 'Mannai' is curious here, since Mannaëi is the name of the Executioner in Flaubert. In Wilde he is called Naaman (almost an anagram of 'Mannai'), as he is in the opera.

5 This is slightly confusing. It is true that Narraboth is referred to consistently as the Young Syrian, but his name is mentioned on the sixth page of Wilde's text, by Salome herself: 'You will do this thing for me, will you not, Narraboth?' (cf. the opera, Fig. 49/8). And it is only after his death that we learn his family history.

6 That is, in performance.

7 And for Strauss's conception of the performance: see 'Reminiscences of the First Performance of My Operas', in *Recollections and Reflections*, ed. Willi Schuh, trans. L. J. Lawrence (London: Boosey and Hawkes, 1953), p. 151, and below, pp. 166–7.

8 Or in anticipation of the censor (the play had of course been performed uncut, but the censors at the Vienna Court Opera were particularly puritanical).

9 The second passage is also a cross-reference to one of Salome's opening speeches: 'The moon is cold and chaste. I am sure she is a virgin, she has a virgin's beauty', etc.

10 Here, as in some of the examples quoted earlier, one also notices a desire to avoid feminine endings. [Author's note]

11 The example shows how Strauss arranged a passage from Lachmann's text to suit his purposes by reordering the words (the numbers show the sequence of words in the copy of Lachmann's text used by the composer and in the latter's final version). [Author's note]

12 Strauss's predilection for grouping things in threes is discussed below, pp. 89ff.

13 When Sarah Bernhardt saw the manuscript of Wilde's play, she decided to play the title role. Wilde told her that the leading role belonged to the moon. Richard Ellmann, 'The Fatality of Passion' (London: Royal Opera House, Covent Garden, 1988), n.p. 'She was, however, aware that it was Herod who must finally dominate the play,' Ellmann comments.

14 From the Page's first speech.

15 A famous production that 'ignored' the moon was the one by Wieland Wagner, reviewed by Carl Dahlhaus in 'Jochanaans Tod: Wieland Wagner inszeniert *Salome*', *Neue Zeitschrift für Musik*, Vol. 123, No. 5 (1962), pp. 232–3.

16 Here Lachmann goes further than Wilde's simple 'Moonlight'.

17 Fig. 6.
18 Fig. 9.
19 Seven bars before Fig. 79; one before 79.
20 Three bars before Fig. 138; four before 140; six before 141.
21 Fig. 348; two bars after 350.
22 Five bars before Fig. 76. It is not clear from Tenschert's original article whether Strauss actually wrote out the music or simply jotted down the names of the notes above the relevant words. Example 1 must therefore be taken as conjectural. (Tenschert also, and incorrectly, gives 'f sharp' as the first two notes of Ex. 2.)
23 *Richard Strauss (1864–1949): 'Musik des Lichts in dunkler Zeit': Vom Bürgerschreck zum Rosenkavalier*, ed. Gisela Jaacks and Andres W. Jahnke (Mainz: Schott, 1979), pp. 50–1. All eight pages are graced with the Beardsleyesque drawings by Behmer.
24 *Richard Strauss persönlich: Eine Bildbiographie* (Munich: Kindler, 1984), p. 119.
25 On the concept of the *Handexemplar*, see Charlotte E. Erwin, 'Richard Strauss's Presketch Planning for *Ariadne auf Naxos*', *Musical Quarterly*, Vol. 67, No. 3 (July 1981), p. 348.
26 Willi Schuh, 'Hugo von Hofmannsthal und Richard Strauss: Legende und Wirklichkeit', in *Umgang mit Musik* (Zurich: Atlantis, 1970), pp. 178ff.; Charlotte E. Erwin, 'Richard Strauss's Presketch Planning', pp. 348–65; Bryan Gilliam, 'Strauss's Preliminary Opera Sketches: Thematic Fragments and Symphonic Continuity', *Nineteenth-Century Music*, Vol. 9, No. 3 (Spring 1986), pp. 176–88.
27 See Erwin, 'Richard Strauss's Presketch Planning', pp. 349–52.
28 *Ibid.*, pp. 351–2; 364.
29 The page reproduced as Plate 3 (see p. 46) shows 'Cis moll' scrawled alongside Narraboth's first line (with the character gazing sullenly out of Behmer's picture on the opposite page).
30 Cf. Erwin: '[Strauss] consistently fails to note down the initial tonic in a libretto: evidently he finds this a needless exercise, the tonic being secure in his mind'. 'Richard Strauss's Presketch Planning', p. 353. Schuh makes the same point about *Der Rosenkavalier*: 'Hugo von Hofmannsthal und Richard Strauss: Legende und Wirklichkeit', p. 17.
31 On the page reproduced as Plate 3 we can see that 'D moll' applies not simply to the word 'Religion' but to the whole passage beginning with the stage direction 'Lärm im Bankettsaal' ('noise in the banqueting-hall'). The 'noise' immediately provokes the question: 'Who are those wild beasts howling?' and the answer: 'The Jews.' See also below, p. 93.
32 See Robert Bailey, 'The Structure of the *Ring* and Its Evolution', *Nineteenth-Century Music*, Vol. 1 (1977), pp. 51–3. The term has been refined by Bailey and his followers in subsequent writings. There is evidence in Strauss's sketches, though not, unfortunately, in those for *Salome*, that the later composer thought this way. A note in Sketchbook 17, probably referring to *Elektra*, says: 'Purity C major $\frac{4}{4}$[;] heroic theme E flat major $\frac{4}{4}$ $(\frac{3}{2})$', while a note in Sketchbook 10 plots the tonal scheme of the fugue in the *Symphonia Domestica* (F major versus B minor, resolving in D major – as we know from other sources, these keys are

associated with the father, the mother and the child respectively, so that the argument about which of his parents the child will resemble is settled by splitting the interval between them): Franz Trenner, *Die Skizzenbücher von Richard Strauss aus dem Richard-Strauss-Archiv in Garmisch* (Tutzing: Schneider, 1977), pp. 29, 21 (my translation). See also the note on *Also sprach Zarathustra* quoted in Erwin, 'Richard Strauss's Presketch Planning for *Ariadne auf Naxos*', p. 352.

33 See also Jaacks/Jahnke, *Richard Strauss (1864–1949)*, p. 50; Wilhelm, *Richard Strauss persönlich*, p. 119.

34 *Richard Strauss: A Critical Study of the Operas* (London: Cassell, 1964), p. 48.

35 On the Veil of the Sanctuary, the Ark of the Covenant and other matters see *The Annotated Oscar Wilde*, ed. with an introduction and annotations by H. Montgomery Hyde (London: Orbis, 1982), p. 317.

36 The same seems to be true, incidentally, of *Wozzeck*; Berg worked from his copy of the play. See George Perle, *The Operas of Alban Berg: Vol. 1, 'Wozzeck'* (Berkeley: University of California Press, 1980), p. 29.

37 For a discussion of this term, see Carl Dahlhaus, *Richard Wagner's Music Dramas*, trans. Mary Whittall (Cambridge: Cambridge University Press, 1979), pp. 13–14.

38 '*Salome*', notes to EMI recording, EMI SLS 5139 (1978), n.p.

39 This idea will be developed in Chapter 5 below.

40 'Reminiscences of the First Performance of My Operas', in *Recollections and Reflections*, ed. Willi Schuh, trans. L. J. Lawrence (London: Boosey and Hawkes, 1953), p. 150.

4 Synopsis

1 The sections of this chapter correspond to the scenes in the opera. Quotations are given in English only. More detailed synopses can be found in Ernest Newman, *More Opera Nights* (London: Putnam, 1954), pp. 14–37; William Mann, *Richard Strauss: A Critical Study of the Operas* (London: Cassell, 1964), pp. 45–59; Norman Del Mar, *Richard Strauss: A Critical Commentary on His Life and Works*, 3 vols. (London: Barrie and Jenkins, 1978), Vol. 1, pp. 246–80.

2 Strauss later said that, before composing *Salome*, he 'had long been criticising the fact that operas based on oriental and Jewish subjects lacked true oriental colour and scorching sun'. *Recollections and Reflections*, ed. Willi Schuh, trans. L. J. Lawrence (London: Boosey and Hawkes, 1953), p. 150. For Adorno's comments on the opening see below, p. 184, n. 48.

3 As Richard Ellmann notes in his chapter, Wilde combines in his character features of three Herods: Herod the Great, Herod Antipas (his son) and Herod Agrippa. Herod Antipas was Tetrarch of Judaea from 4 B.C. to A.D. 34. (It was his father who ordered the massacre of the new-born children.) 'A Tetrarch was governor of a quarter of a province. Herod the Great was Tetrarch before he became king, and on

his death his kingdom was divided between his sons, Herod Antipas, Tetrarch of Galilee, and Philip, Tetrarch of Idumea (Edom) and Trachonitis in Syria.' *The Annotated Oscar Wilde*, ed. with an introduction and annotations by H. Montgomery Hyde (London: Orbis, 1982), p. 306.

4 Romain Rolland was apprehensive: 'This remark is rather naive, and I'm afraid it might raise a laugh. It might have been omitted altogether, all the more because the same phrase . . . is repeated several times in the course of the piece and almost becomes a refrain, not likely to be taken very seriously.' Letter to Strauss of 5 November 1905, in *Richard Strauss and Romain Rolland: Correspondence, Diary and Essays*, ed. and annotated with a preface by Rollo Myers (London: Calder and Boyars, 1968), p. 69.

5 For more on this subject, see *The Annotated Oscar Wilde*, p. 310.

6 Wilde inscribed the complimentary copy of *Salomé* that he gave Beardsley: 'To the only artist who, besides myself, knows what the dance of the seven veils is, and can see that invisible dance.' *Ibid.*, p. 320.

7 See Appendix A.

8 Rolland balked at this. 'Once again! – for the 4th or 5th time. And this time the expression is altogether comic. It is obvious that "some evil will befall someone" since Jokanaan is about to have his head cut off. I am aware that Herod is not thinking about Jokanaan, but the audience is; and the remark sounds like a joke in very bad taste.' Letter to Strauss of 5 November 1905, in *Richard Strauss and Romain Rolland*, p. 73 (wording slightly changed). One can see his point, but he was forgetting the power of Strauss's music. The remark does not sound at all ridiculous in the opera.

9 Translations of Strauss's instruction to the player usually bowdlerise it. The sound is clearly meant to evoke the gasping of a woman in the act of love.

10 The text for this is given below, pp. 114–15.

5 *Salome* as music drama

1 Quoted in William Mann, *Richard Strauss: A Critical Study of the Operas* (London: Cassell, 1964), p. 43.

2 It is in fact the only one of Strauss's operas to style itself 'music drama'. *Elektra* is a 'tragedy', *Guntram* simply 'in three acts'; all the later stage works avoid the term.

3 See below, pp. 134–5.

4 Andrew Porter, 'Music drama', *The New Grove Dictionary of Music and Musicians*, ed. Stanley Sadie, 20 vols. (London: Macmillan, 1980), Vol. 12, p. 830.

5 *Gesammelte Schriften und Dichtungen*, Vol. 3 (Hildesheim: Olms, 1976), p. 231. This well-known formulation is capitalised in Wagner.

6 Any attempt to sum up Wagner's theory and practice in a paragraph

must fail. Good, up-to-date accounts are found in Carl Dahlhaus, *Richard Wagner's Music Dramas*, trans. Mary Whittall (Cambridge: Cambridge University Press, 1979), especially the chapter on the *Ring*; John Deathridge and Carl Dahlhaus, *The New Grove Wagner* (London: Macmillan, 1984), especially the chapters entitled 'Theoretical Writings' and 'Aesthetics'; Arnold Whittall, 'Wagner's Later Stage Works', in *The New Oxford History of Music*, Vol. 9: *Romanticism*, ed. Gerald Abraham (London: Oxford University Press, 1989). I am grateful to Arnold Whittall for letting me see his article in typescript.

7 Strauss became a 'complete Wagnerian', as he put it, in 1879. As a youth he held Wagner in low esteem, but he was soon converted. Strauss first read *Oper und Drama* in 1892. After that he seems never to have lost his love for Wagner, a fact attested by innumerable fine performances. See Willi Schuh, *Richard Strauss: A Chronicle of the Early Years (1864–1898)*, trans. Mary Whittall (Cambridge: Cambridge University Press, 1982), pp. 30, 53, 116–19, 306, 389. Strauss frequently refers to Wagner in his writings; particularly attractive is his description of the *Liebestod*, 'with its unequalled magic of sound (the last bar is considered to be the most beautifully scored last chord in the history of music) . . .' *Recollections and Reflections*, ed. Willi Schuh, trans. L. J. Lawrence (London: Boosey and Hawkes, 1953), p. 86.

8 'Remarks on Richard Wagner's Work and on the Bayreuth Festival Theatre' (1940), *Recollections and Reflections*, p. 69.

9 'On the Production of *Tannhäuser* in Bayreuth' (1892), *ibid.*, p. 58.

10 See n. 7 above.

11 *Treatise on Instrumentation by Hector Berlioz*, revised and enlarged by Richard Strauss, trans. Theodore Front (New York: Kalmus, 1948), pp. i–iii. Strauss's 'revision' consists largely of adding examples from Wagner's works.

12 *The Correspondence between Richard Strauss and Hugo von Hofmannsthal*, trans. Hanns Hammelmann and Ewald Osers (Cambridge: Cambridge University Press, 1980), p. 30. Quoted in Bryan Gilliam, 'Strauss's Preliminary Opera Sketches: Thematic Fragments and Symphonic Continuity', *Nineteenth-Century Music*, Vol. 9, No. 3 (Spring 1986), p. 187. I am indebted to Gilliam's article for bringing this and the following quotation to my attention.

13 The full quotation is even more interesting: 'It is the symphony in the medium of drama, and is psychological, like all music.' Ernst Krause, *Richard Strauss: The Man and His Work* (London: Collet, 1964), p. 299.

14 I have argued against this interpretation elsewhere. See 'An Introduction to *Der Rosenkavalier*', in *Der Rosenkavalier*, ed. Nicholas John (London: John Calder, 1981), pp. 9–11. For Strauss's own comment on this view, see below, p. 140.

15 'The Musical Influence [of Wagner]', trans. Alfred Clayton, in *The Wagner Handbook*, ed. John Deathridge (Cambridge, Mass.: Harvard, in preparation).

16 This is just one of the three technical aspects mentioned earlier as con-

tributing to the 'new kind of continuity' achieved by Wagner. Each of
the others deserves a chapter to itself, but some brief remarks may be
in order. The mixture of closed and open forms cultivated by Wagner,
whereby compact, self-contained tonal structures (Loge's Narration in
Das Rheingold, Siegmund's 'Spring Song' in *Die Walküre*) alternate or
overlap with open-ended, 'atonal' passages, is found again in *Salome*,
where the three verses of Salome's entreaty to Jochanaan (from Fig.
91/3 to 122/9), or of Herod's to Salome (from Fig. 172/4 to 183/5), each
ending with a firm cadence, are set off against the open-ended, non-
cadential nature of the other character's response. These responses are
good examples of 'musical prose'. But the best examples of the latter
are surely the long passage beginning with Herod's entrance (from Fig.
155 to Fig. 172), with its astonishing succession of concise musical
images, the passage where Herodias takes the ring from his finger (from
Fig. 300 to 304/3) and Herod's final horrified murmurings to his wife
(from one before Fig. 351 to 354/6). Dahlhaus relates the concept of
musical prose to Strauss's self-confessed melodic shortwindedness: see
'Issues in Composition', in *Between Romanticism and Modernism*,
trans. Mary Whittall (Berkeley: University of California Press, 1980),
pp. 40ff.

17 Dahlhaus points out that the term is not Wagner's; it was applied to his
works in 1876 by Hans von Wolzogen (half-brother of Ernst, the
librettist of *Feuersnot*), who may have found it in Jähns's 1871 catalogue
of Weber's works.

18 *The New Grove Wagner*, pp. 111–13.

19 Not the happiest choice of word in the circumstances. *Richard Strauss:
A Critical Commentary on His Life and Works*, 3 vols. (London: Barrie
and Jenkins, 1978), Vol. 1, p. 260.

20 *Richard Strauss*, pp. 48–9.

21 *Ibid.*, p. 47n.

22 Robert Craft makes a valid point in this connection. Mann writes of the
passage beginning at Fig. 91/3: 'The music sinks into a timeless B major
while Salome cries the Prophet's name, and first horn with oboes and
clarinets drag out Ex. 1 [Salome's first motive] as from a sluggish chest
of drawers' (*ibid.*, p. 54). 'What actually happens at this place', Craft
comments, 'is simply that Salome's first motif is heard in a rhythmic
form whose momentary effect is to dissolve or suspend the metronomic
beat. Also, the reader who has followed Mr Mann's elucidations of
motivic usages up to this point may justifiably ask why Salome's, rather
than Jochanaan's, motif is played, since his name, not hers, is being
called.' 'A "Beautiful Coloured, Musical Thing"', in *Current Convictions: Views and Reviews* (London: Secker and Warburg, 1978), p. 132.

23 'The Music', in Lucy Beckett, *Parsifal* (Cambridge: Cambridge University Press, 1981), pp. 61–3.

24 'Elektra's Voice: Music and Language in Strauss's Opera', in *Richard
Strauss: 'Elektra'*, ed. Derrick Puffett (Cambridge: Cambridge University Press, 1989).

25 *Strauss' Salome: A Guide to the Opera* (London: John Lane, 1907).

26 *Richard Strauss: A Chronicle*, p. 421.

27 *Richard Strauss 'Salome': Ein Wegweiser durch die Oper* (Berlin: Bard, Marquardt & Co., 1906).
28 As it was, of course, during Wagner's lifetime. Wagner himself did not use the term 'leitmotive', preferring *Grundthema*. Towards the end of his life he regretted 'that the thematic idea, by now called the leitmotiv, seemed to have absorbed all the attention of his commentators'. See Anthony Newcomb, 'The Birth of Music out of the Spirit of Drama', *Nineteenth-Century Music*, Vol. 5 (1981), p. 38.
29 See Franz Trenner, *Die Skizzenbücher von Richard Strauss aus dem Richard-Strauss-Archiv in Garmisch* (Tutzing: Schneider, 1977), pp. 22–4, and in particular the facsimiles of sketches provided on pp. 157–60.
30 Strauss's 'simplistic' conception of the leitmotive is an example of what Hans Keller used to call 'creative misunderstanding'. It was shared by many other composers of the time, notably Elgar, who allowed his friend Jaeger to give the leitmotives in his oratorios *The Apostles* and *The Kingdom* very precise designations.
31 Kurt Overhoff's book on *Elektra*, for example, simply lists the motives with labels. *Die Elektra-Partitur von Richard Strauss: Ein Lehrbuch für die Technik der dramatischen Komposition* (Salzburg: Pustet, 1978).
32 On these three levels, see Jean-Jacques Nattiez, *Fondements d'une sémiologie de la musique* (Paris: 10/18, 1975).
33 By extension it is also associated with death, horror and the supernatural.
34 Because of the metrical structure (a tamtam stroke would be ineffective on a weak beat) the tamtam has to sound on 'kommt', not 'er'.
35 Of course they have a dramatic function as well (the second figure, for example, tends to bring the music back to C major and whatever associations are implied by that), but this seems secondary in the present context.
36 Their final appearance is at the very end of the opera. The upward-rushing semiquavers one bar before Fig. 362 recall the moment when Hagen murders Siegfried in *Götterdämmerung*.
37 These are also the motives with the most clear-cut tonal associations: see below, pp. 93–5.
38 This is discussed in more detail below, as are the implications of the phrase 'definitive statement'.
39 Indeed they are Strauss's most important means of characterisation.
40 See Gilman, *Strauss' Salome*, pp. 70–4; Roese, *Richard Strauss 'Salome'*, p. 23.
41 According to the orchestral score; Fig. 11 comes one bar later in the vocal.
42 From *Models for Beginners in Composition* (New York: Schirmer, 1943), p. 15.
43 The 'Dance' is numbered separately from the rest of the opera. See Appendix A below.
44 Similarly, the '•' in the intervals column for the statement beginning at Fig. 19/4 is less significant than it might appear, since only the first pitch is changed.

45 A major, of course, is one of Salome's 'keys'. See below, pp. 95ff.

46 Strauss himself said, in a letter to Stefan Zweig, that he had originally wanted to portray Jochanaan as a 'clown': 'A preacher in the desert . . . seems infinitely comical to me. Only because I had already caricatured the five Jews and also poked fun at Father Herodes did I feel that I had to follow the law of contrast and write a pedantic-Philistine motif for four horns to characterize Jochanaan.' *A Confidential Matter: The Letters of Richard Strauss and Stefan Zweig 1931–1935*, trans. Max Knight (Berkeley: University of California Press, 1977), p. 90. See also below, pp. 147–8.

47 See 'On Inspiration in Music' (*c*. 1940), in *Recollections and Reflections*, p. 115.

48 For Adorno this fact was bound up with the construction of the motive itself. Commenting on Strauss's beginnings ('his most brilliant operas have no overtures but begin with the rising curtain'), he adds: 'Certain conductors and directors of *Salome* betray both crass lack of style and little understanding of the Straussian spirit when they timidly allow the scene to become visible without music and only afterwards have the clarinets play their passage, which refers not only to the serpentine gliding of the princess but also to that of the curtain, with which it must be synchronized and yet still clearly audible.' 'Richard Strauss', *Perspectives of New Music*, Vol. 4, No. 2 (Spring–Summer 1966), p. 115 and n.

A sketch of the opening reproduced by Trenner (*Skizzenbücher*, p. 157) has the character of a voice-leading exercise, with the 'ninth chord' on D returning to the C sharp major triad on the word 'heute' (see Plate 4). What is conspicuously absent from this sketch is the chromatically ascending violin line, which 'ties together harmonies which at the time were felt to be disparate' (cf. Schoenberg in 1905: 'Perhaps in twenty years' time someone will be able to explain these harmonic progressions theoretically': quoted in Willi Reich, *Schoenberg: A Critical Biography*, trans. Leo Black (London: Longman, 1971), p. 25) and, incidentally, 'illustrates the course of the moon' (Adorno, 'Richard Strauss', pp. 113–14). Perhaps surprisingly, the moon has no leitmotive in *Salome*. But its chromatically ascending line returns at key points, notably at the moment of Narraboth's death (the six bars around Fig. 126) and at Herod's horrified 'Es wird Schreckliches geschehen' (Fig. 354/4–6).

49 Enharmonic reinterpretation of this kind is discussed in Norman M. Dinerstein, 'Polychordality in *Salome* and *Elektra*: A Study of the Application of Re-Interpretation Technique' (Unpublished Ph.D. Diss., Princeton University, 1974). 'Reinterpretation Technique' (*Umdeutungstechnik*) was Strauss's own term, as transmitted to Dinerstein by Arnold Franchetti, a pupil of Strauss in the 1930s. According to Franchetti, 'Strauss himself often lectured on *Salome* and *Elektra* and explained his basic method of operation in relation to those polychordal moments which employ an enharmonic pivot as Reinterpretation Technique' (p. 29).

50 See above, pp. 47–8.

51 Cf. the closing orchestral postlude of *Die Frau ohne Schatten*. On Strauss and Brahms, see Del Mar, *Richard Strauss*, Vol. 1, pp. 23–4.

52 See Chapter 6, Ex. 10c.

53 See below, pp. 94–9, 113–19.

54 Newcomb on Wagner: see 'The Birth of Music out of the Spirit of Drama', p. 38.

55 'Richard Strauss: The Man', in Ernest Newman, *Richard Strauss* (London: John Lane, 1908), p. x.

56 See Peter Heyworth, *Otto Klemperer: His Life and Times*, Vol. 1, p. 273. Heyworth comments: 'Strauss's remark underlines how deeply his imagination remained rooted in the Lisztian world of the symphonic poem.' On Strauss and the 'poetic idea' see also John Williamson, 'Strauss and *Macbeth*: The Realisation of the Poetic Idea', *Soundings*, No. 13 (Summer 1985).

57 Gary Schmidgall quotes a remarkable series of passages – mostly solo instrumental lines – out of context: divorced of their explanatory text, they remind us how original Strauss's musical language really is. *Literature as Opera* (New York: Oxford University Press, 1977), pp. 275–80.

58 Letter of 5 July 1905, quoted in *Richard Strauss and Romain Rolland: Correspondence, Diary and Essays*, ed. and annotated with a preface by Rollo Myers (London: Calder and Boyars, 1968), p. 29.

59 Arthur Schopenhauer, *The World as Will and Representation*, trans. E. F. J. Payne (New York: Dover, 1958), Vol. 2, p. 450.

60 'The Relationship to the Text' (1912), in *Style and Idea*, ed. Leonard Stein (London: Faber and Faber, 1975). See also Dahlhaus's essay 'Schoenberg and Programme Music', in *Schoenberg and the New Music*, trans. Derrick Puffett and Alfred Clayton (Cambridge: Cambridge University Press, 1987).

61 See Dahlhaus, *Realism in Nineteenth-Century Music*, trans. Mary Whittall (Cambridge: Cambridge University Press, 1985), pp. 37–8.

62 'Things which would have seemed impossible a hundred years ago are done with ease today . . . The representative power of music is growing day by day.' Essay on programme music written in 1905; quoted in Peter Conrad, *Romantic Opera and Literary Form* (Berkeley: University of California Press, 1977), p. 150. Elsewhere Newman cites Strauss himself as saying ('in conversation the other day'): 'Music must progress until it can depict even a teaspoon.' Review of *Feuersnot*, *The Nation* (1910), reprinted in Newman, *Testament of Music* (London: Putnam, 1962), p. 270. And in a 1915 review of the *Alpine Symphony* Newman uses the word 'realism' as synonymous with 'musical illustration', citing 'the cracking of whips in *Elektra* . . . the criss-cross of duelling swords in *Don Giovanni* . . . the tinkling of the thirty pieces of silver in *The Apostles* . . . the hee-haw of the donkey in the *Midsummer Night's Dream* overture'. 'Strauss's New Symphony', *New Witness*, reprinted in *Testament of Music*, p. 182.

63 Letter of 1 June 1925, in *The Correspondence between Richard Strauss and Hugo von Hofmannsthal*, p. 404.

64 On which subject, see Percy Grainger's curious remarks, in which he defends these passages as 'pure music': 'Richard Strauss: Seer and

Idealist', in Henry T. Finck, *Richard Strauss: The Man and the Works* (Boston: Little, Brown and Co., 1917), pp. xxi–xxii. But altogether this is a curious piece of work: ' . . . were Salome's swan song put before us as religious music, I feel sure it would not seem to us incongruous in that character, so noble, so cosmically devout is its whole tenor' (*ibid.*, p. xix). He also praises Strauss as 'a *human being* of the great order' (*ibid.*, p. xvii; his emphasis).

65 See above, pp. 11–20.
66 Richard Ellmann, *Oscar Wilde* (London: Hamish Hamilton, 1987), p. 46.
67 Edward T. Cone has remarked of Strauss's tone poems and operas: 'Are we not moving here toward a musical form of complete stream-of-consciousness, in which *no exact recapitulation is possible because no two moments of our lives are ever alike?*' *Musical Form and Musical Performance* (New York: Norton, 1968), p. 86 (my emphasis).
68 From 'The Musical Influence', p. 24. Dahlhaus's dates are inconsistent (sometimes he gives date of composition, sometimes date of first performance).
69 *The New Grove Wagner*, p. 107.
70 On the uneven quality of Strauss's musical ideas, see below, pp. 146–9.
71 Kenneth W. Birkin, 'The Last Meeting: *Die Liebe der Danae* Reconsidered', *Tempo*, No. 153 (June 1985), p. 15.

6 Tonal and dramatic structure

1 Letter of 5 July 1905 to Romain Rolland, in *Richard Strauss and Romain Rolland: Correspondence, Diary and Essays*, ed. and annotated with a preface by Rollo Myers (London: Calder and Boyars, 1968), p. 29. See above, p. 83.
2 Strauss, 'Reminiscences of the First Performance of My Operas', in *Recollections and Reflections*, ed. Willi Schuh, trans. L. J. Lawrence (London: Boosey and Hawkes, 1953), p. 150.
3 See above, pp. 51ff.
4 See below, p. 93.
5 *De Profundis* (letter to Lord Alfred Douglas of January–March 1897), in *The Letters of Oscar Wilde*, ed. Rupert Hart-Davis (London: Hart-Davis, 1962), p. 475.
6 See, for instance, Ernest Newman, *More Opera Nights* (London: Putnam, 1954), pp. 7ff.; Norman Del Mar, *Richard Strauss: A Critical Commentary on His Life and Works*, 3 vols. (London: Barrie and Jenkins, 1978), Vol. 1, pp. 241ff.
7 See above, pp. 69–72.
8 See Chapter 5, Ex. 4.
9 See Chapter 5, Ex. 6.
10 Cf. Chapter 7, Ex. 2b.
11 For a different interpretation of this passage, see below, pp. 123–6. See also Willi Schuh, 'Zur harmonischen Deutung des *Salome*-Schlusses', *Schweizerische Musikzeitung*, Vol. 86, No. 12 (1946), pp. 452–8. [Ed.]

7 Salome's final monologue

1 Michael Kennedy, *Richard Strauss* (London: Dent, 1976), pp. 143–4. See also Ernest Newman's description of the final moments of the opera in *More Opera Nights* (London: Putnam, 1954), p. 36: 'In a final ecstasy of perversion [Salome's] mind cracks'. Thus Salome is seen as not merely perverse (or neurotic) but psychotic (or mad).

2 For a discussion of Wilde's *Salomé* and Strauss's connections with the Symbolist and Decadent movements of the *fin de siècle*, see Gary Schmidgall, *Literature as Opera* (New York: Oxford University Press, 1977), pp. 249–86.

3 In this chapter quotations from the libretto are given in English only.

4 Newman, *More Opera Nights*, p. 35, n. 1. See above, pp. 4–5.

5 Kennedy, *Richard Strauss*, p. 144.

6 As Newman, Schmidgall and Norman Del Mar (*Richard Strauss: A Critical Commentary on His Life and Works*, 3 vols. (London: Barrie and Jenkins, 1978), Vol. 1) acknowledge, Strauss's treatment of Salome as a character is simplified in his adaptation of Wilde's play. But the apparently incidental events that Strauss retains are sufficient to establish the complex and irrational milieu in which she attempts to maintain her personality. A comparison of the libretto of the monologue and Wilde's original text also reveals the ethical, political and moral impetus for her actions to be obscured by Strauss's cuts and reworkings, which are almost always designed to emphasise the obsessive aspect of her personality. See also above, p. 89.

7 See above, pp. 97ff.

8 See above, pp. 65ff.

9 Although C sharp major is the predominant tonality of *Salome*, it would be difficult to sustain an interpretation of the opera as being controlled by that tonality. C sharp has a referential function in the tonal scheme, but this scheme is determined by the Symbolist associations of key and/ or chord, and by textual circumstance.

10 Norman M. Dinerstein, in 'Polychordality in *Salome* and *Elektra*: A Study of the Application of Re-Interpretation Technique' (Unpublished Ph.D. Diss., Princeton University, 1974), discusses the use of polytonal chords in the operas, but prefers the term 'polychordality', 'for the combinations are not of fully-developed tonalities but of chordal elements that are at most suggestive of components of different tonalities' (p. 5). This description fits exactly the harmonic techniques of the monologue, but in order to avoid confusion I have retained the more familiar, though less precise, terms 'polytonal' and 'bitonal' when referring to chords and chord relations.

Strauss himself used the more familiar terms in his discussion of the harmonic style of *Salome* and *Elektra* in *Recollections and Reflections*, ed. Willi Schuh, trans. L. J. Lawrence (London: Boosey and Hawkes, 1953). Regarding *Salome*, he explains that 'the wish to characterise the *dramatis personae* [of the opera] as clearly as possible led me to bitonality' (p. 150), while '*Elektra* became even more intense [than *Salome*] in the unity of structure and in the force of its climaxes . . . Both operas are unique in my life's works; in them I penetrated to the utter-most limits of harmony' (p. 155).

11 This is Newman's description of the motive (see *More Opera Nights*, p. 35, n. 1). J. Maillard, in '*Salome*' (*L'Education musicale*, No. 207 (April 1974)), p. 12/260, regards it as being derived from an earlier motive denoting desire in Scene 4 (first four bars of Fig. 177), where it accompanies part of Herod's attempted seduction of Salome: 'I love to see in a fruit the mark of thy little teeth'. Newman finds the relationship between what he calls the 'teeth' motive and the 'viper's tongue' motive incomprehensible, but this points to a limitation of his critical aware-ness. The union of the erotic in the 'teeth' episode and death in the image of the 'viper's tongue' (which also 'bites') is an essential theme of the opera and places it within the tradition of Decadent art. Strauss's method of creating this correspondence through motivic transform-ation is conventionally Symbolist and reveals an understanding of the dramatic possibilities of Symbolist techniques. Newman's conclusion that 'we shall often go far astray if we regard the themes of the opera as "motifs", each with a definite and fixed connotation, in the Wagnerian sense of the term' (*ibid.*), is correct as far as it goes; but it must be added that the lack of fixed connotations for the motives (or themes) is precisely Strauss's means of creating correspondences that transfer the verbal symbolic nuances of Wilde's play to the musical structure of the opera.

All other descriptions of the 'meaning' of the leitmotives are taken from Maillard's '*Salome*', *L'Education musicale*, Nos. 202–7 (November 1973–April 1974).

12 Schmidgall, *Literature as Opera*, p. 283.

13 Newman, *More Opera Nights*, p. 37.

14 Del Mar, *Richard Strauss*, Vol. 1, p. 279.

15 Kennedy, *Richard Strauss*, p. 144.

16 Schmidgall, *Literature as Opera*, p. 283.

17 Del Mar, *Richard Strauss*, Vol. 1, p. 279, Schmidgall, *Literature as Opera*, p. 285, and the Kalmus edition of the vocal score, p. 203, to cite only three examples, omit the B sharp in the chord (see full score, flute 2 and B flat clarinet 2). The inclusion of this pitch (the leading note to the tonic C sharp) produces a symmetrical structure for the chord: read-ing from the bass, A–C sharp–E–G is symmetrical with the intervals of the upper notes of the chord read from the top notes down, A sharp–F sharp–D sharp–B sharp. This feature points to the systematic con-struction of dissonant sonorities that is characteristic of atonal music. Strauss alludes to this in his comment on the harmonic language of *Salome* and *Elektra*: 'Both operas are unique in my life's works; in them I penetrated to the uttermost limits of harmony' (see n. 10). Neverthe-less, the chord is given here without the B sharp since it is practically inaudible in performance. The analyst is tempted to conclude that, symmetrical structures aside, the B sharp is present to intensify the dissonance rather than to satisfy the demands of voice leading or inter-val structure. [For two different interpretations of the chord, see above, p. 104, and Willi Schuh, 'Zur harmonischen Deutung des *Salome-*

Schlusses', *Schweizerische Musikzeitung*, Vol. 86, No. 12 (1946), pp. 452–8. Ed.]

18 Newman, *More Opera Nights*, p. 37. Newman goes on to describe the end of the opera as a descent into an empire of misrule: 'The broken Salome has now passed into a strangely mystical sphere in which our everyday concepts of sanity and insanity, the normal and the perverse, cease to have any real meaning' (p. 37). This interpretation, while sympathetic to the dramatic intensity of the passage, is circumscribed by an early twentieth-century morality and a failure to recognise the logic of Strauss's symbolism of key and theme.

19 This reflects Anna Amalie Abert's description of the symmetrical structure of the opera: 'An exposition in which the musical material is presented is followed by two corresponding climaxes separated by an extended central section, through which runs the tension operating between them, submerged yet ever noticeable. The structure of this central section, however, is the same as that of the opera itself, since it also consists of an introduction and two scenes with Salome; the difference being that she is not the wooer, but is herself wooed; and the contrast is provided by the Jews' Quintet' (*'Salome'*, notes to EMI recording, EMI SLS 5139 (1978), n.p.).

20 Quoted in Kennedy, 'Richard Strauss', *The New Grove Dictionary of Music and Musicians*, ed. Stanley Sadie, 20 vols. (London, Macmillan, 1980), Vol. 18, p. 234.

8 Critical reception

1 See *Vom Musikdrama zur Literaturoper* (Munich and Salzburg: Musikverlag Emil Katzbichler, 1983), p. 249.

2 Quoted in Edward Timms, *Karl Kraus: Apocalyptic Satirist* (New Haven and London: Yale University Press, 1986), p. 188.

3 Kraus wrote about *Salomé* in 1903, two years before Hofmannsthal wrote his 'Sebastian Melmoth' (see Hugo von Hofmannsthal, *Selected Prose*, trans. Mary Hottinger and Tania and James Stern (New York: Pantheon Books, 1952), pp. 301–5).

4 *Richard Strauss and Romain Rolland: Correspondence, Diary and Essays*, ed. and annotated with a preface by Rollo Myers (London: Calder and Boyars, 1968), pp. 82–3.

5 Christopher S. Nassar, *Into the Demon Universe: A Literary Exploration of Oscar Wilde* (New Haven and London: Yale University Press, 1974), pp. 80–1, 92.

6 See Chapter 2 above.

7 *Berliner Tageblatt und Handels-Zeitung*, 11 December 1905 (my translation).

8 *Salome* (Wiesbaden: Emil Behrend Verlag, 1907), p. 3 (my translation).

9 *Ibid.*, p. 8 (my translation).

10 Quoted in Michael Balfour, *The Kaiser and His Times* (London: Cresset Press, 1964), p. 162.

11 *Neue freie Presse*, 11 December 1905 (my translation).
12 Letter to Strauss, quoted in *Der Strom der Töne trug mich fort: Die Welt um Richard Strauss in Briefen*, ed. Franz Grasberger (Tutzing: Schneider, 1967), p. 174 (my translation).
13 *Ibid.*, p. 170 (my translation).
14 Paul Marsop, 'Italien und der "Fall Salome", nebst Glossen zur Kritik und Ästhetik', *Die Musik*, Vol. 6 (1906–7), p. 147 (my translation).
15 *Deutsches Opernschaffen der Gegenwart* (Leipzig and Vienna: Leonhardt-Verlag, 1921), p. 138 (my translation).
16 *Illustrirte Zeitung*, 21 December 1905 (my translation).
17 Quoted in Franz Trenner, *Richard Strauss: Dokumente seines Lebens und Schaffens* (Munich: C. H. Beck, 1954), p. 116 (my translation).
18 *Dresdner Nachrichten*, 10 December 1905 (my translation).
19 *Ibid.* (my translation).
20 See Alan Jefferson, *The Operas of Richard Strauss in Britain 1910–1963* (London: Putnam, 1963), p. 48.
21 See Sir Thomas Beecham, *A Mingled Chime* (London: Hutchinson, 1944), p. 103.
22 Rudolf Louis, 'Die erlöste Salome', *Süddeutsche Monatshefte*, Vol. 4 (1907), p. 246; Joseph Kerman, *Opera as Drama* (New York: Vintage Books, 1956), p. 260.
23 *Betrachtungen und Erinnerungen* (Berlin: Allgemeiner Verein für Deutsche Literatur, 1909), p. 193 (my translation).
24 Quoted in Trenner, *Richard Strauss*, pp. 115–16 (my translation).
25 Friedrich von Schuch, *Richard Strauss, Ernst von Schuch und Dresdens Oper*, 2nd edn (Leipzig: Verlag der Kunst, 1953), p. 76 (my translation).
26 *Cosima Wagner–Richard Strauss: Ein Briefwechsel*, ed. Franz Trenner (Tutzing: Schneider, 1978), p. 280 (my translation).
27 *Deutsches Opernschaffen der Gegenwart*, pp. 136–46 (my translation).
28 *Strauss' Salome: A Guide to the Opera* (London and New York: John Lane, 1907), pp. 56–7.
29 *Berliner Tageblatt und Handels-Zeitung*, 11 December 1905.
30 Review in *Le Figaro*, 9 May 1907; reprinted in *Opinions musicales* (Paris: Editions Rieder, 1930), p. 140 (my translation).
31 See Hellmut Federhofer, *Heinrich Schenker: Nach Tagebüchern und Briefen in der Oswald Jonas Memorial Collection* (Hildesheim: Olms, 1985), p. 259 (my translation).
32 *Essays on the Philosophy of Music*, trans. Peter Palmer (Cambridge: Cambridge University Press, 1985), p. 38.
33 *Richard Strauss und sein Werk*, 2 vols. (Leipzig, Vienna and Zurich: E. P. Tal & Co., 1921), Vol. 2, p. 134 (my translation).
34 Arnold Schoenberg, *Theory of Harmony*, trans. Roy E. Carter (London: Faber, 1978), p. 402.
35 *Illustrirte Zeitung*, 21 December 1905 (my translation).
36 Fauré, *Opinions musicales*, p. 140 (my translation).
37 *Strauss' Salome*, p. 55.
38 *Structural Functions of Harmony*, ed. Leonard Stein (London: Faber, 1983), p. 77.

39 *Romantische Harmonik und ihre Krise in Wagners 'Tristan'*, 3rd edn (Berlin: Max Hesses Verlag, 1923), pp. 191–2, 302–4, 355, 362, 365–6, 386–7.
40 Federhofer, *Heinrich Schenker*, p. 258 (my translation).
41 *Opera as Drama*, p. 260.
42 *Richard Strauss and Romain Rolland*, p. 150.
43 *Ibid.*, p. 149. Ravel was also 'very struck by the expressive use of the percussion in *Salome*: it is something quite new to him'. *Ibid.*, p. 150.
44 Quoted in Federhofer, *Heinrich Schenker*, p. 66 (my translation).
45 In *The Essence of Music and Other Papers*, trans. Rosamund Ley (New York: Dover, 1965), p. 174.
46 See Alma Mahler, *Gustav Mahler: Memories and Letters*, trans. Basil Creighton, ed. Donald Mitchell, 3rd edn (London: Faber, 1973), p. 89; also below, Appendix A.
47 *Ibid.*, p. 282 (this is Mahler's own comment).
48 *Ibid.*, p. 284.
49 *Ibid.*, p. 98 (this is Alma's recollection).
50 Quoted in Franz Grasberger, *Richard Strauss und die Wiener Oper* (Tutzing: Schneider, 1969), p. 182 (my translation).
51 Quoted in Erich H. Mueller von Asow, *Richard Strauss: Thematisches Verzeichnis*, 3 vols. (Vienna and Wiesbaden: Doblinger, 1959–74), Vol. 1, p. 380.
52 *Essays* (Leipzig: Insel Verlag, 1912), p. 83.
53 *Sämtliche Werke*, ed. Hans-Egon Hass and Martin Machatzke, 11 vols. (Darmstadt: Wissenschaftliche Buchgesellschaft, 1962–74), Vol. 11, pp. 1021–2 (my translation).
54 Specht, *Richard Strauss und sein Werk*, Vol. 2, p. 105 (my translation).
55 *Deutsches Opernschaffen der Gegenwart*, p. 146.
56 *Richard Strauss und sein Werk*, Vol. 2, p. 162 (my translations).
57 *Hugo von Hofmannsthal–Harry Graf Kessler- Briefwechsel 1898–1929*, ed. Hilde Burger (Frankfurt am Main: Insel Verlag, 1968), p. 215; *The Correspondence between Richard Strauss and Hugo von Hofmannsthal*, trans. Hanns Hammelmann and Ewald Osers (Cambridge: Cambridge University Press, 1980), p. 4.
58 *Hugo von Hofmannsthal–Eberhard von Bodenhausen: Briefe der Freundschaft* (Berlin: Eugen Diederichs Verlag, 1953), p. 98.
59 *The Correspondence between Richard Strauss and Hugo von Hofmannsthal*, pp. 402, 453.
60 Richard Strauss, *Recollections and Reflections*, ed. Willi Schuh, trans. L. J. Lawrence (London: Boosey & Hawkes, 1953), p. 152.
61 Federhofer, *Heinrich Schenker*, p. 259 (my translation).
62 *Diaries 1918–1939*, ed. Hermann Kesten, trans. Richard and Clara Winston (London: André Deutsch, 1983), p. 209; even in 1909, Mann was of the opinion that 'Strauss's so-called "progress" is all twaddle' – he never accepted that Strauss had in any sense gone beyond Wagner (Thomas Mann, *Pro and Contra Wagner*, trans. Allan Blunden (London: Faber, 1985), p. 45).
63 Quoted in Fred K. Prieberg, *Musik im NS-Staat* (Frankfurt am Main: Fischer Taschenbuch, 1982), p. 212. But see above, p. 172, n. 37.

64 Quoted in Mueller von Asow, *Richard Strauss: Thematisches Verzeichnis*, Vol. 1, p. 383 (my translation).

65 *Opera as Drama*, p. 259.

66 Peter Conrad, *Romantic Opera and Literary Form* (Berkeley: University of California Press, 1977), p. 147.

67 *Literature as Opera* (New York: Oxford University Press, 1977), p. 273.

68 Mary Garden and Louis Biancolli, *Mary Garden's Story* (London: Michael Joseph, 1952), p. 119.

69 *Richard Strauss: A Critical Study of the Operas* (London: Cassell, 1964).

70 *Richard Strauss: A Critical Commentary on His Life and Works*, 3 vols. (London: Barrie and Jenkins, 1978).

71 Beecham, *A Mingled Chime*, p. 105.

9 *Salome*: art or kitsch?

1 *Remembrance of Things Past*, trans. C. K. Scott Moncrieff and Terence Kilmartin (Harmondsworth: Penguin, 1981), Vol. 2, pp. 465–6.

2 *Le Figaro*, 9 May 1907, translated in *Composers on Music*, ed. Sam Morgenstern (London: Faber, 1958), pp. 283–4.

3 Quoted in Michael Kennedy, *Richard Strauss* (London: Dent, 1976), p. 45.

4 Stravinsky, in Igor Stravinsky and Robert Craft, *Conversations with Igor Stravinsky* (London: Faber, 1959), p. 75.

5 Four bars before Fig. 228 ('Will you indeed give me whatsoever I shall ask?') the first clarinet trills on A sharp; Salome's voice and harmony convert it into B flat; Herod takes it back to A sharp. At Fig. 229 ('You swear it, Tetrarch?') the same clarinet trills on the same B flat; his answer takes the music to E flat minor, converting it to major; she is inexorable ('By what will you swear?') and the B flat melts into A major. Trilling resumes at Fig. 230/3 as she bores on ('You have sworn, Tetrarch'), now on F sharp (= G flat in E flat minor) and transferred from the A to the B flat instrument. His ardent answer restores E flat major, but the F sharp trills on (both clarinets now) with a crescendo over the arrival at C minor with which he vouches half of his kingdom. All this is held in suspense through a gust of uncanny wind, a few routine words from Jochanaan and the entire 'Dance of the Seven Veils', to be resumed with chilling effect to dog Herod's ever-increasing regret for his rash generosity. Having concluded the 'Dance' itself (fifteen bars of freeze before the five of precipitate wildness that end it) the trills needle on – the very sound of her steely will – throughout her inexorable insistence on her rights. At Fig. 249/5 she teases him ('I would that they presently bring me in a silver charger . . . '), and two clarinets (E flat and A) trill an octave apart. The oboe continues their D dissonantly against Herod's infatuated interruption, but when at 254 he is back to the point ('*What*, in a silver charger?') so is she, and the trill slithers up till it makes a sharp dissonance (G and A flat) with her motive in B major, resolving into the major and minor third of E as, at last, she voices her *real* object.

Trilling resumes three bars before Fig. 256, now below the voice but soon returning high, in octaves (and always on the clarinets) as she keeps him to his word. Every wriggle of would-be escape ends with a cessation of tempo but a prolongation of the maddening oscillation. At two before 261 it is again high on a solo clarinet, then in octaves as she becomes more emphatic; at two before 271 it is low on a solo oboe, the voice (doubled by trumpet) a tritone lower still; but it then veers upwards and back to the clarinet. At 279 and 284 four clarinets trill in two octaves, dissonant with her voice. At 297/7 nine woodwinds trill up on high the open fifth of the D major with which Herod concludes his final desperate extravagance, the Veil of the Sanctuary. Salome sings against this fifth, in E flat, of the one thing only that she craves; and so follows the music from Fig. 298 that has already been discussed. Notice that two low clarinets and the bass clarinet trill uninterrupted (though the pair, at least, is mercifully staggered) for no less than thirty-three bars (!) before their G yields in a sudden spasm to the low E flat of the back desks of the basses, creating with the bass drum the chasm of low vibration from which the solitary high bass will sound so uncannily.

Trilling recommences at Fig. 354/6. Here the dissonance implicit in any semitonal trill is made explicit by the upper strings, tremolandi on both notes. The strings soon disappear, but the A/B flat tingle continues on flutes and clarinets against her motive in piercing E minor (oboe and piccolo) and the murky blur, miles beneath, of C sharp minor (plus F double sharp and A sharp). This evocation of the taste of her ambiguous *Liebesmahl* persists for some twenty-eight very slow bars. Even as (at Fig. 358) the harmony begins to clear and glow through F sharp major, then A major, the A/B flat continues; C sharp/D joins it; and the climax of the whole work (from Fig. 359 to Herod's cry, Fig. 361/5), including its most celebrated scrunch, is swathed in a halo of trills involving sixteen woodwinds, timps, suspended cymbal, tambourine, side drum and – again – both hands of the sonically hapless celeste, sanctifying the unclean act in a nimbus of quasi-mystical joy.

6 'At that time [Strauss's] music reminded me of Böcklin and Stuck, and the other painters of what we then called the German Green Horrors.' *Conversations with Igor Stravinsky*, p. 75.

7 'The chaste Joseph himself isn't at all up my street, and if a thing bores me I find it difficult to set it to music. This god-seeker Joseph – he's going to be a hell of an effort! Well, maybe there's a pious tune for good boy Joseph lying about in some atavistic recess of my appendix.' Strauss to Hofmannsthal, 11 September 1912 (*The Correspondence between Richard Strauss and Hugo von Hofmannsthal*, trans. Hanns Hammelmann and Ewald Osers (Cambridge: Cambridge University Press, 1980), p. 142. See Hofmannsthal's shocked and high-minded response two days later! Strauss so realistic, Hofmannsthal so airy-fairy: little doubt, surely, who has the truer grasp.

8 Noel Coward, *Private Lives*, Act I.

9 The last section of Susan Sontag's 'Notes on Camp', in *Against Interpretation* (London, 1967), p. 292.

10 Compare Glenn Gould: ' . . . at every moment – regardless of the breadth of the score, regardless of its metric complexities, regardless of

the kaleidoscopic cross-reference of chromatic tonality – the bass line remains as firm, as secure, a counterpoise as in the works of Bach or Palestrina.' From 'An Argument for Richard Strauss', in *The Glenn Gould Reader*, ed. Tim Page (London: Faber, 1987), pp. 87–8. As always, Gould (writing about Strauss in general, not any particular work) overstates.

11 'Strauss may charm and delight but he cannot move. That is partly because he was never committed. He didn't give a damn.' Stravinsky after *Der Rosenkavalier* at Hamburg, 2 May 1963, quoted in Robert Craft, *Chronicle of a Friendship* (New York: Vintage Books, 1973), p. 215.

12 Frequently in conversation; and see also 'Unmade History', Part 2, *Music and Musicians*, Vol. 23, No. 11 (July 1975).

13 'What I'd like best of all, time and again, would be to put myself to music'. To Hofmannsthal, 12 July 1927: *The Correspondence between Richard Strauss and Hugo von Hofmannsthal*, p. 436.

14 At the final rehearsal before the first performance of the *Alpine Symphony*: 'At last I have learned to orchestrate. I wanted to compose, for once, as a cow gives milk.' Quoted in Kennedy, *Richard Strauss*, p. 64.

15 Letter to Hofmannsthal, 5 June 1916: further, 'sentimentality and parody are the sensations to which my talent responds most forcefully and productively'. *The Correspondence between Richard Strauss and Hugo von Hofmannsthal*, pp. 250–1.

16 Compare Busoni: 'Richard Strauss who (even in his art) is a cross between an artist and an industrialist . . .', in *The Essence of Music and Other Essays*, trans. Rosamund Ley (New York: Dover, 1965), p. 52.

17 'For my part I say that the unique and supreme pleasure in love-making lies in the certain knowledge that one is doing *evil*. Men and women know from birth that in evil lies all pleasure of the sense.' Charles Baudelaire, *My Heart Laid Bare*, ed. Peter Quennell, trans. Norman Cameron (London: Weidenfeld and Nicholson, 1950), p. 157.

18 Overheard during the supper-interval at a Glyndebourne *Rosenkavalier* (answering the question 'Who wrote the music?'): 'It's Mozart, dear; you can tell by the costumes.'

19 This was well-taken by Hofmannsthal. In his letter of 15 May 1916 he speaks both of 'the contrast between the heroic ideal and its denial' in *Ariadne* and of the 'spicing of the sentimental with its opposite' (for Zerbinetta) that 'is quite in your spirit'. *The Correspondence between Richard Strauss and Hugo von Hofmannsthal*, pp. 246–7.

20 See my essay on 'Strauss's Last Opera', *Music and Musicians*, Vol. 21, No. 12 (August 1973). Some of the notions here are taken from this earlier attempt, some are carried further, some controvert it.

21 Hofmannsthal again (to Strauss, 12 February 1919): ' . . . both my art and yours derive so effortlessly, so naturally from the Bavarian–Austrian baroque with its mixture of different elements and their fusion in music'. *The Correspondence between Richard Strauss and Hugo von Hofmannsthal*, p. 324.

22 See my chapter in *Richard Strauss: 'Elektra'*, ed. Derrick Puffett (Cambridge: Cambridge University Press, 1989).

23 Letter of 11 March 1906 (*The Correspondence between Richard Strauss and Hugo von Hofmannsthal*, p. 3). They both agree upon a *Semiramis* (see Hofmannsthal's detailed description of 22 December 1907, pp. 10–11), and Strauss also mentions a *Saul and David* and a *Dantons Tod* in these early days of their collaboration.
24 See n. 15 above and what it dangles from in the text.
25 Compare Debussy: 'In the cookery book, under Jugged Hare, will be seen this wise recommendation: "Take a hare." Richard Strauss proceeds otherwise. To write a symphonic poem he takes anything.' Quoted in Edward Lockspeiser, *Debussy* (London: Dent, 1951), p. 241.

Postlude: images of Salome

1 See above, pp. 24ff.
2 Dennis Barker, 'Salome Leads a Wilde Dance', *The Guardian* (London), 18 June 1988.
3 Interview on 'Kaleidoscope', BBC Radio 4, April 1988.
4 Reproduced in Appendix A below.
5 'The Veils Stay on', *The Observer* (London), 3 April 1988.
6 'Lust for Power', *The Guardian*, 29 March 1988.
7 'Reminiscences of the First Performance of My Operas', in *Recollections and Reflections*, ed. Willi Schuh, trans. L. J. Lawrence (London: Boosey and Hawkes, 1953), pp. 151–2.
8 See the pictures in *The Annotated Oscar Wilde*, ed. with an introduction and annotations by H. Montgomery Hyde (London: Orbis, 1982), pp. 316–22.
9 See the photos reproduced in Robert Orledge, *Debussy and the Theatre* (Cambridge: Cambridge University Press, 1982), pp. 129–38.
10 See above, pp. 2–3.
11 See above, p. 49.
12 *Current Convictions: Views and Reviews* (London: Secker and Warburg, 1978), p. 135. See also my article 'Strauss as Conductor', *Music and Musicians*, Vol. 25, No. 12 (August 1977).

Appendix A

1 The sketches for *Salome* are contained in Sketchbooks 11–14, held in the Richard-Strauss-Archiv, Garmisch. Most of the sketches for the 'Dance', however, are in Sketchbook 15 (Nos. 22b–30), along with material for *Ariadne auf Naxos*, *Der Bürger als Edelmann* and *Die Frau ohne Schatten*, though there are some isolated 'Dance' sketches in earlier books. See Franz Trenner, *Die Skizzenbücher von Richard Strauss aus dem Richard-Strauss-Archiv in Garmisch* (Tutzing: Schneider, 1977), pp. 21–6.
2 'Strauss . . . had finished *Salome*, and asked Mahler whether he might play it through to him from the manuscript score . . . We came to the dance – it was missing. "Haven't got it done yet," Strauss said and played on to the end, leaving this yawning gap. "Isn't it rather risky,"

Mahler remarked, "simply leaving out the dance, and then writing it in later when you're not in the same mood?" Strauss laughed his light-hearted laugh: "I'll fix that all right." But he did not. The dance is the one weak spot in the score – just botched-up commonplace.' Alma Mahler, *Gustav Mahler: Memories and Letters*, trans. Basil Creighton, ed. Donald Mitchell, 3rd edn (London: Faber, 1973), pp. 88–9.

3 See Willi Schuh, 'Zum Tanz der Salome', in *Straussiana aus vier Jahrzehnten* (Tutzing: Schneider, 1981), p. 93.

4 *Theaterzeitung des Stadttheaters Basel*, 25 September 1952; article reprinted in *Straussiana aus vier Jahrzehnten* (reference given in n. 3 above), pp. 91–5.

5 Reproduced from Rudolf Hartmann, *Richard Strauss: The Staging of His Operas and Ballets*, trans. Graham Davies (Oxford: Phaidon Press, 1982), pp. 41–5. Reproduced by kind permission of the Office du Livre, Fribourg. Some errors in the translation have been corrected.

6 Gaston Vuillier, *La Danse* (Paris: Hachette, 1898).

7 Actually the third and fourth bars if the first bar of O is included.

8 The dancer in this picture (reproduced by Schuh, 'Zum Tanz der Salome', p. 95) is in the pose known as the 'bridge', bending over back-wards until her hands touch the ground behind her, so that her body forms an arch. The same pose crops up repeatedly, according to Schuh, in medieval representations of Salome. Strauss evidently wanted the performance of his 'Dance' to be very stylised.

9 'Reminiscences of the First Performance of My Operas', in *Recollections and Reflections*, ed. Willi Schuh, trans. L. J. Lawrence (London: Boosey and Hawkes, 1953), p. 151. See also his letter of 30 September 1930 to Erich Engel, in which he emphasises that he wants 'a pure oriental dance, as serious as possible and thoroughly decent, as if on a prayer mat'. Quoted in Kurt Wilhelm, *Richard Strauss persönlich: Eine Bildbiographie* (Munich: Kindler, 1984), p. 124 (my translation).

10 See above, pp. 43ff.

11 See above, p. 95.

12 On the association of Salome and the moon, see above, pp. 47–8.

13 Schuh, 'Zum Tanz der Salome', p. 91.

14 For an answer to this question see Patricia C. Tate, ' "The Dance of the Seven Veils": A Historical and Descriptive Analysis' (Unpublished D.A. Diss., University of Northern Colorado, 1985).

Appendix B

1 Reprinted from *Dallapiccola on Opera* (*Selected Writings of Luigi Dallapiccola*, Vol. 1), trans. and ed. Rudy Shackelford (London: Toccata Press, 1987), pp. 126–8.

2 At the Staatsoper am Platz der Republik, 4 February 1930.

3 Pietro Grossi (b. 1917), electronic music composer and experimenter.

Bibliography

Abert, Anna Amalie, *Richard Strauss: Die Opern* (Hanover: Friedrich, 1972)

'*Salome*', notes to EMI recording, EMI SLS 5139 (1978) (English translation of *Salome* chapter from above)

Adorno, Theodor W., 'Richard Strauss', *Perspectives of New Music*, Vol. 4, No. 1 (Fall–Winter 1965), pp. 14–32; No. 2 (Spring–Summer 1966), pp. 113–29

Arnold, Denis, 'Strauss and Wilde's *Salomé*', *Monthly Musical Record*, Vol. 89, No. 992 (March–April 1959), pp. 44–9

Asow, Erich H. Mueller von, *Richard Strauss: Thematisches Verzeichnis*, 3 vols. (Vienna and Wiesbaden: Doblinger, 1959–74), Vol. 1 (Opp. 1–59), pp. 346–86 (on *Salome*)

Banks, Paul, 'Richard Strauss and the Unveiling of *Salome*', in '*Salome' and 'Elektra*', ed. Nicholas John (London: John Calder, 1988)

Beecham, Sir Thomas, *A Mingled Chime* (London: Hutchinson, 1944), pp. 102–5 (on *Salome*)

Birkin, Kenneth W., 'The Last Meeting: *Die Liebe der Danae* Reconsidered', *Tempo*, No. 153 (June 1985)

Brosche, Günter, *Richard Strauss: Bibliographie* (Vienna: Brüder Hollinek, 1973)

'Richard Strauss und Arnold Schoenberg: Mit unveröffentlichen Briefen', *Richard Strauss-Blätter*, Vol. 2 (December 1979)

Brosche, Günter, and Dachs, Karl, *Richard Strauss: Autographen in München und Wien: Verzeichnis* (Tutzing: Schneider, 1979)

Conrad, Peter, *Romantic Opera and Literary Form* (Berkeley: University of California Press, 1977)

Craft, Robert, *Current Convictions: Views and Reviews* (London: Secker and Warburg, 1978), especially the essays 'A "Beautiful Coloured, Musical Thing"' (on *Salome*), '*Der Rosenkavalier*: "Something Mozartian"?', '*Elektra* and Richard Strauss'

Dahlhaus, Carl, 'Jochanaans Tod: Wieland Wagner inszeniert *Salome*', *Neue Zeitschrift für Musik*, Vol. 123, No. 5 (1962), pp. 232–3

Die Musik des 19. Jahrhunderts (Wiesbaden: Akademische Verlagsgesellschaft Athenaion, 1980)

'The Musical Influence [of Wagner]', trans. Alfred Clayton, in *The Wagner Handbook*, ed. John Deathridge (Cambridge, Mass.: Harvard, in preparation)

Daviau, Donald G., and Buelow, George J., *The 'Ariadne auf Naxos' of Hugo von Hofmannsthal and Richard Strauss* (Chapel Hill: University of North Carolina Press, 1975)

Del Mar, Norman, *Richard Strauss: A Critical Commentary on His Life and Works*, 3 vols. (London: Barrie and Jenkins, 1978)

Dinerstein, Norman M., 'Polychordality in *Salome* and *Elektra*: A Study of the Application of Re-Interpretation Technique' (Unpublished Ph.D. Diss., Princeton University, 1974)

Ellmann, Richard, 'Overtures to Wilde's *Salomé*', *School of Letters: Twentieth Anniversary 1948–1968* (Bloomington: Indiana University, 1968); repr. in *Tri-Quarterly*, Vol. 5, No. 1 (Spring 1969), pp. 45–64

Oscar Wilde (London: Hamish Hamilton, 1987)

'The Fatality of Passion', Covent Garden programme note (London: Royal Opera House, Covent Garden, 1988)

Erwin, Charlotte E., 'Richard Strauss's Presketch Planning for *Ariadne auf Naxos*', *Musical Quarterly*, Vol. 67, No. 3 (July 1981), pp. 348–65

Finck, Henry T., *Richard Strauss: The Man and the Works* (Boston: Little, Brown and Co., 1917)

Forsyth, Karen, *'Ariadne auf Naxos' by Hugo von Hofmannsthal and Richard Strauss: Its Genesis and Meaning* (London: Oxford University Press, 1982)

Gerlach, Reinhard, *Don Juan und Rosenkavalier: Studien zu Idee und Gestalt einer tonalen Evolution im Werk Richard Strauss* (Berne: Haupt, 1966)

Gilliam, Bryan, 'Strauss's Preliminary Opera Sketches: Thematic Fragments and Symphonic Continuity', *Nineteenth-Century Music*, Vol. 9, No. 3 (Spring 1986), pp. 176–88

Gilman, Lawrence, *Strauss' Salome: A Guide to the Opera* (London: John Lane, 1907)

Gilman, Sander L., 'Strauss and the Pervert', in *Reading Opera*, ed. Arthur Groos and Roger Parker (Princeton: Princeton University Press, 1988)

Disease and Representation: Images of Illness from Madness to AIDS (Ithaca: Cornell University Press, 1989)

Gollob, H., *Richard Wagner und Richard Strauss in der musikalischen Malerei* (Vienna: Gerold, 1957)

Gould, Glenn, 'An Argument for Richard Strauss', in *The Glenn Gould Reader*, ed. Tim Page (London: Faber, 1987)

Grainger, Percy, 'Richard Strauss: Seer and Idealist', in Finck, Henry T., *Richard Strauss: The Man and the Works* (Boston: Little, Brown and Co., 1917), pp. xvii–xxv

Grasberger, Franz, ed., *Der Strom der Töne trug mich fort: Die Welt um Richard Strauss in Briefen* (Tutzing: Schneider, 1967)

Grasberger, Franz, *Richard Strauss und die Wiener Oper* (Tutzing: Schneider, 1969)

Hartmann, Rudolf, *Richard Strauss: The Staging of His Operas and Ballets*, trans. Graham Davies (Oxford: Phaidon Press, 1982)

Holloway, Robin, 'Strauss's Last Opera', *Music and Musicians*, Vol. 21, No. 12 (August 1973)

Jaacks, Gisela, and Jahnke, Andres W., eds., *Richard Strauss (1864–1949): 'Musik des Lichts in dunkler Zeit': Vom Bürgerschreck zum Rosenkavalier* (Mainz: Schott, 1979)

Jefferson, Alan, *The Operas of Richard Strauss in Britain 1910–1963* (London: Putnam, 1963), pp. 43–61 (on *Salome*)
The Life of Richard Strauss (Newton Abbot: David and Charles, 1973)
Richard Strauss (London, 1975)

Kennedy, Michael, *Richard Strauss* (London: Dent, 1976)
'Richard Strauss' (with worklist by Robert Bailey), in *The New Grove Dictionary of Music and Musicians*, ed. Stanley Sadie, 20 vols. (London: Macmillan, 1980), Vol. 18, pp. 218–39

Kerman, Joseph, *Opera as Drama* (New York: Vintage Books, 1956)

Klein, Walter, 'Die Harmonisation in *Elektra* von Richard Strauss: Ein Beitrag zur modernen Harmonisationslehre', *Der Merker*, Vol. 2, Nos. 12–14 (1911), pp. 512–14, 540–3, 590–2 (of relevance to *Salome*)

Kohler, Stephan, '"Warum singt der Franzose anders als er spricht?": Richard Strauss und die französische Fassung seiner Oper *Salome*', unpublished (revised version of 'Warum singt der Franzose anders als er spricht?', *Jahrbuch der Bayerischen Staatsoper*, Vol. 2 (1978/9))

Kralik, Heinrich, *Richard Strauss: Weltbürger der Musik* (Vienna: Wollzeilen, 1963)

Krause, Ernst, *Richard Strauss: The Man and His Work* (London: Collet, 1964)

Mahler, Alma, *Gustav Mahler: Memories and Letters*, trans. Basil Creighton, ed. Donald Mitchell, 3rd edn (London: Faber, 1973)

Gustav Mahler–Richard Strauss: Correspondence 1888–1911, ed. with notes and an essay by Herta Blaukopf, trans. Edmund Jephcott (London: Faber, 1984)

Maillard, J., '*Salome*', *L'Education musicale*, Nos. 202 (November 1973, pp. 4/48–8/52), 203 (December 1973, pp. 12/100–23/111), 204 (January 1974, pp. 16/144–18/146), 205 (February 1974, pp. 26/194–30/198), 206 (March 1974, pp. 10/218–13/221), 207 (April 1974, pp. 8/256–13/261)

Mann, William, *Richard Strauss: A Critical Study of the Operas* (London: Cassell, 1964)

Marek, George R., *Richard Strauss: The Life of a Non-Hero* (London, 1967)

Marsop, Paul, 'Italien und der "Fall Salome", nebst Glossen zur Kritik und Ästhetik', *Die Musik*, Vol. 6 (1906–7), p. 139

McMullen, Sally, 'Sense and Sensuality: Max Reinhardt's Early Productions', in *Max Reinhardt: The Oxford Symposium*, ed. Margaret Jacobs and John Warren (Oxford: John Warren, 1986)

Newman, Ernest, *Richard Strauss* (London: John Lane, 1908; repr. 1970)
More Opera Nights (London: Putnam, 1954)
Testament of Music (London: Putnam, 1963)

Overhoff, Kurt, *Die Elektra-Partitur von Richard Strauss: Ein Lehrbuch für die Technik der dramatischen Komposition* (Salzburg: Pustet, 1978)

Panofsky, Walter, *Richard Strauss: Partitur eines Lebens* (Darmstadt: Deutsche Buch-Gemeinschaft, 1965)

Praz, Mario, *The Romantic Agony*, trans. Angus Davidson (London: Oxford University Press, 1970)

Puffett, Derrick, 'Strauss as Conductor', *Music and Musicians*, Vol. 25, No. 12 (August 1977)

'An Introduction to *Der Rosenkavalier*', in *Der Rosenkavalier*, ed. Nicholas John (London: John Calder, 1981)

Puffett, Derrick, ed., *Richard Strauss: 'Elektra'* (Cambridge: Cambridge University Press, 1989)

Roth, Ernst, ed., *Richard Strauss Stage Works: Documents of the First Performances* (London: Boosey and Hawkes, 1954)

Schmidgall, Gary, *Literature as Opera* (New York: Oxford University Press, 1977)

Schuch, Friedrich von, *Richard Strauss, Ernst von Schuch und Dresdens Oper*, 2nd edn (Leipzig: Verlag der Kunst, 1953)

Schuh, Willi, 'Zur harmonischen Deutung des *Salome*-Schlusses', *Schweizerische Musikzeitung*, Vol. 86, No. 12 (1946), pp. 452–8

Über Opern von Richard Strauss (Zurich: Atlantis, 1947)

The Stage Works of Richard Strauss (London: Boosey and Hawkes, 1954) (includes plates of 1937 Munich *Salome* production)

Hugo von Hofmannsthal und Richard Strauss: Legende und Wirklichkeit (Munich: Hanser, 1964); repr. in *Umgang mit Musik* (Zurich: Atlantis, 1970), pp. 173–202

Straussiana aus vier Jahrzehnten (Tutzing: Schneider, 1981)

Richard Strauss: A Chronicle of the Early Years (1864–1898), trans. Mary Whittall (Cambridge: Cambridge University Press, 1982)

Schuh, Willi, and Roth, Ernst, *Richard Strauss: Complete Catalogue* (London: Boosey and Hawkes, 1964)

Shewring, Margaret, and Mulryne, Ronnie, 'Max Reinhardt's *Salome*', Welsh National Opera programme book (Cardiff: Welsh National Opera, 1988)

Smith, Patrick J., *The Tenth Muse: A Historical Study of the Opera Libretto* (London: Gollancz, 1971)

Specht, Richard, *Richard Strauss und sein Werk*, 2 vols. (Leipzig, Vienna and Zurich: E. P. Tal & Co., 1921), especially Vol. 2, pp. 103–64 (on *Salome*)

Steinitzer, Max, *Richard Strauss* (Berlin: Schuster and Loeffler, 1911)

Strauss, Richard, ed., *Treatise on Instrumentation by Hector Berlioz*, trans. Theodore Front (New York: Kalmus, 1948)

Strauss, Richard, *Recollections and Reflections*, ed. Willi Schuh, trans. L. J. Lawrence (London: Boosey and Hawkes, 1953)

Richard Strauss: Briefe an die Eltern 1882–1906, ed. Willi Schuh (Zurich: Atlantis, 1954)

Richard Strauss: Briefwechsel mit Willi Schuh, ed. Willi Schuh (Zurich: Atlantis, 1969)

[*Richard Strauss:*] *Salome*, About the House, No. 5 (1980) (pp. 59–62 reprint Ernest Newman's *Sunday Times* review of 20 November 1949)

Richard Strauss and Romain Rolland: Correspondence, Diary and Essays, ed. and annotated with a preface by Rollo Myers (London: Calder and Boyars, 1968)

Richard Strauss und Ludwig Thuille: Briefe der Freundschaft 1877–1907, ed. A. Ott (Munich, 1969)

Richard Strauss und Hugo von Hofmannsthal: Briefwechsel: Gesamtausgabe, ed. Willi Schuh, 5th edn (Zurich: Atlantis, 1978) (includes letters not in the English edition)

The Correspondence between Richard Strauss and Hugo von Hofmannsthal, trans. Hanns Hammelmann and Ewald Osers (Cambridge: Cambridge University Press, 1980)

Tate, Patricia C., '"The Dance of the Seven Veils": A Historical and Descriptive Analysis' (Unpublished D.A. Diss., University of Northern Colorado, 1985)

Tenschert, Roland, *Dreimal sieben Variationen über das Thema Richard Strauss* (Vienna: Frick, 1944)

'Richard Strauss' Opernfassung der deutschen Übersetzung von Oscar Wildes "Salome"', *Richard Strauss Jahrbuch (1959–60)*, ed. Willi Schuh (Bonn: Boosey and Hawkes, 1960), pp. 99–106

Trenner, Franz, *Richard Strauss: Dokumente seines Lebens und Schaffens* (Munich: C. H. Beck, 1954)

Die Skizzenbücher von Richard Strauss aus dem Richard-Strauss-Archiv in Garmisch (Tutzing: Schneider, 1977), pp. 21–6 (on *Salome*)

Wilde, Oscar, *Salomé* (London: Methuen, 1908 (1st edn); repr. Dawsons, 1969)

Salome, trans. Hedwig Lachmann (Leipzig: Insel Verlag, n.d.)

'The Importance of Being Earnest' and Other Plays (includes English translation of *Salome*) (Harmondsworth: Penguin, 1954)

The Letters of Oscar Wilde, ed. Rupert Hart-Davis (London: Hart-Davis, 1962)

The Annotated Oscar Wilde, ed. with an introduction and annotations by H. Montgomery Hyde (London: Orbis, 1982), pp. 305–25 (*Salomé*)

Wilhelm, Kurt, *Richard Strauss persönlich: Eine Bildbiographie* (Munich: Kindler, 1984)

Williamson, John, 'Strauss and *Macbeth*: The Realisation of the Poetic Idea', *Soundings*, No. 13 (Summer 1985)

'Salome and the Orchestra', *Newsletter of the Friends of Welsh National Opera*, No. 10 (May 1988)

Winterhager, Wolfgang, *Zur Struktur des Operndialogs: Komparative Analysen des musikdramatischen Werks von Richard Strauss* (Frankfurt: Lang, 1984)

Discography

MALCOLM WALKER

S	Salome	(m)	mono recording
H	Herodias	(4)	cassette version
Her	Herod	CD	Compact Disc version
N	Narraboth	*	78 rpm record
J	Jochanaan	CDV	Compact Disc Video

All recordings in stereo unless otherwise stated. The dates quoted relate to the year of recording.

Complete recordings

1948   Goltz *S*; Karen *H*; Aldenhoff *Her*; Dittrich *N*; J. Hermann *J*; Dresden State Opera Orch / Keilberth
Olympic (m) OL9101/2
Concert Hall (m) MMS2027

1949   (public performance: Metropolitan Opera House, New York) Welitsch *S*; Thorborg *H*; Jagel *Her*; Sullivan *N*; Janssen *J*; Metropolitan Opera Orch / Reiner
Golden Age of Opera (m) EJS158

1952   (public performance: Munich) Borkh *S*; Barth *H*; Lorenz *Her*; Fehenberger *N*; Hotter *J*; Bavarian State Opera Orch / Keilberth
Melodram (m) MEL106

1952   (public performance: Metropolitan Opera House, New York) Welitsch *S*; Höngen *H*; Svanholm *Her*; Sullivan *N*; Hotter *J*; Metropolitan Opera Orch / Reiner
Metropolitan Opera (m) MET9

1952   Wegner *S*; von Milinkovic *H*; Szemere *Her*; Kmentt *N*; Metternich *J*; Vienna SO / Moralt
Philips (m) 6747 406

1953   Varnay *S*; Klose *H*; Patzak *Her*; Hopf *N*; Nissen *J*; Bavarian Radio Orch / Weigert
Estro Armonico (m) EA35
Discocorp (m) IGI289
Bruno Walter Society (m) BWS289

1954   Goltz *S*; Kenney *H*; Patzak *Her*; Dermota *N*; Braun *J*; Vienna PO / Krauss
Decca (m) GOM549/50
Richmond (m) RS62007

1955 (public performance: Metropolitan Opera House, New York)
Goltz *S*; Thebom *H*; Vinay *Her*; Sullivan *N*; Schoeffler *J*;
Metropolitan Opera Orch / Mitropoulos
Historical Opera Productions Edition (m) HOPE238

1956 (public performance: Metropolitan Opera House, New York)
Borkh *S*; Thebom *H*; Vinay *Her*; Sullivan *N*; Harrell *J*; Metropolitan Opera Orch / Mitropoulos
Cetra (m) LO82

1961 Nilsson *S*; Hoffman *H*; Stolze *Her*; Kmentt *N*; Waechter *J*;
Vienna PO / Solti
Decca SET228
CD: 414 414–2DH2
London OSA1218
CD: 414 414–2LH2

1963 Goltz *S*; Eriksdotter *H*; Melchert *Her*; Hoppe *N*; Gutstein *J*;
Dresden State Orch / Suitner
EMI Electrola STE91320/1
Eterna 825 375/6

1968 Caballé *S*; Resnik *H*; Lewis *Her*; King *N*; Milnes *J*; London
SO / Leinsdorf
RCA (UK) SER 5582/3
(US) LSC7053

1970 (public performances and rehearsal: Staatsoper, Hamburg)
G. Jones *S*; Dunn *H*; Cassilly *Her*; Ochman *N*; Fischer-Dieskau *J*;
Hamburg State Opera Orch / Böhm
DG 2721 186

1977 Behrens *S*; Baltsa *H*; K.-W. Böhm *Her*; Ochman *N*; van Dam *J*;
Vienna PO / Karajan
EMI/Angel EX7 69246–1
(4) EX7 69246–4
CD: CDM7 69246–2

1981 (Unitel film, 1974) Stratas *S*; Varnay *H*; Beirer *Her*; Ochman *N*;
Weikl *J*; VOP / Böhm
CDV: DG 072 109–1

Abridged recordings

1934 (public performance: Metropolitan Opera House, New York)
Ljüngberg *S*; Manski *H*; Lorenz *Her*; Clemens *N*; Schorr *J*;
Metropolitan Opera Orch / Bodansky
Golden Age of Opera (m) EJS506

1942 (two separate public performances: Vienna State Opera)
Schulz *S*; Bugarinovic *H*; Witt/Sattler *Her*; Dermota *N*;
Schoeffler/Hotter *J*; Vienna State Opera Orch / R. Strauss
Golden Age of Opera (m) EJS463

Final monologue

c. 1910	(in Italian: heavily abridged) Adorni *S*; orch / Sabajno
	Voce del Padrone 53600*; 053241*
1921	Kemp *S*; Berlin State Opera Orch / ?von Schillings
	Preiser (m) LV13
1924	Ljüngberg *S*; T. Davies *Her*; SO / Coates
	HMV D910*
1929	Ljüngberg *S*; Berlin State Opera Orch / Blech
	Preiser (m) LV176
	Rococo (m) 5252
1933	(public performance: Vienna State Opera) Jeritza *S*; Vienna State Opera Orch / Reichenberger
	Golden Age of Opera (m) EJS334
1934	(in French) M. Lawrence *S*; Pasdeloup Orch / Coppola
	Preiser (m) LV133
	Camden (m) CAL216
1930s	(?public performance) Pauly *S*; orch
	IRCC L7018*
1941	(broadcast performance) Cebotari *S*; Berlin Radio Orch / Rother
	Acanta (m) 22179
c. 1943	Enck *S*; Berlin State Opera Orch / Heger
	Telefunken (m) KBM8030
	Capitol (m) L8036
1944	Welitsch *S*; Austrian Radio Orch, Vienna / von Matačić
	EMI/Angel CD: (m) CDH7 61007–2
1948	Welitsch *S*; Schuster *H*; Witt *Her*; Vienna PO / Karajan
	EMI (m) SH286
1949	Welitsch *S*; Metropolitan Opera Orch / Reiner
	CBS (m) 61088
	CBS Odyssey (USA) (m) 32 16 0077
1951	Goltz *S*; Plümacher *H*; Windgassen *Her*; Württemburg Staatsoper Orch / Leitner
	DG (m) LPM18090
1951	Varnay *S*; Niederöst Tonkünstler Orch / Weigert
	Acanta (m) 22645
1956	Borkh *S*; Chicago SO / Reiner
	RCA CD: 5603–2–RC
1956	Borkh *S*; Vienna PO / Krips
	Decca 411 669–1DM
	(4) 417 339–4DA
	London OS25102
1965	Tynes *S*; Budapest PO / Varga
	Hungaroton SLPX1074
1965	L. Price *S*; Boston SO / Leinsdorf
	RCA (UK) LSB4083
	(US) LSC2849

1972   (public performance: Metropolitan Opera House, New York)
Nilsson *S*; Metropolitan Opera Orch / Böhm
DG 2530 260

1973   Silja *S*; Vienna PO / Dohnányi
Decca SXL6657
London OS26937

1977   Caballé *S*; French National Orch / Bernstein
DG 415 446–1GS
(4) 415 446–4GS

1983   Migenes *S*; Monte Carlo PO / Valdes
Apache 240295–1
Eurodisc 40.29401AS

1985   (public performance) Marton *S*; Toronto SO / A. Davis
CBS IM42019
(4) IMT42019
CD: MK42019

Index